ENGLISH DIAL CLOCKS

Ronald E. Rose

Antique Collectors' Club

Published for the Antique Collectors' Club
by the Antique Collectors' Club Ltd.

British Library CIP Data
Rose, Ronald E.
    English dial clocks. — 2nd ed.
    1. English clocks, ca 1730-ca 1920
    I. Title   II. Antique Collectors' Club
    681.1'13'0942

Printed in England by the Antique Collectors' Club Ltd.,
5 Church Street, Woodbridge, Suffolk

The frontispiece shows a tavern clock, c.1790, by Francis Perigal of Bond Street, London.

The Antique Collectors' Club

The Antique Collectors' Club was formed in 1966 and now has a five figure membership spread throughout the world. It publishes the only independently run monthly antiques magazine *Antique Collecting* which caters for those collectors who are interested in widening their knowledge of antiques, both by greater awareness of quality and by discussion of the factors which influence the price that is likely to be asked. The Antique Collectors' Club pioneered the provision of information on prices for collectors and the magazine still leads in the provision of detailed articles on a variety of subjects.

It was in response to the enormous demand for information on ''what to pay'' that the price guide series was introduced in 1968 with the first edition of *The Price Guide to Antique Furniture* (completely revised, 1978), a book which broke new ground by illustrating the more common types of antique furniture, the sort that collectors could buy in shops and at auctions rather than the rare museum pieces which had previously been used (and still to a large extent are used) to make up the limited amount of illustrations in books published by commercial publishers. Many other price guides have followed, all copiously illustrated, and greatly appreciated by collectors for the valuable information they contain, quite apart from prices. The Antique Collectors' Club also publishes other books on antiques, including horology and art reference works, and a full book list is available.

Club membership, which is open to all collectors, costs £15.95 per annum. Members receive free of charge *Antique Collecting,* the Club's magazine (published every month except August), which contains well-illustrated articles dealing with the practical aspects of collecting not normally dealt with by magazines. Prices, features of value, investment potential, fakes and forgeries are all given prominence in the magazine.

Among other facilities available to members are private buying and selling facilities, the longest list of ''For Sales'' of any antiques magazine, an annual ceramics conference and the opportunity to meet other collectors at their local antique collectors' clubs. There are over eighty in Britain and more than a dozen overseas. Members may also buy the Club's publications at special pre-publication prices.

As its motto implies, the Club is an amateur organisation designed to help collectors get the most out of their hobby: it is informal and friendly and gives enormous enjoyment to all concerned.

For Collectors — By Collectors — About Collecting

The Antique Collectors' Club, 5 Church Street, Woodbridge, Suffolk

A rare and finely decorated tavern clock in a lacquered case of unusual teardrop design, which has an oak backboard and door with pine sides and a bulbous base. The decoration on the base is of extremely fine execution and design. The dial surround is one piece of wood with the dial which has outside minute numerals and a double circle minute track without difference in five minute markings. The movement has tapered plates 7¼ in. tall and a five wheel train giving a full week duration to this small case. Circa 1785.

Dimensions: *Height 45½ in., surround diameter 21in.*

Maker: *Thomas Fordham, Braintree, the son of Joseph Fordham. He was at Braintree in 1779 having moved from Bishop's Stortford.*

Strike One (Islington) Ltd.

Contents

Acknowledgements

For cooperation, help and knowledge acquired over the years I am especially grateful to a good friend with a private collection of wall clocks and also to my many colleagues in the trade.

I am also indebted to Thwaites and Reed Ltd. for the use of their records, and indeed for my training and apprenticeship days.

I am fortunate in having had access to the many wall clocks which passed through the workshops of Strike One Ltd., and without this the book could not have been written.

My thanks also to Biggs of Maidenhead and private collectors for making available a number of the photographs in this book; these are acknowledged in the text. The remainder of the photographs are by courtesy of Strike One Ltd.

In this second edition my thanks also go to Gillett and Johnston, Croydon, to the many extra private collections I have visited and to F.W. Elliott of Hastings for the history and background of their company.

Throughout my research I have been made most welcome with many cups of tea coming my way so I thank you all not only for the information but also the hospitality.

Ronald E. Rose

Introduction

It has always concerned me that the English dial clock has been unfairly discriminated against in that there is very little reference material in existence. The need to put the evolution of the dial clock into perspective, together with that other neglected area — tavern and English cartel clocks, gave me the idea to write this book. But the actual decision to do so spiralled from an article written sixteen years ago; it then took six years to find time to write the text, do the drawings and gather together the photographs.

I am not a writer but a clock repairer and. since words are not my favourite medium, a fair number of drawings and photographs are included which I hope will speak for themselves. So that the layman will not be overwhelmed by detail, I have tried to avoid the use of too much technical jargon, though it has not been possible to avoid this entirely.

Since completing the book more facts and interesting clocks have come to light and it is hoped this trend will continue. Although the dial clock story will never be fully told, I hope I have succeeded in scratching the surface and whetting a few appetites. Certainly I have enjoyed the time-consuming work and the knowledge it has given me.

An early 19th century mahogany tavern clock typical of the end of the tavern clock era, which is mahogany veneered on to a mahogany carcase with simple earpieces, has a curved top to the trunk door matching the contour of the dial and a chisel foot base with an access door to the pendulum. The dial is one piece with the surround and is a shallow convex form with a narrow moulded edge. It has brass spade hands and is signed on the dial itself. The movement has tapered plates with cutouts on the base, four pillars and the normal anchor escapement. Circa 1815.

Dimensions: *Height 44¼ in., surround diameter 21½ in., dial diameter 20¼ in.*

Maker: *Desbois & Wheeler, Gray's Inn Passage.*

Britten observes that 'several generations of the Desbois family have carried on business in the neigbourhood of Holborn'. Desbois & Wheeler were at 9 Gray's Inn Passage from 1790-1835.

Strike One (Islington) Ltd.

Chapter 1

People and Clocks

In England at the start of the eighteenth century the need to know the correct time was confined almost entirely to the wealthy ruling classes. The poor who represented the bulk of the population and made their living mainly from the land had no need of timekeeping. Work on the land was governed by what needed to be done; it was more often a battle against the weather than against the time. Dawn and dusk provided the main divisions of the day. Apart from the sun only the church clock striking the hours gave the illiterate labourers an indication of the passage of time.

The clock was thus a rich man's possession and even by 1700 it remained relatively expensive. By then, thanks to the application of the pendulum and anchor escapement, the new longcase domestic clocks were attaining a degree of accuracy and reliability phenomenal by the standards of earlier eras and astonishing even to the expectations of contemporaries. An idea of the unreliability of public clocks at the end of the seventeenth century is provided by a query sent to the *Athenian Mercury,* VI, 1692/3:

> '*I was in Covent Garden when the Clock struck two, when I came to Somerset-house by that it wanted a quarter of two, when I came to St. Clements it was half an hour past two, when I came to St. Dunstans it wanted a quarter of two, by Mr. Knib's Dyal in Fleet-street it was just two, when I came to Ludgate it was half an hour past one, when I came to Bow Church, it wanted a quarter of two, by the Dyal near Stocks Market it was a quarter past two, and when I came to the Royal Exchange it wanted a quarter of two: This I averr for a Truth, and desire to know how long I was walking from Covent Garden to the Royal Exchange?*'

Clearly even in the capital, knowledge of the exact time was not counted of paramount importance.

After the religious and political disruptions and upheavals of the second half of the seventeenth century a stable pattern of government emerged in Britain at the start of the eighteenth century. Attention now focused on material possessions. Daniel Defoe disarmingly summed up the philosophy in the 1720s: 'Getting money,' he remarked, was 'the main affaire of life'.

A busy urban community, engaged in commerce and providing the ancillary services necessary for trade, needs a more accurate measure of the passage of time than a rural community with a fixed job of work to be done. Newly made wealth required the flaunting of suitable prestigious possessions, of which expensive clocks were one, but there was now also a need for inexpensive, trouble free, accurate measure of time to ensure the smooth running of the manufactory, office, shop and public services.

By 1720-1740 the prices of clocks had settled down at the levels they would retain for most of the century. For a locally made eight-day movement without case, a man might expect to pay between £3.10s. and £5. Samuel Roberts of Llanfair-Caereinian, Wales, charged about £4 each for the six eight-day movements which he made between 1755 and 1774. An eight-day clock supplied for use at Castle Howard in 1771 cost 5 guineas for the movement and 1 guinea for the case. Clockwork weighing 60lb at 14d. per lb ran out at £3.10s. in 1756, while rival clockmakers in Newcastle in 1776 were charging respectively £3.13s.6d. and £4.4s. for eight-day movements. Movements for thirty-hour movements cost approximately half this amount. A note on the inside of the trunk door of a clock by William Roberts of Otley records that 'This clock was settled the 7th Oct 1758 prise £2.3s.6d.', although it is unclear whether 'settled' means that the clock was put in position, the full bill was paid, or that the price was agreed after haggling. Prices of goods in the eighteenth century were generally not fixed and each buyer made the best price that he could. In a high cost field such as clockmaking however there may not have been as much room for manoeuvre as there was in other fields. The greatest variation probably occurred in the price of the case which would start at £1 or £1.10s. for a plain oak or walnut case. Painted, inlaid or decorated cases cost more according to their complexity. Gillows clock cases in 1771 ranged from £2.5s. to £10.

The prices of clocks by London makers, as of all clocks with such refinements as month duration, maintaining power, repeating work, calendar indications, and the like, was considerably higher. The trade price for an eight-day movement seems to have been about the same as the provincial retail price. Thus in 1781 Thwaites and Reed charged Andrew Fouldes £19 for five eight-day movements and £3.18s. for another. In the same year a 'New spring Clock' cost Viscountess Downes £12.12s. Prices such as these compare interestingly with those charged by the same makers for dial clocks which were sold complete with case. In July 1781 Dwerrihouse was charged £3.10s. for a 'New Spring Diall'. A 'New Timepiece' cost Matthew French £2.2s and weight dials were charged to Dwerrihouse at £2.5s. each. In the provinces spring driven dial clocks retailed at about the same as the London trade prices, Chaplin of Bury St. Edmunds advertising them 'exceeding neat... in mahogany cases' at £3.13s.6d. in the *Ipswich Journal* in 1791. If this seems high it was still competitive given that the case was included and that the movement would be of rather better quality than that of the cheapest thirty-hour clocks which alone, after the cost of the case had been added, could rival it.

If dial clocks had only had a competitive, though not markedly lower, price to recommend them in the face of the established styles of clocks, it is doubtful if they would ever have attained much popularity. With their relative cheapness however, they combined an attractive, even elegant appearance, suggestive of solid prosperity without being flamboyant, and reliable performance. At the same time they were more convenient. They could be bought in one transaction not two since they were ready cased, and being mounted on the wall they required no floor space. They could easily be seen and were not subject to interruption or damage from the brooms of careless housemaids or the mischievous tamperings of others. It was the combination of these advantages which gave them a wide appeal. For an elegant, solid, reliable clock was exactly suitable for a middle class market. At the same time it was also right for the subsidiary clocks needed in large households to regulate the activities of servants in the stables, the kitchen or elsewhere below stairs. Dial clocks, because they could be mounted high and could have large clear dials with large easily read numerals, were also perfectly adapted for use in semi-public places such as banks and counting-houses, insurance offices, factories, coffee houses and taverns. Because they were entirely enclosed they were guarded against dirt, and because they could be mounted high up they were safe from damage.

But it was the industrial revolution toward the end of the eighteenth century which made time keeping even more essential. A factory must be constantly manned if it is to work properly, industrial processes take predictable times and above all labour is paid by the hour. A large number of reliable clocks which told the same correct time became vital.

Time consciousness extended to communications. The great growth in coaching services, both for goods and passengers, which took place in the 1750s and 1760s, led to the attempt to introduce regular time schedules and also to coordinate land services with those of coastal and water transport. Advertisements for coach services now announced specific times of departure and arrival instead of merely stating the place and the day. In 1774 the York and Newcastle post coach which ran three times a week was advertised to leave at twelve o'clock at night. It 'breakfasts at Darlington, dines at Easingwood, and will be at the George in Carey Street, York at six, where six places will be kept in the London Fly, which sets out at eleven o'clock that night'. Soon afterwards in 1783/4, John Palmer introduced the practice of timing the mail coaches to hours and minutes, and by 1800 the post office at Gosport was announcing that London letters, 'must be put in the Letter-box a quarter before six o'clock in the afterternoon [sic], as the bag is sealed exactly at six o'clock'. In the decades that followed, the coaching services not only became increasingly complex, but increasingly precisely timed and exact. Printed time-bills were produced and the times of arrival and departure at set points were recorded by the coach timepiece, these times being checked against those shown by the office clock at those points.

The coaching service, which enjoyed its heyday between about 1800 and 1840, is one of the clearest examples of the growth of a time-disciplined and synchronised industry. Once the idea of regular running times and coordinated services was established, it must have helped greatly in strengthening the idea of time as a measured quantity determined by clocks, in much the same way as it led to a demand for showy, but reliable clocks for taverns whence the coaches normally departed and, less flamboyant but equally reliable, timepieces in the stables and offices of their owners. The dial clock, both as the grandiose 'tavern clock' and in its simpler everyday form, was generally the clock employed, and, like the whole concept of the timetabled, interlocking service, it was later taken over by the railways. The railway clock from the earliest period has been a dial clock, cheap, durable and accurate.

The increasing public awareness of time during the middle and latter part of the eighteenth century led to the clocks like the one shown in Plate 1 being put up in taverns for the convenience of patrons. The name 'Act of Parliament' being an obvious misnomer as this clock dates from around the 1760s whereas the Act of Parliament referred to was passed in 1797. In any event by that time this particular design had ceased to be made.

The possible predecessor of the tavern clock was the black dial clock, first made in the 1720s. It had a simple circular case without a trunk and the dial was usually quite large, around sixteen inches in diameter, and made basically of oak with a pine moulded surround (Plate 2). It was lacquered black and had gold leaf Roman figures with outside minute numerals and brass hands.

Roman hour figures were used on all the early clocks with conventional Arabic numbering for the minutes. In fact, Roman numeral marking was far simpler for ordinary people to understand as there is a combination of only three different numerals used on the dial as against a combination of ten different numerals for conventional numbering.

The early black dial clock changed its lines towards the tavern clock over a period of not more than fifty years. Probably only a few were ever made, which may explain their extreme rarity today.

The movement which had been spring driven with a verge escapement was changed to weight driven with an anchor escapement and a long pendulum (Plate 3), and this made necessary a short trunk to the case. The dials became shield shaped and, with one or two exceptions, did not revert back to circular (Plate 3 again) until the middle of the century. The sizes varied but all were large, as the main function of such clocks was for public timekeeping — hence their common use in inns, churches and halls. The dials were usually black with gilt numerals and the cases decorated with chinoiserie on a black background, this decoration being at its peak of popularity at the time. However, these clocks were not cheap by any means and only a few taverns (in which these clocks were probably most widely used) could afford them. To imply that these clocks were made in any great numbers would be wrong; a tavern which could afford one would gain a considerable amount of prestige, and the clock itself would have been quite a topic of conversation and interest.

Just as the black dial clock evolved into the tavern clock, so the English cartel clock evolved into the dial clock. The English cartel clock first appeared in the houses of the wealthy about 1730. It was an almost direct copy of the French counterpart, the major difference being that it was made from carved wood and then watergilded whereas the French cartel was solid cast brass. The movement (Plate 4) was on the same lines as the black dial clock, being spring driven with a verge escapement. The style, however, did not catch on as it did in France — the flamboyant features just weren't English. The case was quite large, often asymmetric and sometimes surmounted by an eagle, but after a very short life of about forty years it went out of fashion. In spite of its early demise the English cartel did play a very important role in the development of English horology being the immediate predecessor of the English dial clock. The movement and dial style were taken intact and used in a much simplified case (Plate 5) to form the most popular style of clock ever produced.

It was the William Pitt, who was in office from 1783 to 1801 and from April 1804 until his death in 1806, who was responsible for passing the 1797 Act which taxed the possession of clocks and watches. Although it was repealed in the following year it had the effect of cutting the numbers employed in the horological trade by half. After the end of the Napoleonic wars and the industrial depression which followed the dial clock industry gradually revived. The huge prosperity of Victorian England resulted in a large demand for dial clocks, indeed more of these clocks were produced than any other single type up to that date. It was not until the industrial electric master clock and its 'slaves' began to be installed that the dial clock lost its place as the leading type of clock.

PLATE 1

Surround section

This clock is typical of the type used in taverns during the middle fifty years of the eighteenth century.

The black dial has gold leaf Roman figures with outside minute numerals and is decorated on the two lower corners of the shield shaped dial. The hands are brass with heart shaped tips and both are counterbalanced. The moulding around the dial is made like a picture frame with the dial, which is constructed of three vertical boards, put into the frame from the back. It is signed 'Thomas Smith, Norwich.'

The short trunk has a moulding around the top and bottom and has an arched top door and a shaped base. This is fully decorated with chinoiserie on a black background. Circa 1760.

Additional details: Two side doors. Movement with tapered plates, non friction hour wheel, five wheel train, four pillar construction, anchor escapement, eight day duration.

Dimensions: Outside of surround 36½ in. by 30½ in., dial diameter 24in., hour numerals height 3in., minute numerals height 1⅝ in., total length 57in.

Maker: Thomas Smith, Norwich. Baillie records as before 1769.

PLATE 2

A rare black dial clock. The dial constructed from horizontal boards and black lacquered with gilt numerals. It has outside minute numerals and single stroke minute divisions between two circles with no difference in five minute markings. There is a gilt circle within the hour numerals. Brass hands with a counterbalanced end to the minute hand. The concave sectioned surround has two gilt bands around it and is attached to a back box with salt box style projections. The whole of the case is of simple oak construction.

The eight day fusee, timepiece movement has a verge escapement with tapered plates.

A late eighteenth-century tavern clock by Francis Perigal, Bond Street. It has a white dial and black Roman numerals with triangle five minute divisions. Brass spade hands with the minute hand only counterbalanced.

The long trunk has a shaped base, fancy fretted ears and a trunk door with the top edge following the line of the dial. The original decoration has no raised gesso work except for very slightly raised figures. It is signed, above the door, 'Frans. Perigal, Bond Street.' Circa 1790.

Additional details: *Two side doors. Dial made from three horizontal boards. The hands, although old and of the correct pattern, are probably not original — the hour hand is, in fact, made from an old barometer scale.*

Dimensions: *Dial diameter 19½in., surround diameter 21in., hour numerals height 2¼in., total length 45¼in.*

Maker: *Francis Perigal, New Bond Street, London. Baillie records as 1770, Clockmakers Company 1781, Master 1806, died 1824.*

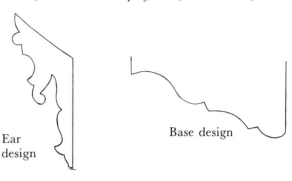

Ear design

Base design

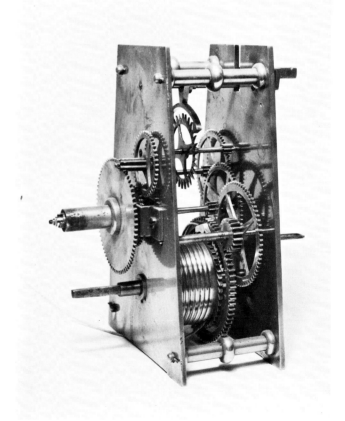

Pillar design

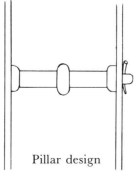

Surround section

This typical tavern clock movement shows the anchor escapement and a five wheel train. The clock winds anti-clockwise and the barrel wheel gears into a large brass pinion. The two lower pillars have tapped holes for the seatboard fixing screws.

Additional details: *Tapered plates, four pillars, five wheel train, four spoke wheels, second wheel with eighteen leaf pinion, barrel with eight turn groove. Friction hour wheel.*

PLATE 4

Right: This fine example of an English cartel clock by Wintmills, London, has a carved case of shell and leaf scroll design. The original water gilding has obviously suffered due to its age.

The silvered brass dial has small Roman hour numerals with outside minute numerals. The minute divisions are single strokes between two circles, without difference in five minute markings. Low down, but above the centre, is the false pendulum aperture and the full signature is below the winding square. The hands are not original and of the wrong design.

This particular clock is fairly unusual in being symmetrical. Circa 1755.

Additional details: *Shallow, concave sectional bezel with soldered and bent over clips to hold a flat glass. Push button sprung bezel catch on left side of case. Dial set ½in. deep from front edge and put in from the back as usual.*

Dimensions: *Height 23½in., width 15in., bezel diameter 8¼in., dial diameter showing 7in. but actually 7⅜in.*

Maker: *Wintmills, London. Unrecorded.*

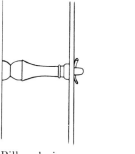

Pillar design   Bezel section

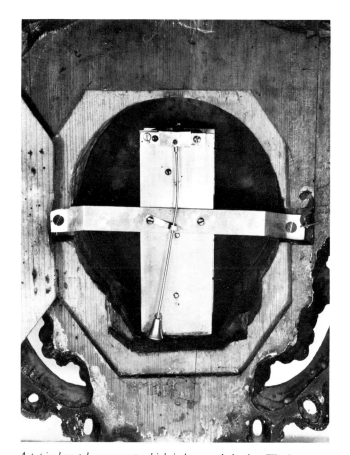

A typical cartel movement which is long and slender. The bar across the centre is screwed to the backplate and in turn screwed to the case. The pendulum bob of the verge escapement is quite small and at the moment is hooked up into a spring loaded catch. The back door is the only access to the movement and is hinged on the left side.

Additional details: *Size of plates 7¹⁄₁₆in. by 2⁹⁄₁₆in., distance between plates 1⁷⁄₁₆in. Verge escapement with plain apron. Small fusee and barrel. Barrel diameter 2in., width 1⅜in. Five elaborate pillars.*

PLATE 5

This early dial clock by Thomas Wynn, London, has a mahogany case with a moulded mahogany bezel.

The silvered brass dial bears close resemblance to the cartel clock in Plate 4, except that this is larger and has triangle five minute divisions. The false pendulum aperture has disappeared and the signature has taken its place. The place name takes the usual position with fine scrolled letters. The winding hole is offset at III. The fancy blued steel hands would have been a similar style suited to the cartel clock. Circa 1780.

Additional details: *Dial feet riveted. Verge escapement. Tapered plates. Four pillar construction. One side door. Flat bottom to box without a door. No projection from box. Dial screwed in from front with four screws.*

Dimensions: *Dial diameter 11 in., bezel diameter 12¾ in., surround diameter 13½ in., hour numerals height 1¼ in., minute numerals height ⅝ in.*

Maker: *Thomas Wynn, London. Unrecorded.*

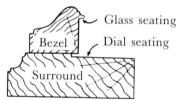

Glass seating
Dial seating
Bezel
Surround

Bezel and surround section

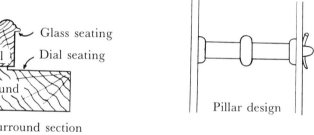

Pillar design

The dial signature although quite worn shows the fine scrolls used in the name with the s in Thos. set higher and underlined. Also shown is the engraver's mistake of a double line on the inner ring of the chapters.

Chapter 2

The Retailers

Throughout the eighteenth century it was customary for the vast majority of clockmakers to buy as many as possible of the parts they required, and so although they were fully capable of making complete clocks many, especially in the cities, were actually clock finishers.

In outlying districts, due to the availability of parts, the clockmakers made more finished clocks by themselves and indeed many made the complete article. At this time there were also plenty of retailers, so it was not difficult to find somewhere to buy a clock.

Virtually every town or village had a clockmaker or watchmaker — or one fairly locally. However the village clockmakers did not always have sufficient work for a full time occupation and many undertook any type of work that came their way, often advertising for different types of work as well. They were not only clockmakers but also locksmiths, braziers, ironmongers, tinsmiths, etc., and also sold any item that was even remotely connected with the trade.

It was inevitable with the flow of the population into cities that the country clockmaker had to move with the times. He began to deal less and less with clocks and so was forced either to take up his allied trades more seriously or move to a larger town where he could obtain more clockmaking work.

Eventually by the end of the eighteenth century most towns had at least one clockmaker and more often two or three, which in turn made it necessary for a person in an outlying district to travel into the nearest town to purchase a clock or have one repaired.

Some of the more prosperous clockmakers in the country travelled around their areas setting up their goods in a hired room in the village inn at a pre-arranged date from where they could sell their clocks and watches to the public. Since the place where a clock was sold was often written on the dial this explains why a clockmaker is sometimes noted as working in several different places at the same time.

Tavern clocks, although made elsewhere as well, appeared most popular in East Anglia, where some makers virtually specialised in this type of clock. One such person was William Mayhew of Parham and Woodbridge who, apart from making a number of watches and longcase clocks in lacquered cases, possibly made more tavern clocks than any other clockmaker (Plate 6).

These clocks were probably made almost entirely by the clockmaker, as it is doubtful that the demand was ever sufficient to warrant the parts being industrially made; even the cases were locally made.

Although virtually all clockmakers were retailers as well, there were also some retailers who did not have any dealings with the manufacture of the clocks at all, and were solely retailers. These were found mainly in the cities and had a wide range of clocks and watches from which to choose, but one could also order a clock to be made specially. Sometimes clocks are to be found with the owner's name on the dial. This happened fairly frequently in the nineteenth century, as is noted in a letter to Thwaites and Reed Clockmakers dated 26 May, 1866, from 32, King Street, Southwark.

'Dear Sir,
    I should like the name 'WESLAKE, LONDON' on the dial but not too large. I suppose they are called block letters.

I remain yours truly
WESLAKE.'

The majority of English dial clocks were bought, even by the country clock-makers, as ready-made items direct from the factories and the name of the retailer appearing on the dial was commonplace (Plate 7). Often the name was put on at the factory in which case the retailer had nothing to do when he received the clock except sell it.

Once clocks could be bought in this way many clockmakers turned to retailing as their main business — undertaking repairs but no manufacturing at all.

It is apparent that the majority of private trade dealt through the retailers and not direct with the factories. It is unlikely that the retailers dealt with anything other than direct payment — hire purchase as such did not exist until late in the nineteenth century, though money-lending did take place throughout the eighteenth and nineteenth centuries, with a statutory maximum interest imposed by the Government of five per cent. Money-lending activities were carried out quite independently of the retailer. Occasionally, however, there would have been deals worked out in which payment was received over a period of time or in some other form than cash.

The retailers however were not just shop keepers; they would have had considerable knowledge of clocks themselves and would often have to deliver purchases to the house, hang them on the wall and set them up, also possibly continuing to call every week to keep them in good order and wind them — a quite commonplace practice as most people were not familiar with the workings of a clock.

Winding was contract work which, for a yearly sum, included the winding and regulation of the clock, the occasional reoil, and any slight adjustments that could be attended to on the spot. A visiting card dated 11 March, 1865 quotes 'BELL & SON, The only survivors of the late firm of Dwerrihouse, Carter, Ogston and Bell. Watch and Clockmakers, 131, Mount St. Clocks wound up and kept in repair by the year. EST 1760.'

Many private houses and most of the banks, offices and churches (Plate 8) had the clockwinder call on them regularly once a week. He carried a selection of keys with him — using one of these in preference to the one with the clock, which was usually missing anyway, a small selection of tools and some oil. If the clock required more attention than he could give on the spot or if it needed overhauling he would then take it back to the shop and the customer would be charged the repair as an extra cost on top of the winding contract. Sometimes the contract would include overhauling but this was only done when a set rotational pattern could be arranged and coupled with a yearly reoiling session. This arrangement usually required the clocks to be wound by the clockwinder every week with a separate visit annually to reoil and check over all the clocks and a set number to be taken away for complete overhaul.

Clocks were, of course, then guaranteed after any repairs and it is probable that one year was the normal period. An invoice for the sale of a three train bracket clock on 28 November, 1882 by M. & S. LYON, 135, High Holborn, states 'We guarantee this chime clock of first class mechanism in perfect order. Any fault with its performance to be certified free of expense. Accident excepted'. It was then signed and certified paid over a 1d. Victorian stamp.

There were, of course, so many clocks to be wound especially in a big city like London that full time clockwinders were necessary and some of the larger firms towards the end of the last century had as many as seven or eight.

Some of the large organisations had literally hundreds of clocks which ranged from three train turret clocks to carriage clocks which all had to be wound, although undoubtedly with such numbers most of them would have been English dial clocks. St. Pancras Station had around four hundred clocks (Plate 9) earlier this century as also did the Bank of England. In fact the winders went to many places which were not normally open to the public. Clocks wherever they were had to be wound and since they were required in most places the clockwinder's day was often full of interest. From the gold vaults of the Bank of England the next stop may have been the Mansion House and then to round off the day he may have finished up winding the Mortuary clock at St. Bartholomew's Hospital. Sometimes there were so many clocks at one place that the winder needed a full day to wind them; for example at the Imperial Institute in Kensington, it took a man eight full hours to wind for which he was paid 12s.6d. about twenty-five years ago.

With the increase in mechanical knowledge and the gradual changeover to electric and battery clocks, clockwinders began to decrease from the 1920s but they have by no means died out and still exist in small numbers even today.

During the time when clockwinders were commonplace back in the nineteenth century the clocks generally were far better looked after and were serviced much more frequently. On the other hand the oil that was used was not as good as today's oil and so congealed more quickly, and with coal fires and smoky chimneys the air was not as clean either. It was therefore necessary to have clocks frequently overhauled and the public accepted this fact in order to protect their treasured possessions. It seems sad nowadays that clocks are not kept up to that standard but are kept going until they are absolutely exhausted of life.

PLATE 6

Right: A late eighteenth century tavern clock with a white dial by William Mayhew. No outside minute numerals; the minute markings are single strokes across a single circle and diamond shaped five minute markings. The brass hands are both original and of quite an elaborate design, although extensively repaired which accounts for their short length. The dial is made from three horizontal boards and put into the moulded surround from behind. It is then pegged onto the trunk with four wooden pegs. The clock is decorated with gilt chinoiserie on a black background. The scene in the door depicts two Japanese workers in front of houses and trees, above which are two birds. The lacquer has been restored on the ear pieces, since the design should be foliage scrolls as in Plate 3. Circa 1785.

Additional details: *Shaped base. Case decorated as normal on the sides. Two side doors with wooden toggles. Hanging hole as usual in the backboard. Uncounterbalanced hands.*

Dimensions: *Dial diameter 24½ in., surround diameter 29in., length 56in.*

Maker: *Suffolk clocks and clockmakers record Mayhew in considerable detail. He was born in 1725, taking up his apprenticeship in Woodbridge in 1741. After completing this, he returned to his birthtown of Parham but returned to Woodbridge to continue his business in 1751. He died in 1791 and was buried at Martlesham.*

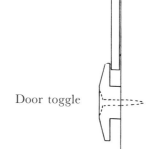

Surround section

Door toggle

The eight day, weight driven movement shows the second wheel on the left hand side with barrel winding anti-clockwise. The intermediate wheel on the motion work is crossed out with three wheel crossings and is mounted on a stud which is conventional practice in tavern and longcase clocks, but not in dial clocks where the pinion has pivots bearing in the plate and a cock.

Additional details: *Anchor escapement. Shorter than usual pendulum with a total length of only 32½ in. Tapered plates. Hour wheel without friction. Five wheel train. Large brass pinion on second arbor. Flat rectangular weight.*

PLATE 7

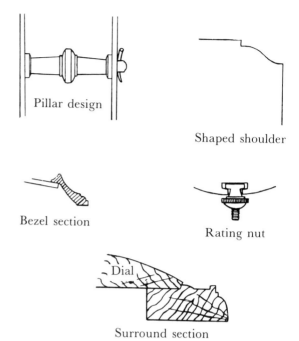

Pillar design

Shaped shoulder

Bezel section

Rating nut

Dial

Surround section

*Above: A striking English trunk dial signed Dwerrihouse, Carter &
Son. As in many of the English dial clocks, this one is signed on
the dial by the retailer. The movement is a factory-made Thwaites
clock.*

 *The dial is made from wood secured to the surround by two screws
through the side locating strips. It is painted with diamond five
minute divisions and is signed 'Dwerrihouse Carter & Son, Berkeley
Square.' The blued steel hands, although heavy in appearance,
indicate on close inspection that they are in fact original. It has a
concave sectioned brass bezel with a convex glass and a very narrow
mahogany surround. The trunk has unfortunately been subjected to
the addition of brass inlay. Circa 1806.*

Additional details: *Bezel lock. Convex sectioned surround.
Circular falseplate on the back of the dial with four dial feet. Flat
trunk moulding. Curved foot base with access door. Two side doors
with glass but probably had sound frets originally.*

Dimensions: *Dial diameter 14½ in., bezel diameter 15½ in.,
surround diameter 16¼ in., length 26½ in., height of hour
numerals 1⅜ in.*

Maker: *Baillie records Dwerrihouse & Carter as 1802-1823 with
Dwerrihouse, Carter & Son as being 1808-1815. Although the
movement number of 3809 suggests that this was made in 1806, it
could been in stock for a few years before it was cased up.*

*A typical two train movement by Thwaites, with shaped
shouldered plates and the number 3809 stamped with
unmatching punches above the bottom edge of the front plate.
The hour and minute tubes and the winding squares are longer
than usual to go through the deep convex wooden dial.*

Additional details: *Steel rod pendulum, 3¼ in. diameter bob
with rating nut let in. Separate striking snail. Anchor
escapement. Five pillars. Winding square 1½ in. long to plate.
Plates 6¾ in. by 4⅞ in. Also numbered in typical Thwaites
fashion on the inside of both barrel caps.*

PLATE 8

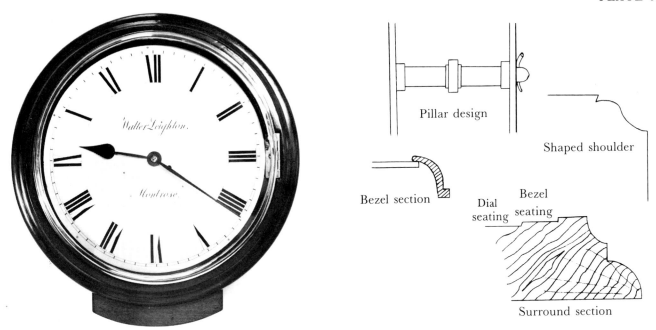

Dial clock by Walter Leighton, Montrose. This interesting dial clock was almost certainly first built into a church gallery. The large silvered brass dial has the maker's signature above the centre and the town name below. The minutes are straight lines between two circles without difference in five minute markings. The reason the dial is considerably smaller than the bezel and shows a gap of about ¼ in. all round is because it has been put into a surround which is too big for it. Both surround and bezel are probably about 1870 but the back box is not at all old and has a solid side door without beading and a back door to allow access to the pendulum. Circa 1840.

Additional details: *Late convex sectioned brass bezel with large hinge and flat glass. Offset winding hole. Three threaded dial feet screwed into the back of the dial.*

Maker: *Recorded 1830.*

Left: This large movement shows the shaped shouldered plates, unusual pillar design and the later style of ratchet wheel made all in the same thickness. The motion work shows the cannon pinion in the centre of the front plate gearing to a wheel on its left: this is mounted on an arbor pivoting between the plates to which is attached the set hand on the backplate. The wheel to the right of the cannon pinion lifts the hammer of the passing strike which sounds one blow at each hour. It can also be seen that the bell stand is unusually screwed to the inside of the backplate.

Right: The back view of the movement shows the cutout shape of the bottom of the plates and the set dial. This is silvered brass with engraved Roman hour numerals and minute divisions and is secured by two screws into the backplate. The blued steel minute hand and brass collet are fitted onto the squared arbor and pinned through.

Additional details: *Non friction hour wheel but a friction cap on the hour hand. Anchor escapement.*

Dimensions: *Plates 7¼ in. by 5¼ in., hour wheel diameter 2⅜ in., set dial diameter 2 in., fusee wheel diameter 2½ in., depth of barrel 3 in.*

27

PLATE 9

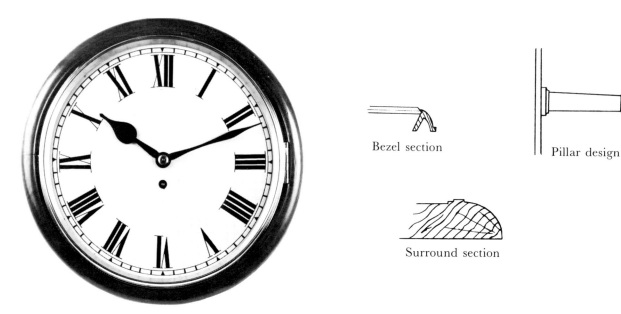

Bezel section

Pillar design

Surround section

This particular English dial clock was typical of those used most commonly in stations, offices and hospitals, etc.

The 12in. white painted iron dial is plain and very clear with bold Roman numerals, triangle five minute divisions and blued steel spade hands. The cast brass, convex sectioned bezel has a silvered sight ring cast in one piece and has a flat glass, bevelled around its edge which is snapped into the bezel. The mahogany surround is also convex sectioned and perfectly plain. This type of clock was probably produced in larger numbers than any other design. Circa 1900.

Additional details: Bezel catch at the back of the surround. One side door on the right hand side which is solid mahogany and rebated. Bottom door with side moulding attached. A fixing plate on either side of the bottom of the case to secure it to the wall. Surround made from one piece of wood.

The movement is also a very standard design with rectangular plates, plain ratchet wheel to the barrel set down low on the left side. Chain fusee. Plain pillars and an anchor escapement. The centre scribed line on the front plate is clearly visible and so are the three large holes for the dial feet.

Chapter 3

The Manufacturers

Towards the later part of the eighteenth century the manufacturers, especially in the large cities, grew more important, often employing thirty to fifty employees, most of whom were skilled or semi-skilled.

The conditions of employment were not acceptable by today's standard: although the employees worked long hours with low pay, they always feared unemployment and so had to be fairly content with what they had. Once a worker was in a job it was paramount that he should keep it, so long-service was common providing the employee's health could last out. There was little consideration to sickness and no retirement plans. A man worked from the age of twelve until he was incapable of doing a day's work, in which case he was lucky to get a pat on the back and a word of thanks for fifty or more years faithful service. He was then told not to come in any more as he was no longer required. This situation continued throughout the century and when a worker was inconsiderate enough to die midweek his pay was docked accordingly. Times were hard for these workers but they were in other industries too, often more so.

Concessions were made which eased working conditions. The Factory Act of 1802 limited apprentices to a maximum of twelve hours work a day. Although apprentices started their time as little more than children, it seems unlikely that actual child labour was used to any great extent in the clock factories even though it was cheap at a farthing an hour in 1817. The main reason for this was probably because most operations in the manufacture of the movements demanded a certain standard of skill which could not be achieved by children.

Many clockmaking factories felt the brunt of the tax on clocks and watches in 1797 and eventually were forced to close or at least cut back. After the tax was repealed it seems as though the factories which had taken up dial clock manufacturing increased production rapidly to take advantage of the improved market.

Manufacturers virtually always held a stock of standard movements which may have been in stock for some considerable time. This probably might explain the situation where a numbered dial clock predates the retailer whose name is on the dial (see Plate 10 for an example). Sometimes the predating can be by several years.

The clock factories usually concentrated on making movements only, the cases being ordered directly from the casemakers. Although many parts used in the manufacture of movements themselves were also bought out they were not mass-produced. Standard parts and most castings were extremely similar from one clock to another, except that they were all finished and assembled as individual items which explains why parts seldom, if ever, are exactly interchangeable on early clocks.

Some factories made all types of timekeepers from turret clocks to watches, although it was normal to keep within slightly closer boundaries than this. They had their standard lines but would also make up any clock to a customer's specification. All orders were made in the same fashion whether the order was for one clock or one hundred. The movements were very individual pieces — pride was taken in their work by both the employers and employees and, of course, there was a compulsory quality to achieve as well. This pride in the finished product and the refusal to accept poorer quality probably started the long decline of the British clock industry.

Foreign imported clocks began to make their mark firstly with the Black Forest clocks which started to appear as early as 1810. These were vastly cheaper and, although nowhere near the quality of English work, were just as effective to the general public as well as requiring few repairs. The timekeeping was adequate for the type of market which they covered and although most were only of thirty hour duration this did not detract from the most popular attraction — the price. In fact, people did not mind having to wind their clocks daily as they probably enjoyed the involvement with their new possessions.

The clocks were imported to England in bulk, often with the dials in separate containers and usually without weights. The movement was then assembled to the dial and the hands and chains put on. The weights were generally made in this country and seem to differ in design from the weights that stayed in Germany.

However, the Black Forest clocks were superseded around the middle of the nineteenth century by the even more popular American ogee clocks and replicas of English dial clocks (Plate 11). The movements of these clocks were almost entirely mass-produced and the quality probably very offensive to English clockmakers. The English public however could not see inside to the movement and if they did it probably did not mean much to them, so the clocks sold on appearance and price only. The price was far cheaper than the English counterpart and the performance was adequate although, again, most were of thirty hour duration. Probably the most important factor in the enormous sales of these clocks was that they looked very good indeed. The cases were well veneered onto rather poorer quality carcases, they were exceedingly well finished from the exterior point of view and sometimes had decorated tablets. The popularity of these American clocks right up into this century finished off the English clock factories which were still endeavouring to manufacture their quality goods. Inevitably most either closed down completely or settled down to repairs as their major source of income.

One factory which survived through all these troubled times, and still exists today manufacturing clocks, is Thwaites and Reed Ltd (Plate 12). The firm was originally founded in 1740 as Aynsworth Thwaites, later becoming Aynsworth and John, John Thwaites and then Thwaites and Reed.

Fortunately the firm's excellent records still exist with many interesting facts recorded about tavern and dial clocks. These records show that probably the majority of repair work and fifty per cent of the new work by Edward Ellicott was carried out by John Thwaites in Ellicott's name. Also that more than three quarters of the new clocks and repairs were carried out for other clockmakers by Aynsworth and John Thwaites. Such records show that the majority of private individuals did not go straight to a factory but tended to deal through other clockmakers who were basically retailers (Plate 13). See also Appendix V.

Following are extracts taken from the order books of Thwaites and Reed which may be of interest. They have been taken at random and have been limited to those relating to dial clocks. Some of the terms and spellings used by Thwaites have changed since the books were kept, so a short explanation follows the extracts.

1780 Feb 5 DWERRIHOUSE, John. A new spring striking diall with 12 in copper plate, made ready to japan.

1781 Oct 22 BRAY. Thos. A new spring diall.

1782 Mar 20 ELLICOTT. A new large spring diall with the minute hand balanced behind, a strong rise and fall to the pendlum and a copper diall plate with hammered moulding at the edge of 1 ft 9 in diameter. £5 15s 6d.

1784 Aug 19 ELLICOTT. Two new spring dialls with flat pendlums £6 6s 0d.

1785 Jun 7 ELLICOTT. A new spring diall to a 12 in Japaned Plate £4 0s 0d.

1785 Aug 17 ELLICOTT. A new 8 day clock with 12 in diall plate, dead scapement etc £6 6s 0d.

1787 Apr 28 ELLICOTT. A new spring diall with a copper diall plate 1 ft 8 in dia. Japaned white with black figures and a gilt moulding round the edge with rise and fall to the pendlum. Fitted up by Messrs Denis Snows in the Strand £6 16s 6d.

1787 EVIL of Bath. To a new spring diall to strike a single blow at the hour with a 2 ft mahogany board painted white with a gilt moulding round the edge and mahogany box at the back.

1787 Aug 1 UNDERWOOD. Robert. A new spring diall in a black case with a 14 in board Japaned black with gilt figures.

1790 Apr 15 CRIBB. William. A new large spring diall to shew through a wainscott and to wind up behind with a swing wheel and pallats and a large bob and with a 2 ft mahogany diall board.

1790 May 5 THOROGOOD. Stephen. A new spring diall to a 16 in board with flat pendlum large bob, to a diall case mahogany board of 16 in dia black and white and round bottom. Delivered to Mr. Drinkall at Porters Key to be shipped on Capt Rowe, The Hope.

1790 Aug 31 VALENTINE. John. A new spring diall with round pendlum and knife edge in a case with 12 in diall board and mahogany ring and glass.

1790 Sept 17 SELBY, Peter. A spring diall with rise and fall to the pendlum, a case to do with 16 in board painted white with black figures made to fit into a hole in the wall.

1791 Feb 24 FLADGATE. John. A new spring diall to a 13 in silvered plate with flat pendlum, etc.

1791 Apr 23 PEACHEY. A new large spring diall with the diall work in a distinct frame with long minute arbor and universal joint to pass through one upright with a copper diall plate of 2ft dia Japaned and to strike a single blow at every quarter. Fixed in the gallery of St. Andrews church.

1791 May 7 SPENCER. William. A new spring diall to a 14 in round plate silvered and with rise and fall to the pendlum.

1791 Jun 9 FIELD. Thos. Bath. A new weight diall in a Japaned case to a seconds pendlum and with large board sent by Wilshires Waggon to Bath.

1792 Jan 23 BUNYON. Robert. To a spring diall with 16 in Birmingham Japaned plate with swing wheel and pallats and flat pendlum.

1792 Jun 29 MASON John. To a new weight timepiece to shew the hours and minutes on a diall of 2 ft diameter and painted and gilt the diall plate and gilt the hands.

1794 Oct 9 HEDGE. Nathaniel. To a new spring dial with 14 in brass plates.

1795 Apr 6 JONES. William. To a new spring diall with best rise and fall and a leaver to set it going in a mahogany case 16 in convex diall board and glass.

1799 Aug LE COQ and Son. 4 spring clocks with 7 in dials in mahogany cases numbered 1619, 1649, 1642, 1744.

1799 Sept LE COQ and Son. 6 spring quarter clocks with 7 in dials numbered 1632, 1726, 1747, 1750, 1742, 1758.

LE COQ and Son weight 2 tune clock, quarters on 8 bells, 12 in round convex dial number 1756.

1800 Feb 8 BECK Christopher (app. Francis Perigal).
To a large spring diall with a 20 in board and gilt moulding in a large mahogany truss case.

1800 Feb 26 CADE & ROBINSON. To a spring diall with 20 in board japaned and gilt moulding in a mahogany case short trunk.

1800 Nov 17 SCOTT and IDLE. To a spring striking diall with 16 in copper diall plate japaned and best rise and fall to the pendlum and brass hands with a mahogany front brass ring and convex glass.

1801 Mar 3 HARRISON. Thos. To a spring diall with brass hands.

1801 Dec 29 WALL John. To a large striking weight diall with 2 feet japaned board in a very large mahogany sweeped case with brass ring and convex glass according to directions sent.

1802 Apr EARNSHAW. Cleaned a spring diall named Earnshaw, stopped up the centre and 3rd wheel pivot holes and set the 3rd wheel deeper.

1802 June 14 LEROUX Jno. To a spring diall with 14 in silvered diall plate, steel hands and in a mahogany case with long trunk and brass ring and flat glass.

1804 May 30 LINDLEY. To a spring dial with brass hands.

1804 Sept 20 BOWEN. Thos. To a spring diall to a 13 in board.

1804 Oct 3 LAMBERT. John. To a spring diall with 13 in Jappaned board in a mahogany case brass ring and flat glass.

1804 Nov 23 MITCHELL AND RUSSELL. To a best spring striking diall with 24 in Jappaned board in a black case brass ring and flat glass.

1843 25 March Mr. MASON Lime Street, 4 spring dialls, 12 inch plate in mahogany cases for St. James' Gt Pollards Row and St. Barts, Cambridge Rd. Bethnal Green.

30 March BRITISH MUSEUM. To make a striking plate and an alarum to the new double diall in the reading room for order of Sir Robt Smirke. To be completed by 6th May.

3 May Rt Honble LORD SEFTON. The best spring clock, 16 inch plate, chains, rise and fall to case to be in the Hall for order of Mr. Hardwick.

13 May GUILDHALL. 12 inch spring diall trunk case to fix in Controllers office £7 0s 0d.

8 June LONDON AND BIRMINGHAM RAILWAY. 12 inch spring diall. chain for engine room, Rugby.

12 June Mr. GATWORD, Hitchin. Spring diall 12 inch plates, 16 in Drum Case outside £6 2s 0d.

23 June COMRS OF THE MODEL PRISON. A large spring diall 10 inch plates, flat rise and fall chains to fusee complete with oak board, bronzed ring glass and box at the back. For order of Major £12 12s 0d.

23 June As above, large spring diall chain with triangle wood plates complete as per estimate £30 0s 0d Pr order of Major.

28 June Mr W.P. ACKLAND. 5% off for cash.

1 August MODEL PRISON, 2 weight noctuaries in wainscott cases. £7. 0s 0d. each.

3 August Major JEBB. A double diall 15 inch flat plates, mahogany boards, rings, glasses pack'd complete £15. 15s 0d.

12 August. Messrs COMBE AND DELAFIELD. Spring diall 10 in flat plate oak, drum case, ring, glass chain complete. Price not given.

17 August EAST INDIA COMPANY. Spring striking dial, 12 inch plate, chain, to Warley Barracks £10 10s 0d.

30 August Mr. FRENCH 12 in double diall convex plate, wall 9 inches.

1844 24 Jan W. BROWN. Spring diall, 12 in plates and cash.

25 Jan Mr. LEWIS The Queens Mews, Pimlico. 12 inch spring diall complete (cash) £5 0s 0d.

15 Jan LONDON AND BIRMINGHAM RAILWAY. 3 spring dialls 12 in with chains £6 0s 0d each.

1844 8 March DUTTON Robt 14 in Grey spring diall flat plate VR Oak trunk case, bronzed ring £4 8s 0d.

27 April BANK OF ENGLAND. Spring diall for 3 foot plate and hand, chain. Oak box to be fitted at the back of the dial (no diall or hands wanted) £12 12s 0d.

One guinea per year to be paid for winding.

23 May MILBANK PRISON. Spring diall 12 in cox plate in mahogany case. £5 0s 0d.

30 May 4 spring dialls, chains 12 in flat top, ditto plates, mahogany cases, bezil rings te chains.

1 June LONDON AND BIRM. RAILWAY. A spring diall, 12 in plate chain in mahog case for order of Mr. Chapman to be sent to stores.

1851 11 Dec Mr. DUTTON. A Gray striking diall C3, 12 in plate engraved 'Record Office' 1 secs pendulum: A short trunk case to do.

1852 6 Jan LONDON AND N.W. RAILWAY COMP. An extra large size spring striking diall 2 ft 6 in flat jappaned plate chain to fusees. A mahog trunk case, brass ring, glass.

16 Feb SURREY NEW PRISON. A spring diall 14 in flat plate chain to fusee. Mahg circular case. £6 10s 10d.

A 12 in ditto £5 0s 0d.

8 April HOUSE OF OCCUPATION. A spring diall 12 in plate in trunk case for the school £5 12s 0d.

2 June A grey spring double dial 18¼ chains, balancing hands, rise and fall 15s 0d. Seat board 2s 0d Total £6 6s 0d. + 17s 0d.

1858 31 July NORTH LONDON RAILWAY. A 12 in diall chains, Mahg case to fixed at Stoke Newington Station.

1859 8 OCT ST. BARTS HOSP. A spring diall 12 in oak case £4 0s. 0d.

1863 3 Dec C.N. TAYLOR. 12 best spring clocks 12 in flat jappaned plates chains to fusees in mahg round cases, brass rings, plate glass polished edges as before £60 0s 0d Packing do.

Explanation of terms used in order books.

BARRELL) BARRIL)	Barrel
BEZIL	Bezel
BRONZED RING	Bronze plated bezel
COX	Convex
DEAD SCAPEMENT	Dead beat escapement
DIALL	Dial
DO	Ditto
FLAT PENDLUM	Lenticular Pendulum Bob
GULLS	Worn grooves
JAPPANED	Painted
LACKERED	Lacquered
LAURUM) ALARUM)	Alarm
LEAVER	Lever
NOCTUARY	Night Watchman's Clock
PALLATTS	Pallets
PENDLUM	Pendulum
PLATE	Dial
RING	Bezel
ROUND PENDLUM	Verge type bob pendulum
SPRING DIALL	Dial clock
STOPPED UP	Rebushed
SWING WHEEL	Verge crown wheel
TE	Abbreviation of complete
WAINSCOTT	A superior quality of foreign oak imported from Russia, Germany and Holland

Several interesting features arise even from this comparatively short list of clocks mentioned. It is also readily apparent that Thwaites worked for some of the very important clockmakers of the time which included Dwerrihouse, Ellicott and Earnshaw.

In the entry of 1780 there is mention of a striking dial clock with a copper dial. Although only a few dial clocks were made with copper dials, which were then painted, it seems that Thwaites did use them fairly frequently in the early dial clock years for double dials and inset dials — another is mentioned in 1782. It tells us that this had a rise and fall regulation which was most commonly used for dial clocks inserted into the wall as often the only access to the pendulum was by removing the dial. These generally large clocks seems to have been very much a Thwaites speciality.

In June 1785 a 12in. dial was made for Ellicott, for which £4 was charged; in August of the same year a similar clock cost £6. 6s. This one had a dead beat escapement and so cost an extra £2. 6s although it is quite possible that the standard of movement may have been higher as well.

The clock made for Evil of Bath in 1787 is an example of a passing strike clock which has a time train only and sounds a single blow on each hour by directly lifting the hammer from the motion work. The fact that the white dial was 2ft. with a gilt moulding round the edge could imply that this was an early mahogany tavern clock, but as there are few descriptions which are complete or accurate enough this can only be speculation. Another example which raises a query is that made for John Valentine in 1790; it seems that the 12in. wooden dial clock had a mahogany bezel, verge escapement and a bob pendulum. However, a wooden dial combined with a wood bezel is normally out of keeping, in which case the lack of a comma combined with the brief note form could make for confusion, and it may have been intended to say a 12in. dial of mahogany with bezel and glass.

For Thos. Field of Bath in 1791 it seems as though the clock mentioned was almost certainly a tavern clock as also was the one for John Mason the following year. In 1794 Thwaites made a dial clock for the well known Colchester clockmaker Nathaniel Hedge.

The clock made for William Jones in 1795 is interesting to note as this was probably a clock inserted into the wall. As such a positioning presented a problem when starting the pendulum after the clock stopped, it was normal practice to make a tiny hole in the dial around the figure VI (Plate 14), through which a piece of wire was poked to give the pendulum a swing. In this case it seems as though a lever was incorporated to do the job instead.

In 1799 the four spring clocks made for Le Coq and Son may not have been dial clocks, especially as they had only 7in. dials. But either way their numbering implies that they were supplied from old stock, numbers 1619, 1649 and 1642 being made in 1793 with number 1744 in the year 1795. The same thing appears to have happened with the following entry for six spring quarter clocks, as number 1632 was made six years previously with numbers 1726, 1747, 1750 and 1742 being made in 1795 and number 1758 in the year 1796.

It is worth noting the entry for 28th June, 1843, which implies that cash speaks as loudly as it does nowadays (also in the entries for 24th Jan 1844 and 25th Jan 1844).

The entry for 8th March, 1844 has written VR, a frequently used feature painted on the front of the dial in bold letters standing for Victoria Regina. The following clock for the Bank of England gives a winding fee of one guinea per year.

In several entries, when the words 'best spring diall' are used, it would appear that different grades of movement were available; in the entry for 2nd June, 1851 the breakdown is quite precise. The fusee chains were $18\frac{1}{4}$ in. long and were probably priced up per inch, and so, with the rise and fall mechanism and balancing the hands, cost an extra 15s., the seatboard costing 2s. These amounts being added to the basic movement cost of six guineas.

The final entry of 1863 shows the mention of bezels with presumably bevelled glasses which would have been in a cast bezel with sight ring made in one piece.

Wages at this time appeared to be extremely stable. Again the fine records of Thwaites and Reed are used in the following list of wages paid, chosen at random over a twenty-three year period.

Date	Total Wages Bill	Total Number of employees	Max. paid to any one person	
1828 22nd March	£46.11s.8d.	37	£2. 1s.11d.	Total of 40 employees. Three presumably sick. Boy paid 5s.0d. Average about £1.10s.0d.
1828 29th March	£54. 3s. 5d.	38	£2. 4s. 0d.	
1830 20th March	£38. 7s. 2d.	32	£1.16s. 0d.	

Date	Total Wages Bill	Total Number of employees	Max. paid to any one person	
1832				
17th March	£23. 9s. 6d.	19	£1. 16s. 0d.	Boy paid 4s. 0d.
1834				
15th March	£21. 13s.7d.	18	£1. 16s. 0d.	
1836				
26th March	£23. 15s. 5d.	20	£1. 16s. 0d.	
1840				
29th February	£27. 0s. 8d.	23	£2. 5s. 0d.	Boy paid 5.s 8d.
1844				
23rd March	£28.18s. 4d.	18	£2. 0s. 0d.	
1848				
25th March	£22. 1s. 3d.	15	£2. 0s. 0d.	
1851				
15th November	£21. 1s. 8d.	15	£2. 0s. 0d.	

It can be seen from these figures that wages were virtually stable and in some cases actually decreased. The staff too decreased from forty employees down to fifteen. This suggests that there was a decrease in the volume of work available, leading to the laying off of staff rather than failure to recruit more. The boy being paid was almost certainly an errand boy, not to be confused with an apprentice. It was customary then and up till early this century for an apprentice to be paid very little. In 1927 an errand boy for the same company was paid 12s. 6d. per week, but on taking up an apprenticeship it meant a drop in wages to 10s. per week. Qualified clock repairers were at this time averaging about £3 per week or about 1s. 3d. per hour.

A substantial amount of stock was held during the boom years and although it is difficult to decide from Thwaites and Reed's lists exactly what basic description applies to which type of clock, the following list shows approximately the amount of stock held.

STOCK LIST 1 January, 1815

COUNTING HOUSE

Spring clock and case	Probably a dial clock
Spring clock and case	ditto
Timepiece with alarm	
2 small cases	
1 ditto	
3 cases	
6 small cases	
9 cases	
4 ditto	
4 spring clocks	Probably dial clocks
11 spring dial movement	Dial clocks
5 best eight day movements	Probably dial clocks
17 Common ditto	ditto
3 Best spring movements	ditto
46 Common ditto	ditto
7 cases	
6 ditto with clocks	
2 timepiece cases	
Water gilt case and movement	Probably a cartel clock
Alarm clock and case	
4 cases	
2 spring quarter clocks and cases	

continued

1 spring clock and case	Probably a dial clock
12 eight day clocks	Probably dial clocks
7 spring clocks in white	
IN HOUSE	
Timepiece and case	Could be a dial clock
PARK PLACE	
Small clock	
Small eight day clock	
AT HAWLEYS	
Spring clock and case	Probably a dial clock
MAKEPEACES	
Spring clock and case	Probably a dial clock
WORKHOUSE	
Spring dial and case	Dial clock
GALLINGTON'S SHOP	
1 spring clock and case	Probably a dial clock
Spring clocks	Probably dial clocks
Ditto in white	
Spring dial in case	Dial clock
Ditto Alarm	Dial clock with Alarm
10 clocks	
UPPER SHOP	
1 best 8 day movement gilt	
3 spring movements	Probably dial clocks
1 timepiece	
6 clocks	
COPPER SHOP	
Spring dial and case	Dial clock
UPPER LARGE SHOP	
Old clock	
BRASS ROOM	
200lbs Lead	
295lbs Yellow Brass	
103lbs of new ditto	
67lbs Copper	
Pewter and solder	
351lbs of Wrought Brass	
2207lbs of Cast Brass	
BACK PREMISES	
Straw and Corn	
Chaise and harness	
Cart and harness	
Horse	
Saddles	

Total value of stock at this date £2,517.11s.9d.

From these figures we can deduce that Thwaites and Reed had in stock at this point possibly around 120 dial clocks. Some were movements only and some were complete, although empty cases were also probably in stock. Of course many other types of clock would have been held in stock at this time as well as dial clocks. It is also very likely that some would have been out on loan to companies having their dial clocks repaired. This was a quite commonplace arrangement which lasted through until about 1960 when dial clocks began to become a bit scarce and increase in value.

Left: A fine black dial clock. See Plate 25 for details.

It is interesting to note that a very large amount of metal was in stock, including three different types of brass. The fact that the list mentions 103lbs of new yellow brass implies that the 295lbs was secondhand and was either melted down or used again as sheet or rod, etc. This could perhaps explain some of the rough falseplates used on the back of wooden dials made by Thwaites and Reed around this date. They often had rough edges, unaccountable holes, patches of engraving or perhaps were an odd shape.

By far the greatest type of brass used was cast brass, of which the firm held nearly 1½ tons — about half of the total metal stock mentioned and enough in weight to make over five hundred dial clocks. There is, however, no mention at all of iron or steel of which they must have had substantial stocks.

The firm also had their own transport, included in the stock list, and would have made their own deliveries by horse and cart.

The company was a large concern, and although the £2,500 worth of stock may not seem much by present day standards, it would probably, as a direct money equivalent,be around £100,000 nowadays, perhaps even more. This, as with any stock list, represents the actual cost price and would not take into consideration the selling value.

PLATE 10

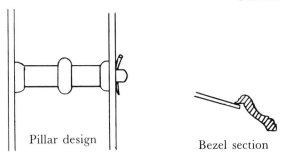

Pillar design

Bezel section

Dial

Surround section

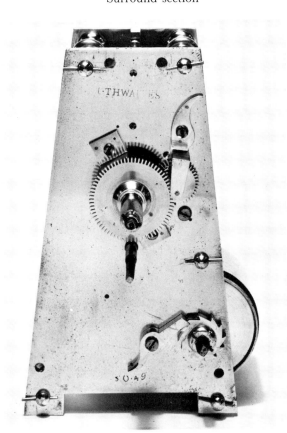

This early trunk dial clock is signed on the convex wooden dial 'Yonge & Son, Strand, London' and is recorded as after 1820. Yet the movement was made by John Thwaites in 1803. This would most likely be explained by the movement being old stock. The dial is from a separate piece of wood to the surround and has small Roman numerals with triangle five minute divisions. The brass hands are the typical design of Thwaites clocks. The cast bezel of concave section has a plastered in convex glass and a bezel lock secured to the bezel itself. The mahogany case has a long trunk with a veneered front inlaid with boxwood edging following down the sides through to the curved foot base. The curved bottom door has the usual cockbead around its edges and there is a fine moulding separating the trunk from the base. The side ear pieces are rather large and more crude than usual but almost certainly original.

Additional details: Side door on right hand side with veneered side strips. Very deep convex to dial.

Dimensions: Surround diameter 17in., dial diameter 14 1/8 in., hour numerals height 1 5/16 in., dial 7/8 in. thick in the centre.

Maker: Britten records George Yonge as 1798 at 131, Strand; Yonge succeeded the celebrated Holmes (the shop was pulled down to make the entrance to Waterloo Bridge in 1824). George Yonge and Son, 156, Strand, 1823. However, Baillie records George Yonge as 1776-1815 and George & Son, London 1820-25. Thwaites is known to have made twenty-seven clocks for George Yonge.

The 8in. high tapered plates are another typical Thwaites sign with the stamp of I (J) THWAITES on the top of the front plate and numbered 3049 with unmatching stamping set on the lower edge of the front plate, the right hand top edge of the front plate and inside the barrel cap. The ratchet wheel is the early form in that it is thicker at the centre. The two holes at the top are unusually close together for the pillars on the dial plate, the other two dial pillar holes being at the bottom near the outside edges. The anchor escapement has a very long pendulum and an escape wheel of only twenty teeth. Five pillar construction.

39

PLATE 11

This type of clock was typical of the kind of American clock which cornered the market in the mid-1890s. This particular example is better than most, with scalloped edges to the surround and a trunk which has a shaped window through which the small brass pendulum bob can be seen. The decoration is very finely executed in many colours with flowers and leaves on a black background with gilt lines around the edges. The zinc, painted dial has bold Roman numerals with the minute divisions between two circles with dots at five minute intervals. The blued steel hands are stamped out with a fairly elaborate design. The bezel is spun brass with a silvered sight ring and a flat glass. This type of case is not as deep as with English fusee dial clocks and has a very small side door, low down the trunk to enable the pendulum bob to be hooked on. The movement is timepiece only with thin square skeletonised plates with the mainspring not enclosed in a barrel as it is with fusee clocks. As is normal with most American clocks, there are no side doors through which to view the movement.

PLATE 12

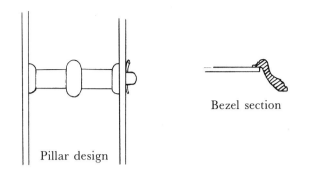

Pillar design

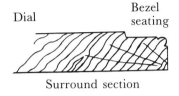

Bezel section

Dial

Bezel
seating

Surround section

An early nineteenth century wooden dial clock signed 'Thwaites and Reed, Clerkenwell, London'. The flat wooden dial is made in one piece of wood with the surround, and has typical brass hands of Thwaites design with the minute hand counterbalanced. The signature has been overpainted and in doing so the scroll at the end of 'Reed' has been mistaken for an 'e', a common mistake with overpainted signatures. The concave sectioned brass bezel has a large hinge which is dovetailed and soldered into it; the lock is missing but a latch passes through the extremely narrow mahogany surround. The box has a rounded bottom with a conventional door except that it has a turncatch instead of a lock. The side door has strips around its edge and is high up to give access to the top of the pendulum. Circa 1823.
Dimensions: *Dial diameter 14⅛ in., surround diameter 15¾ in., hour numerals height 1½ in.*

The tapered plated movement has a cutout on the bottom edge, a deep ratchet wheel and a central barrel directly underneath the fusee. The hour wheel pipe and the winding square are very long so as to pass through the thick wooden dial. It has a friction hour wheel with a friction collet on the hour hand as well. The plates are stamped on the front, above the ratchet wheel, T & R 6982 and the number is repeated on the back of the rectangular falseplate in paint. The movement also has an anchor escapement and is of five pillar construction.

PLATE 13

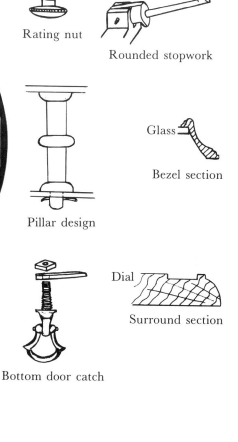

Rating nut

Rounded stopwork

Pillar design

Glass

Bezel section

Bottom door catch

Dial

Surround section

Pendulum rod

Above: A clock extremely similar to Plate 12 with a wooden dial signed 'C.H. May, Swanwick' and Roman numerals. The minute markings are between two circles with triangles at five minute intervals and diamonds at the quarters. The brass hands are identical to those in Plate 12 except that the minute hand has no counterbalance due to the smaller size of this clock. Again the bezel is concave sectioned and has a narrow wooden surround. The dial and surround are made from one piece of wood (as with all one piece dials it is pegged onto the box). The box has a rounded bottom with a larger than usual access door with a turncatch and is unusually hinged from the left hand side. The bottom only is veneered but not the sides. Circa 1817.

Dimensions: *Dial diameter 12in., surround diameter 14¼in., hour numerals height 1⅛in.*
C.H. May was a repairer in Swanwick by the river Hamble, close to Bursledon near Southampton, who died in the 1960s. He is known to have put his name on dial clocks that he worked on. The true maker is Thwaites and Reed.

Left: The movement is also very comparable with that in Plate 12. Note the position of the pillars, the same shaped plates, position of the barrel and the ratchet wheel. The plates are 7¾in. high and 4¾in. across the bottom. The escape wheel is screwed onto its collet with three screws. The movement is stamped just below the winding square T & R 5809; the number also repeating itself on the inside of the barrel cap. The stopwork and pendulum rod are finished to a higher degree than normal.

PLATE 14

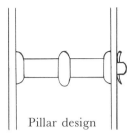

Pillar design

Bezel section

Surround section

Above: An inset dial clock made by Thwaites, which now has a back box and is hung as a conventional dial clock. The signs of an inset dial are clear: a square arbor in the hole just above the signature and S — F for regulation of the clock through the dial, a tiny hole just above the figure VI through which was put a wire to swing the pendulum. So that the pendulum was not pushed out of the crutch pin when this was done, it was normal practice to make a hole in the end of the crutch pin through which a taper pin was put. The flat iron dial has diamond five minute markings and Thwaites brass hands with the minute hand counterbalanced because of its size. The dial is screwed into the mahogany surround with four screws, screwed into brass plates set into the wood. The heavy convex sectioned, cast brass bezel previously had a bezel lock but the clock is now latched through the back. Circa 1818.

Dimensions: *Dial diameter 18in., surround diameter 21in.*

Movement: *The eight day gut fusee movement is mounted on a seatboard and has tapered plates with the rise and fall regulation block mounted on the top. It is of five pillar construction with an anchor escapement and a shaped pendulum rod with the bob screwed directly to the rod without a rating nut. This bob fixing is usually incorporated on inset dials. The front plate is stamped underneath the minute wheel bridge T & R 6147.*

Left: This shows the back box from the left hand side. The obvious signs that the box is an addition are that it is made of oak (note the grain against that of the surround) and that it has no pegs. The door is secured by only one hinge and is on the left hand side of the case instead of the right. The back of the case is fixed onto the sides as opposed to the sides going the full depth and being fixed onto the back. The method of the backboard showing from the sides was only ever conventionally used in early salt box case construction.

PLATE 15

A large English dial clock of exceptional quality. The deep convex wooden dial has diamond five minute divisions and blued steel hands with heart shaped tips. The bezel is convex sectioned with a very deep convex glass and has the bezel lock riveted on. The surround is of dark mahogany and is a separate piece of wood to the dial which is secured by screws through the locating strips which are in turn pegged onto the back box. The trunk is well veneered and is inlaid with brass. It is further decorated by a darker strip along the length of the front edges and a turned moulding above the curved foot base. The ears are of the highest quality, carved from solid mahogany and supported from the back. Circa 1824.

Additional details: *Large bottom door with cockbead 6⅜ in. by 5⅝ in., two side access doors with a glass in each but these were probably originally wooden, silked sound frets. The clock was hung by two hanging plates secured on the backboard which have since been replaced by a central hanging hole in the backboard itself.*

Dimensions: *Dial diameter 16¼ in., bezel diameter 17¼ in., surround diameter 19¼ in., height 31in.*

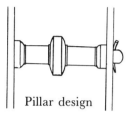

Pillar design

Rating nut

Bezel section

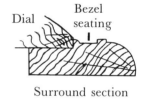

Dial   Bezel seating

Surround section

Right: This front view shows the stamp of Thwaites and Reed, the manufacturer, which has been double stamped T & R and numbered 7389 with unmatching number punches. The ratchet wheels are of the early design with the centres thicker than the teeth.

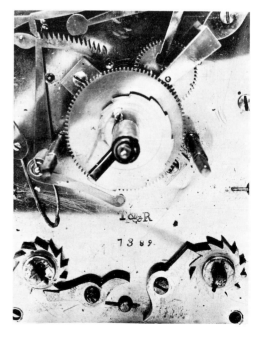

This shows the backplate of the striking movement which has concave shouldered plates, shaped backcock and line fusees. The counterbalance for the minute hand is on the backplate on the extended arbor of the intermediate motion work pinion and passes behind the crutch.

The movement has five unusually shaped pillars and an anchor escapement with a long flat steel pendulum rod with a deep lenticular shaped pendulum bob of 3⅜ in. diameter and 1¼ in. thick.

PLATE 16

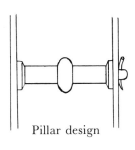

Pillar design

Bezel section

Surround section

An English dial clock by the well known maker Frodsham, London. The flat iron dial has triangle five minute divisions, typical shaped Frodsham blued steel hands and is signed 'Frodsham, Gracechurch St., London'. The convex sectioned bezel has a convex glass and a bezel lock set in the mahogany surround. The back box has a rounded bottom with the usual access door but with a turncatch and not a lock. It also has a right side door with side strips as conventional. Circa 1845.
Dimensions: *Dial diameter 12in., surround diameter 14¼in.*
Maker: *According to Baillie, John, grandson of the first William Frodsham, was born in 1785, was admitted to the Clockmakers Company in 1822 and worked in Gracechurch Street. He also had a partner named Baker. John Frodsham died in 1849.*

Left: The fusee movement has shaped shouldered plates, shaped backcock, four pillars and an anchor escapement. The backplate is stamped in full, with the Frodsham manufacturer's stamp, just below the pivot hole of the fusee.

There are two large holes and three small holes in the backplate which are not being used at the moment. This is because the movement was originally made with a pendulum fixing block which was screwed to the plate and had a steady pin on either side. The pendulum was secured by a large brass knurled knob screwed into the fixing block. When the pendulum was free the large knob was screwed, out of the way, into the plate which accounts for the large hole on the extreme left.

It is also supposed that these fixing blocks were only used on bracket clocks, but it is fairly common to see the evidence of them on dial clocks, though virtually all have since been removed. Most were probably taken off as the pendulum fouled the block if hung on a wall that was not perpendicular. The only remaining spare hole is in the centre at the bottom edge of the plate and this is repeated on the front plate. This was used when manufacturing the movement: the plates were pinned together for marking out and drilling the pivot holes and were then separated and the holes used for the pins were seldom filled up.

45

PLATE 17

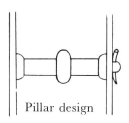

Pillar design

Bezel section

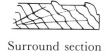

Surround section.

Private Collection

Above: This English dial clock is signed 'Grant, Fleet Street, London' but the movement was manufactured by Handley & Moore. The brass silvered dial has small Roman numerals, triangle five minute divisions and fine blued steel spade hands. It is signed, in typical Grant fashion, in a semi-circular plane. The concave sectioned bezel has a flat glass and a lock set in the left hand side. The surround is very narrow and is convex sectioned and pegged onto the back box which has a rounded bottom with an access door hinged on the left side, and a turncatch. Circa 1815.

Additional details: *The four outside screw holes in the dial secure the dial to the surround. The four screws in the dial centre secure the movement to the dial.*

Dimensions: *Dial diameter 12in., bezel diameter 13⅜in., surround diameter 14in., hour numerals height 1³/₁₆ in.*

Maker: *John Grant was born in 1796 and was admitted to the Clockmakers Company in 1817, and was master five times between 1838-67. He left Fleet Street in 1852 and for some years carried out a pawnbroking business. He died in 1882 aged eighty-five.*

Handley & Moore were both apprentices of John Thwaites and carried out their business nearby in 39 Clerkenwell Close from 1798. G. Handley died in 1824 and John Moore carried on as John Moore & Sons from 1824-42.

Right: The movement has shaped shouldered plates cut away at the bottom edge and has the four dial feet riveted as a permanent fixture to the front plate. The wheel train is planted in a straight line except for the barrel which is set high up on the left side. The front plate is stamped 21 above the barrel ratchet wheel and Handley & Moore 3521 just below the stopwork screw.

Chapter 4

Manufacturing

The sub-division of labour into various production processes in the horological trade increased tremendously from the mid-eighteenth century until it reached its height in the mid-nineteenth century. Some of the allied trades were as follows: manufacturers of balances, barrels, cases, dial plates, escapements, fusees, hands, keys, pallets, pinions, springs and wheels to name but a few. As well as these there were also the finishing trades such as gilders, polishers, carvers, dial painters, glaziers, locksmiths and all the dealers who supplied the raw materials. The network of these different trades was enormous, each playing its own individual role towards the final manufacture of clocks.

Dial Clocks

Cases. Virtually all manufacturers of English dial clocks bought their cases ready-made and completely finished. Up until about 1870 nearly all of these cases were made entirely from mahogany. Later, mainly due to cost, oak became very much more popular and occasionally simulated walnut was used.

Some of the cases were carved (Plate 18) with perhaps an oak leaf surround, and many trunk dials had carved ear pieces. Some were very crudely done while others were of exceptionally fine quality. The wood used for carving did not usually differ from the basic type used for the main construction. For rounded bottom cases, usually only the base was veneered in mahogany; the surround and sides being finished in the solid wood. The trunk dials were veneered on the front of the trunk as well as the base. The exceptions to general veneering were that the octagonal dial clocks had a veneered front surround and often sides as well; and the drum dial which was veneered to the front and completely around the sides. The grain of the veneer usually followed through over the door. Trunk dials were often inlaid with either other types of wood in the form of stringing or crossbanding, brass for stringing and pattern forms, or mother-of-pearl which was usually used for circles and occasionally for designs. Plate 19 shows a decorative use of mother-of-pearl very similar to that seen on tea caddies and writing boxes of the period.

Bezels. Apart from the later spun bezels, they were cast in yellow brass to the appropriate design from a wooden pattern. The rough cast bezels were then turned in a lathe when the details of the moulded shape were brought out. After turning and finishing the hinge and lock were fitted or, in the later type, a catchplate which went through the surround. The hinges were dovetailed in and then soldered, often being pinned as well. The locks were generally screwed onto the bezel with two screws. After these were fitted, the glass was put in and then the completed bezel was polished before being given a finish of bronze, gilt or lacquer.

Locks and Keys. Most dial clocks have only two locks, one for the bezel and one for the bottom door; except on better quality clocks the side door usually has a turn catch. The locks were quite simple requiring only a single lever key and consisted of an iron bolt attached to a brass plate with an iron cover plate, though the bezel locks did not always have this. The keys usually had a bow shaped end and were ringed along the shank itself.

Glass. The glass fitted to the bezels could be either flat or convex. Early glass is usually detectable by trapped air bubbles or ripples in the surface, sometimes only visible from a certain direction, for glass manufacture was seldom perfect in the early nineteenth century. The main reason for the imperfections was that the glass could not be cooled in a uniform manner and large sheets often warped. The molten glass was poured from the furnace onto a table and was confined to certain dimensions by adjustable iron rulers. It was then smoothed out to an even thickness by manually-operated rollers and transferred to the annealing furnace where it took about ten days to cool. Convex glass was poured into a mould, generally of a deeper convex than replacements available today. On cast bezels with sight rings attached, the flat glasses had their edges bevelled by grinding and polishing. The bezel was then slightly heated so it would expand and the glass was sprung into the recess. When the bezel cooled and contracted it gripped the glass on the bevel and so prevented it falling out.

Dials. Three basic materials were used in the making of dials: brass, wood and iron.

Brass dials were made from wrought brass and finished on the front surface, with the back either left untouched or occasionally roughly cleaned off. The dial was then hand engraved with numerals, maker's signature, town name (Plates 20 and 21) and sometimes with decoration on the centre. Next hard black wax was melted onto the engraving and it was then silvered. Although several methods of silvering were used, the general method was to rub onto a cleaned dial a paste mixure of silver dissolved in cyanide and mixed with salt. This was washed off and the treatment repeated using cream of tartar, followed by a coat of lacquer. The silvering eventually wears through and many dials are now brass coloured, but resilvering is a simple process and ready-made silvering pastes are now available. The dial feet were either riveted to the dial and virtually unnoticeable from the front, or were secured by four screws with polished heads.

Wooden dials were either made in one piece with or separately from the surround, and were either flat or convex. Generally the dials were turned from a solid slice of mahogany and not jointed at all. They were then gessoed with a chalk based plaster and painted on top. To the back of the dial was attached a falseplate with pillars for attaching the movement and the centre was sometimes chiselled out to allow freedom for the motion work.

Iron dials had the dial feet riveted on the back first and were then painted on the front only.

Proportions for dial painting differed not only from maker to maker but also throughout the dial clock period. It is interesting however to note that Thwaites had a general rule at one stage. 'Proportions for painting dials without minute figures. The divisions and hour figures to take $\frac{1}{3}$ of the whole plate. The divisions to be $\frac{1}{4}$ of that or $\frac{1}{3}$ of the length of the hour figures. The hour figures to be near $\frac{1}{6}$ of their length in thickness. The minute divisions to be $\frac{1}{4}$ of their length in thickness. The space between the hour figures and minute divisions to be taken out of the figures and divisions an equal part from each. The space between the parts of the hour figures viz. between the two strokes of the 2 to be $\frac{2}{5}$ of the thickness of the figures.'

Hands. The early hands were drawn on paper, the drawing stuck onto a metal sheet and holes drilled where spaces were to appear on each hand. A piercing saw was

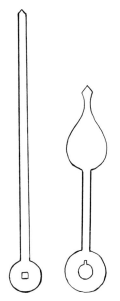

Straight minute hands and spade shaped hour hands such as these were manufactured in large quantities and are frequently found.

then passed through each hole and the shape fretcut out. After the design was cut the edges were filed square with a needle file and faceted on the top surface (Plate 22), and the back sometimes ground down towards the tip to reduce the weight. The hands were then polished and blued in a tray of sand or brass filings. The blueing of hands is a heat treatment in which the sand is heated while the hand rests on the surface. The hand would become straw colour, then blue and as soon as an even colour was reached the hand was removed and quenched in oil.

Later hands, with less elaborate designs, were stamped out from thinner metal and could be made in large numbers, designs were few and used by virtually all manufacturers. The most common design was a straight minute hand and a spade hour hand, see left.

Plates. These were cut to shape, the surfaces cleaned up, and then pinned together on the top and bottom edges and filed up. The front plate was marked out for the wheel train and the position of the pillars. To ensure accuracy pilot holes were drilled straight through both plates while they were still pinned together, after which they were separated and the pivot holes opened out to the correct size. As a general rule the small pinning holes were not filled and can usually be seen.

Wheels and Pinions. Early wheels were made from cast brass blanks which had the crossings already cast into them. These were machined and the teeth cut on a wheel cutting machine. The later wheels were made from standard brass blanks and after the teeth were cut the crossings were either fretcut or stamped out. There were also two methods of producing pinions; one was to use a solid rod which was turned down to form the arbor with the pinion being cut on a pinion cutting machine. The arbor was then finished and the pivots turned and polished. The other method was to use pinion wire. This was a long length of pinion which was marked out for the true pinion position and the rest chiselled off to form the arbor. This method was much preferred by clock manufacturers and was used on most standard size pinions. The wheels were attached to the pinions either by being riveted onto a brass collet which had already been fitted and turned on the arbor, or by direct riveting onto the pinion which had been turned down to form a shoulder (movement in Plate 23).

The wheels and pinions were then set up in a depthing tool and adjusted for a perfect mesh. The ends of the tool were used to scribe the positions of the pivots onto the plates.

Fusees. The fusee is the device which evens out the power of the mainspring from the fully wound to unwound position. The tapered form enables the chain to pull on the smallest diameter when the mainspring is fully wound and works up to the largest diameter by the end of the week.

Fusees were cut on special fusee engines to the correct contour and were matched to the mainspring power. Ready-cut fusees made from cast brass blanks were probably produced by individual fusee makers who supplied most of the dial clock manufacturers and they in turn had only to fit the arbors and finish them.

Fusee chains. The manufacture of fusee chains was an entirely separate industry largely carried out by outworkers paid on a piecework basis. The links were stamped out, riveted together and then hardened and polished. The full details and history of this fascinating industry is described in a remarkable book by Allen White called *The Chain Makers*.

The chains had two hooks fastened to them, one for the fusee and one for the barrel. It was a time consuming task to make these and, although the labour used was cheap, the chains were far more expensive than gut or wire. Throughout most of the dial clock period the movements were graded and chains used only on the best grade clocks, the cost of the chain being calculated by the inch.

Gut Lines. These were used especially in early clocks and were made from sheep's intestines slit into strips. A number of these strips were then twisted together and sulphur treated. Unfortunately the quality of gut lines has deteriorated so much so that nowadays wire line is usually used as a replacement on dial clocks, although wire line was originally used on lower grade clocks when they were manufactured this century.

Castings. Most of the brass components were cast for dial clock movements including wheel blanks, cocks, pillars and fusees. The larger manufacturers probably cast most pieces themselves but inevitably castings of all kinds were readily available at the foundries. Yellow brass contained a percentage content of copper and zinc and after it had been melted in the furnace it was poured into sand moulds. Since castings were usually quite rough a good deal of finishing was involved, which explains why the castings were generally quite a lot larger than the finished articles.

Pendulums. Pendulum bobs were made from two spun brass discs with ground flat edges. A hole was made in one disc and a recess for the flat of the rod. Then the rod was bound with thin oiled paper and the two halves of the bob placed together over it, after being tinned on the inside. The bob shells were bound together and molten lead was poured in through the hole in the back shell. When cool the rod could be removed and the bob finished and polished.

Tavern Clocks

Weights. Most weights used on tavern clocks seem to have been lead and were probably rectangular or oval in shape (see left), but since so many have been replaced with longcase cast iron or lead circular weights it is difficult to say whether or not some of these were originally used. The weights were sand cast and the hooks inserted while still molten, though occasionally lead was poured into brass shells, usually oval, with a centre thread cast into the weight. The top hook was also made in brass and screwed onto the thread.

Lacquering. Virtually all tavern clocks were lacquered on a black background. Other colours are exceptionally rare and usually suspect as, generally speaking, the use of other colours (for instance on longcase clocks) predated the tavern clock.

The lacquering of the cases is not perhaps as romantic as is sometimes thought, in fact the lacquer is not genuine Oriental lacquer at all. Oriental lacquer was spread over a very thick layer of plaster on top of cheap wood. It was often more than ¼ in. thick and, although imitated by European artists, the original lac from a lacquer tree was not used on clock cases at all. English case artists used an oil-based paint for backgrounds with the raised work either built up with gesso, a mixture of chalk and size, or a made-up composition of the artist's own recipe. The front and dial were sized where they were to be gilded and gold powder was brushed on. Burnished gilding involved a slightly different process in that it had to have a gesso base; gold leaf was then put on and finally rubbed with an agate stone to obtain the burnished finish. Silver, too, was used to a great extent on the linework but smoke and dirt have now turned this a yellow colour which is difficult to tell from gold.

The sides of the case were not considered to be so important, and generally these were decorated with bronze powder mixed with gold size, which explains why the sides always deteriorate to a greater extent than the front. Similarly, comparing the quality of workmanship between the front and the sides, it is very likely that the master craftsmen decorated the front, leaving the rest to apprentices. The finished work was finally polished over to protect the case and then waxed to bring it up to the desired degree of polish.

Three original tavern clock weights, typical of the type generally used. The rectangular lead weight at the top has a shaped top; the two oval weights are lead filled and brass covered. The loop on the top of each weight, through which the 'S' hook passes, screws onto a thread set in the lead and secures the top cover plate.

PLATE 18

A carved English trunk dial clock in mahogany. The surround is decorated with leaf scrolls and flowers with matching ear pieces and a carved surround to the trunk glass. The trunk itself is veneered on the front and base onto solid mahogany.

The flat iron painted dial has long Roman numerals and dots at the five minute divisions. It is signed 'Jones, New Town' in two different styles of lettering and has moon hands.

Additional details: One access door on each side, aperture on top of box probably originally with a silked sound fret, curved door in the base has the side strips attached to the case itself instead of the door. Plain half round moulding to trunk. Spun bezel with plastered-in sight ring and latched through surround for catchplate. Circa 1875.

Dimensions: Hour numerals height 1¾in., dial diameter 12in., height 29½in.

Maker: Since the name is so common in Wales it is difficult to be definite. However it could be David Jones, Horse Market, Newtown 1856-90.

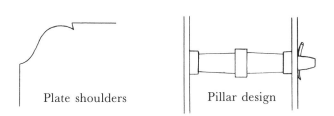

Plate shoulders   Pillar design

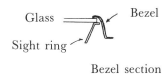

Glass   Bezel

Sight ring

Bezel section

Right: The hour striking fusee movement is of only average quality but has the interesting feature in the position of the dial feet holes. The frontplate has a projection at the bottom to take the lower dial foot hole and the other dial holes are very near the edges. The normal position for dial feet are at the 2, 4, 8 and 10 positions but here they are more or less at 3, 6, 9 and 12. Note also the disappearance of the tail on the clicks and the ratchet wheels with the same thickness centres — signs of a late nineteenth century clock. The plates are 6⅞in. by 5in. and have shaped shoulders with a cutout on the base.

PLATE 19

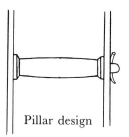

Pillar design

Glass

Bezel and sight ring
section

Dial seating

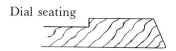

Surround section showing
deep dial seating to take
sight ring

*Above: An attractive circular dial clock with a flat surround,
chamfered at the edge. The front veneered with mahogany in sections,
coinciding with the mother-of-pearl inlaid circles. The inlaid line
between the circles is pewter. The flat, painted iron dial has dot five
minute markings and blued, steel fleur-de-lys style hands. It is
signed in three different styles of lettering 'Ball & Edwards, NEW-
ST; Birmingham'. The bezel is of an early spun type with a very
shallow convex and a plastered in sight ring with a flat glass. Circa
1860-70.*
Additional details: *Very small bottom door without side strips but
bordered by a gauged line. Two side doors.*

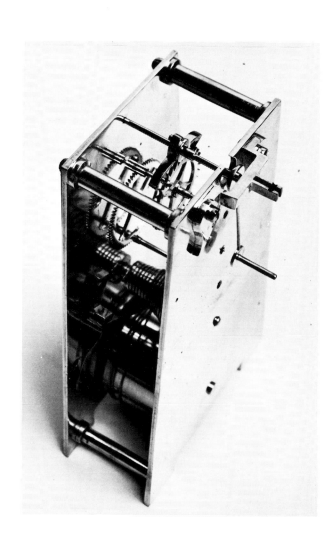

*Right: The movement has some peculiar early features such as the
tall tapered plates, 8¼ in. high, cut out at the bottom. The straight
line wheel train including the barrel has shaped cocks. However, it
also incorporates the signs expected of a clock of this period, including
the long pinions. ratchet wheel with the same thickness centre and
the late style of the pillars.*

PLATE 20

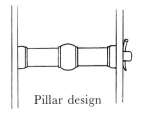
Pillar design

Bezel section

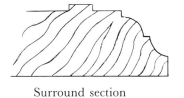
Surround section

Above: This large late eighteenth century English dial clock has an excellent, well proportioned brass silvered dial. It has outside minute numerals with minute divisions between two circles and triangle five minute markings. There are also two other engraved lines, one on the extreme outer edge and the other within the Roman hour numerals. The winding hole is engraved around its circle and has an engraved cartouche of leaf scrolls enclosing the signature 'Conyers Dunlop, London'. There are four steel screws with polished heads screwed through the front to secure the movement to the dial. The hands are replacements but probably in the correct style. The clock has a heavy, concave sectioned cast brass bezel and a mahogany surround. The salt box back has a projection of the backboard on both the top and bottom and has one side door and a bottom door both with locks and moulded side strips. Circa 1790.

Dimensions: *Minute numerals height 1in., hour numerals height $1^{15}/_{16}$ in., dial diameter $17\frac{1}{2}$ in., bezel diameter $19\frac{1}{4}$ in., surround diameter 22in.*

Maker: *Conyers Dunlop, London 1790-93.*

Right: This shows the dial feet permanently riveted to the frontplate, the shaped top on the pallets and the pendulum fixing block on the backplate. The crutch pin has a small hole drilled at the end for a pin to keep the pendulum in position. Four pillar construction. The stop work has been replaced as the original square fixing hole is in the frontplate and the position has been shifted.

PLATE 21

Left: This early dial clock has a brass silvered dial with outside minute numerals, single engraved circle within the hour numerals and minute divisions between two circles with triangle five minute markings. It has a concave sectioned wooden bezel with the lock set into the left hand side. The surround is also concave sectioned and is screwed directly onto the mahogany salt box style back. It has a side and bottom door with side strips and a projection of the backboard at the bottom only.

The movement has tapered plates, four pillars and a verge escapement. Circa 1785.

Dimensions: *Dial diameter 11in., bezel diameter 13⅞ in., surround diameter 15in., hour numerals height 1in., minute numerals height ½ in.*

Maker: *William Gostling, Diss, recorded between 1774-1791.*

This photograph shows the detail of the town name of Diss. The engraving is typical of many town names of this period with the horizontal hatched lines, although the semicircles are not usually incorporated.

PLATE 22

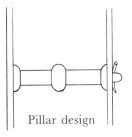

Pillar design

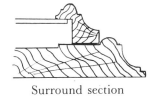

Surround section

Private Collection

This clock has a fairly simple silvered brass dial with outside minute numerals, small Roman hour numerals and dot minute divisions. It is signed 'Chas. Penny, Bristol'. The hands are original and blued steel. The mahogany bezel is of concave section and has a matching surround. The salt box back is unusual in being virtually fourteen inches square instead of rectangular. The backboard projects at the bottom only and is constructed to overlap the sides slightly and is then rounded off. The doors are not central but towards the back, measuring only 5 ⅝ in. by 2 ¼ in., which is quite small for this size of clock. Circa 1795.
Dimensions: *Minute numerals height ¹³/₁₆ in., hour numerals height 1⁷/₁₆ in., dial diameter 15 ⅞ in., bezel diameter 17 ¾ in., surround diameter 20 ⅛ in.*
Maker: *Charles Penny was the son of James Penny, silversmith and clockmaker of Bath, and was apprenticed to James Burr in July 1772. He is recorded between 1772-1801.*

Right: The rack striking movement has rectangular plates without any cutouts, a nicely shaped intermediate motion wheel bridge and very pronounced centres to the ratchet wheel. Both barrels project well below the bottom edge of the plates. Anchor escapement, five pillar construction. The movement is mounted on a seatboard which has been cut away to take the projecting barrels. A long square headed bolt is screwed into the centre pillar, which is 1 ⅜ in. up from the bottom of the plates, through the case and seatboard. Apart from this fixing it is also conventionally pinned onto the four dial feet.

PLATE 23

Left: An early painted iron dial clock. The dial has small hour numerals with the minute divisions between two circles, triangle five minute marks and diamond markings at the quarters. It is signed 'Massey, Bridge Road, Lambeth'. It has its original fine blued steel hands. The concave bezel has a convex glass and original bezel lock. The mahogany surround is very narrow, typical of early nineteenth century dial clocks, and has a rounded bottom box with an original turncatch on the bottom door. Circa 1825.

Dimensions: *Hour numerals height 1⅛ in., dial diameter 12in., bezel diameter 13⅜ in., surround diameter 13⅞ in.*

Maker: *John Massey appears to have worked at the Strand from 1810-23 when he moved to 40 Bridge Road, Lambeth until 1835.*

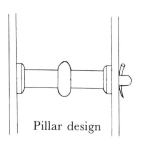

Pillar design

Bezel design

Surround section

A very conventional movement with tapered plates cut away at the bottom and the wheel train laid out in the normal fashion with the fusee, centre wheel, escape wheel and pallets set on the centre line. The third wheel is slightly offset to the right and the barrel planted to one side. It has an anchor escapement and is of four pillar construction.

Chapter 5

The Tavern Clock

The tavern clock, or Act of Parliament clock as it is more widely called, possibly started its life as early as 1720. It may well have been a progression from the very rare black dial clock. This particular clock was fairly large with a dial diameter of between fourteen to twenty four inches (Plate 25). The numerals were gold leaf with outside minute numerals and large Roman hour numerals. The surround also had a couple of gilt bands around the mouldings and the hands were brass with the minute hand counterbalanced. The whole clock was lacquered black and had a salt box style back box. Salt box cases of this early date would have had projections of the backboard at both top and bottom and the side and bottom doors were large and hinged from the backboard. The movements of these clocks had tapered plates, verge escapements and were of eight day duration.

The first true tavern clock was very large and had a square dial with a low half round shape on top to form an arch (Plate 26). The trunk was fairly short and would be expected to have a cushion shaped base. Between the trunk and the dial were the fretwork ear pieces formed from the front panel of the trunk and bearing the signature moved up to this space (Plate 24), though it was still written in one line. The actual decoration remained similar, the dial itself having large outside minute numerals and being decorated in the corners with gold leaf, vase or flower decorations (Plate 27). On the corners of the surround was a single leaf pattern decoration and the fretwork ear pieces under the dial were attached separately. The trunk itself remained basically the same as its predecessor.

The first major change in tavern clock design came when the dial, although retaining the same shape at the top, became slightly deeper at the bottom and the signature moved up to this space, though it was still written in one line. The actual decoration remained similar, the dial itself having large outside minute numerals and being decorated in each of the four corners with gold leaf, vase or flower decorations. On the corners of the surround was a single leaf pattern decoration and the fretwork ear pieces under the dial were attached separately. The trunk itself remained basically the same as its predecessor.

Following this, the appearance changed considerably by the simple alteration in which the bottom corners of the dial curved inwards and down to meet the trunk and any ear pieces were discarded (Plate 30). There was now less room for the signature, so this was concentrated into two lines and a concave moulding was added below the dial. The shape at the top of the dial remained but the top was often ornamented with two gilt wooden finials (Plate 28). The shape of the base also altered, being deeply moulded, and continued in this style for the rest of the tavern clock period.

Square and shield shaped dials were generally constructed from three vertical boards glued together. The dial was then put into the surround from the back and secured by wooden strips nailed down. In turn the surround was pegged onto the side boards of the trunk. The front trunk panel butt joined onto the sides so that the end grain of the wood was not visible from the front. The base, moulded on the outside only, had the joints covered at the front by the bottom trunk moulding which showed the end grain at the sides.

At this stage, around the middle of the eighteenth century two other styles made their mark. One was the hexagonal dial and the other the bulbous base, quite often found together.

Hexagonal dial tavern clocks were usually in lacquered cases with either white or black dials. The figures were gilt on a black background or black on a white background. Occasionally they were also made in oak and then veneered in walnut with solid walnut mouldings and, normally, black dials (Plate 29). The trunks had broken arched top doors, small ear pieces and moulded bases. The lacquered examples sometimes had a bulbous base which had straight sides to the trunk and then bulged out onto a circular bottom. The bulbous base, however, was used on the later circular dials but these are few.

Around 1760 circular dial tavern clocks were introduced, appearing first with black dials (Plate 31). The dials were usually constructed of three horizontal boards with the surround usually built up onto the dial itself. The numerals became slightly smaller although the outside minutes still remained. The trunk, although actually remaining the same length *overall,* appeared to be much longer, though it was only the visible part that became longer due to the dial shape becoming smaller. The trunk door also altered, with the top of the door following the line of the surround and now there was no moulding around its edge (Plate 32). The ear pieces were fairly small and the deeply moulded base predominated. The lacquer work became much simpler with less and less raised gesso. Signatures, between the surround and the trunk door, were in two lines following the line of the surround and were bordered by foliage leaves flowing up into the ear pieces.

Within a short time the dials also became white (Plate 33) and, at the same time, flamboyant brass hands appeared although there were limitations on the size of the hands to avoid an increase in weight. Whereas with plainer hands the counterbalance was not essential, with fancy pierced hands it became compulsory.

Occasionally the trunk doors on the circular dial tavern clocks were decorated with prints which were as wide, though not as high, as the door itself (Plate 34). The print was lacquered and decorated with very fine gilt leaf and foliage scrolls above and below. These prints enhance the beauty of the clocks tremendously and one wonders why they were not perhaps used more often; they virtually always depict people in either country or tavern scenes (Plate 36) and some of them appear to be quite well known paintings or subjects.

During the latter years of the lacquered tavern clock, within the last quarter of the eighteenth century, the style known as the teardrop trunk or keyhole trunk appeared (Plate 35). This design is extremely attractive but obviously more difficult to make, so they were never common though the shape continued through the mahogany tavern clock and Norwich clock stages. The trunk door on such a clock followed the line of the outside of the trunk and did not have a moulding around it, nor did it have ear pieces.

About 1790 or thereabouts lacquered tavern clocks gradually declined and gave way to mahogany clocks. These were better quality and made with sharper lines than the earlier clocks since the wood offered more scope to the case maker. Dials were usually white and minute numerals had become very much smaller and eventually disappeared altogether. The hands still remained brass and if the clock was signed at all it was on the dial centre. The trunks had fairly plain ear pieces but were often veneered with flame mahogany veneer in one sheet following right through into the base which was still deeply moulded and later became convex, sloping back to the wall. An additional feature of the base was that it either opened completely or had a smaller door; this was extremely useful for regulation when the rating nut disappeared below the trunk door level.

During the hundred years it was fashionable the movements of tavern clocks changed hardly at all. They are virtually always timepieces only, with an occasional passing strike and, very rarely, a two train strike. The timepiece movements had tapered plates with four pillars and an anchor escapement and either a four wheel train winding clockwise or a five wheel train winding anti-clockwise. The duration fluctuates widely from about five days to one month but the majority run for between seven to ten days. It seems as if there was very little attempt to make them a standard eight day duration as with other clocks of the period and therefore the wheel trains are seldom the same. All tavern clocks appear to be weight driven on a double line and the weights most usually, if original, are oval in shape and either bare lead or brass covered lead. Sometimes the movements incorporated a passing strike. The hammer was lifted directly from a pin on the intermediate motion wheel which let it drop when the pin passed, and so sounded one blow on a bell at every hour. This arrangement of striking was very easy to incorporate since there was no need for an extra train and the arrangement only consisted of the hammer, hammer arbor, bell and bell stand. It was therefore used in most clocks over the years and especially in nineteenth century skeleton clocks. The full striking tavern clock movements are extremely rare and desirable and have rack striking with the train on the left hand side. It is curious to note that with the few clocks that have come to light all have had a plugged hole in the dial where a timepiece winding hole would normally be situated. At first sight it appears that the movement had been changed, but it is more likely that such a dial was made up to take a normal timepiece movement and the maker plugged the hole in the first instance when he decided to do the unconventional. Certainly the few strikes available show nothing to deter from their originality, have no dial feet holes in the front plates and show the tavern clock characteristics of few turns on the barrel and the correct distances between the plates.

Following the tavern clock, around the first quarter of the nineteenth century, came a very similar type of clock generally called a Norwich clock or East Anglian wall clock (Plate 38). Both names are misleading and suggest that this was the only place they came from; in fact they were found all over the country, although they seem to have been most popular in the counties of Norfolk and Suffolk. Except on very odd occasions tavern clocks were expected not to have a bezel, but these Norwich clocks did have a bezel which was usually wood. The dials were a lot smaller, usually ranging from twelve to sixteen inches, and at first were silvered brass and later ones painted. Most of the dials either had very small outside minute numerals or often none at all. The hands were usually blued steel and tended to copy the longcase styles of the period. The case usually had a slide off hood which was round topped and little bigger than the dial itself. The trunk was straight sided or teardrop shape and, if the former, had a shaped design to the top of the door and either a moulded or convex base. Mahogany veneer was used on the trunk, base and also on the bezel itself as this was flat and not usually moulded. It was often inlaid with boxwood and other woods and crossbanded on the edges of the door and the corners.

The movements were often full strikes and closely resembled a longcase movement with the usual distance between the plates and fairly long arbors. The weights were often rectangular, sometimes rounded off at the bottom towards the back to get as much duration as possible. To increase duration the pulley was sometimes set inside the top of the weight into a channel and had a removable centre which could be pulled out from the front.

Since even the smaller ones were quite large, tavern clocks tended to be situated high up on a wall, well out of the way of bustling people. They were used therefore in large places like churches, halls and, naturally taverns, and were made large so as to be visible from a distance. Today there are many in perfectly ordinary homes, on wall spaces barely large enough to take them yet, even though cramped, they still fit perfectly into the surroundings.

The advantages of the tavern clock over other clocks of the period was that it was robust, readily visible and had a simple mechanism. With its weight driven movement, anchor escapement and long pendulum it was an extremely accurate timekeeper which was more than adequate for normal usage. The movement was affected little by changes of temperature and took smoke and dirt in its stride. The main disadvantage, however, was the lacquerwork on the case which did not take too kindly to being knocked about and dry atmospheres. Present day central heating is not at all good for lacquering and humidity control is virtually essential. Lacquerwork on most of these clocks has suffered to some extent, sometimes simply through bad restoration. Another easily and commonly damaged area is the hands which have often been repaired many times or replaced completely, mainly because of the absence of a bezel and glass which would have offered some kind of protection. Fairly often the bases have been replaced — due to the weight falling through the bottom of the case — and repaired with a board to make the base chisel shaped but, with virtually all these clocks, such a repair is entirely wrong in style. Ear pieces are another commonly damaged feature and are seldom repaired but often removed. As they make a natural point at which to lift the clock, but are not at all strong, it is fairly obvious how such damage occurred. Otherwise, tavern clocks have borne the times well and few other clocks have escaped marriages the way these have, basically because there was never sufficient quantity to swop around movements and dials. Again, they did not change hands as frequently as other clocks, since they tended not to belong to individuals but were owned by companies and, if they belonged to a public house, might well form part of the fittings and fixtures. Until recent years they were not considered very saleable due to their size and appealed only to a small number of people who intended to put them up in places similar to those from which they had originally come.

As I have already said, the tavern clock is perhaps more often named an Act of Parliament clock because of the tax imposed on clocks and watches in July 1797. The original Act of Parliament granting to His Majesty certain duties on clocks and watches was hand-written on a scroll. Part of the scroll is shown opposite.

As can be seen it is extremely difficult to read, so for that reason the whole of the text is given in Appendix I.

To sum up the very lengthy Act, it imposed a duty of 5s. on every clock, 10s. on every gold watch and 2s.6d. on every silver or other metal watch. The appointed assessors had to have a notice at every place where a clock or watch might be used to require its occupiers to make a list of all clocks and watches held by them within fourteen days. If the householder neglected to make out the list, the assessors had the right to assess him by any information they could obtain; this assessment was final unless proved wrong. If an omission was found in a list then the assessors could charge double the duty as a surcharge on top of the normal rate and the assessor was entitled to keep half of the surcharge. It was intended that the first assessment should be made for three quarters of a year from 5th July until 5th April and thereafter yearly, although the actual payments were quarterly. The penalties for not delivering a list or declaration, or for not declaring the owning of a clock or watch, were heavy, the fine being £10 for every offence. The duty, however, did not extend to clocks that were sold for less than 20s. or to the royal family, ambassadors, the House of Parliament, hospitals or churches. Pawnbrokers, dealers and makers of clocks and watches were exempt but had to register and pay an annual licence (Plate 39). The fee was 2s.6d. in the City of London, Westminster, Mary-le-Bone, Saint Pancras or Southwark, but for some reason was only 1s. elsewhere. The penalty for not registering was £5.

However the Act was very difficult to enforce and led to a catastrophic decline in the horological trades. After intense lobbying it was repealed, nine months after it had been enforced and at the end of the three quarter period on April 1798.

Most Gracious Sovereign

We your Majesty's most dutiful and loyal subjects the commons of Great Britain in parliament assembled towards raising the necessary supplies to defray your Majesty's public expences and making a permanent addition to the public revenue have freely and voluntarily resolved to give and grant unto your Majesty the duties hereinafter mentioned and do most humbly beseech your on to the public revenue have freely and voluntarily resolved to give and grant unto your Majesty the duties hereinafter mentioned

PLATE 24

This very early tavern clock has large gilt Roman numerals, minute divisions between two circles without difference in five minute markings, and large outside minute numerals. It is decorated with leaf scrolls on the bottom dial corners and signed in one line at the base of the dial. The brass hands, although old, are probably not original. The surround is convex sectioned and has faint traces of the single leaf decoration at the corners. The trunk itself has a break arch topped door with a replacement moulding of the wrong design. It has large side ear pieces, excellently decorated with leaves and fruits, which are certainly perfectly original even though the top trunk moulding originally carried on round the sides. The cushion shaped base, although basically correct, has been subjected at some time to alterations.

The movement has a five wheel train, four pillars and unusually shaped tapered plates. It is driven by its original tapered weight. Circa 1735.

Dimensions: *Width of surround 29½ in., height of surround 36in., total height 60½ in., hour numerals height 2⅞ in., minute numerals height 1⅝ in.*

Maker: *Abraham Perinot, London.*

Private Collection

PLATE 25 (shown in colour on page 36)

A fine example of a black dial clock. The dial is made from three horizontal boards as with tavern clocks and is put into the surround from the back. It is simply marked with large gilt Roman numerals, an outside minute band and triangle five minute divisions. Brass hands have heart shaped tips; the minute hand is counterbalanced. The pine surround is decorated with two gilt bands.
Dimensions: *Dial diameter 22in., surround diameter 28¼in., hour numerals height 2¾in., length of salt box back 24½in.*

Right: Side view showing dial construction and how it fits into the surround. The salt box back is unusually fixed to the dial with two locating pieces cut from the solid top and bottom, which enter the holes in the vertical side strip. The other side is then secured with two conventional pegs. (Here the locating pieces are out of their correct position.) The side and only door runs the height of the back box and is fitted with a lock. Movement is eight day fusee with verge escapement and tapered plates.

PLATE 26 (shown in colour on page 62)

The earliest style of tavern clock with a virtually square dial surround and arched top. The dial has large gilt Roman numerals with large outside minutes and minute divisions with no difference in five minute markings. The brass hands have arrow shaped tips and both minute and hour hands are counterbalanced. The horizontal construction of the dial is unusual; normally in this shape of dial the boards are vertical.

The signature of John Dewe, Southwark (the J appearing as an I) is on the trunk itself which is constructed with the ear pieces in one board across the top jointed at the top corners of the door. The criss cross designs indicate the lower part of the ears have been broken off in the past. The clock has also lost its (probably cushion shaped) base. The trunk door is unconventional in not having a moulding around its edge, a feature which normally only occurs with circular tavern clocks. The lacquer work is exceptionally fine on the surround corners, below the signature and in most of the area of the trunk door. The lock area has

Private Collection

been damaged with the addition and removal of two locks and a turncatch. Circa 1730.
Dimensions: *Actual dial diameter 23½in., surround height 30in., surround width 30½in., height without base 56½in., hour numerals height 3½in., minute numerals height 1⅞in.*
Maker: *John Dewe, Gravel Lane, Southwark, was an apprentice in 1726 and member of the Clockmakers Company 1730-64.*

Pillar design

Dial

Surround section

Above right: The movement is typical of most tavern clocks, except for the plates which are less of a taper than normal, being 3¼in. wide at the top and 4in. at the bottom over a height of 7in. It has four pillars, anchor escapement and a five wheel train with a large brass pinion on the second arbor. The extra heavy lead weight is tapered oval, though the clock has a normal wheel train and a duration of just over eight days.

PLATE 27

This early tavern clock has gilt Roman numerals and bold outside minute numerals with a gilt outer circle. The minute divisions have no difference in the five minute markings and only the lower corners of the dial are decorated with vase and leaf scrolls. The signature takes up the full width of the dial and is written in a single line. These brass hands are original except for the tip of the minute hand which has had the final three inches replaced and would probably have been a design matching the heart shaped tip of the hour hand. The surround has single leaf decoration on its corners which has now quite faded and is barely visible, though the trunk has retained its original lacquer very well. The door has a moulding around it and the trunk terminates in a cushion shaped base. It is possible that this clock originally had ear pieces but if so they have been missing for such a long time as to erase any trace of them. Circa 1740.

Additional details: *Dial constructed of three vertical boards, original lock and hinges.*

Dimensions: *Surround width 31in., surround height 36in., full length 60½in., hour numerals height 2⅞in., minute numerals height 1¾in.*

Maker: *Richard Duck was born in London in 1711 but was in Ipswich by 1731. He died in 1762 having been primarily a watchmaker.*

Right: This movement has unusual shaped plates for a tavern clock with concave shoulders about two thirds of the way up. It has typical motion work with an uncrossed hour wheel with friction cap and the intermediate wheel with three crossings mounted on a stud. The five wheel train has a large brass pinion on the second arbor and an uncrossed escape wheel which certainly appears original although most unorthodox. The barrel has eleven turns on the groove and there are five pillars — more than usual; the extra one is not visible but is on the left underneath the hour wheel.

PLATE 28 (shown in colour on page 70)

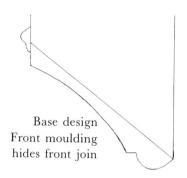

Base design
Front moulding
hides front join

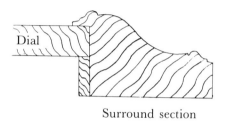

Dial

Surround section

This shield dial tavern clock has a conventionally marked out dial but with triangle five minute divisions and decoration on only the lower two corners of the dial. It has a fine elaborate signature with the 'w' in Matthew written more like an 'n' which is fairly common (see also Plate 31). The dial surround is surmounted by two spherical gilt wooden finials, a traditional feature of this shape of dial. The hands are quite fancy and both have counterbalanced ends. The dial surround slightly overhangs the top trunk moulding and the trunk itself has a rather small door, bordered by a concave sectioned gilt moulding. Circa 1765.

Dimensions: *Actual dial diameter 24 ¼ in., width of surround 30 ½ in., height of surround 37in., total height 58 ½ in., hour numerals height 3 ⅛ ., minute numerals height 1 ⅝ in.*

Maker: *Matthew Worgan, Bristol 1754-94.*

Right: The movement appears to be substantially later than the case although there is no evidence other than indications which suggest early Victorian. The plates are rectangular in shape and all the motion work wheels are uncrossed. The five wheel train has a large pinion on the second arbor which is steel instead of the usual brass.

Private Collection

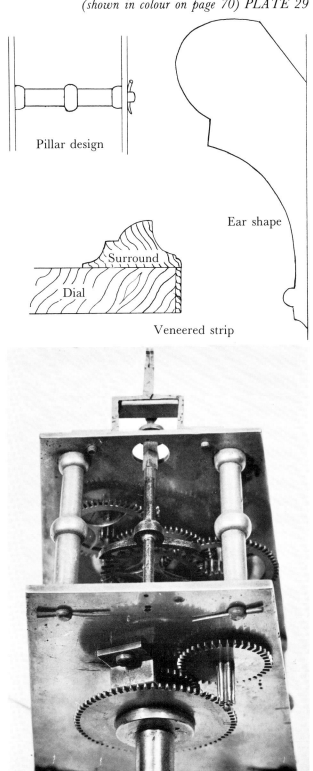

Pillar design

Ear shape

Surround

Dial

Veneered strip

An unusual walnut veneered clock with an octagonal dial. The black dial has Roman numerals, large outside minute numerals and no difference in five minute markings. The hands, although basically original are in bad condition and several sections have been replaced. The dial construction is of two horizontal boards cut to octagonal shape with the surround built up with mouldings applied on top of the dial. The raw edges of the dial are then veneered over. The trunk has a long, broken arch topped door with a moulding around its edge and is walnut veneered with an inlaid border. The ear pieces are very simple and applied to the sides of the case behind the top trunk moulding. The base is chisel shaped but almost certainly a replacement. Circa 1760.

Dimensions: *Actual dial diameter 23 ½ in., surround diameter across the flats 28 in., total height 59 ¾ in., hour numerals height $2^{15}/_{16}$ in., minute numerals height $1^7/_{16}$ in.*

Maker: *John Harrison, Norwich. Second half of the eighteenth century.*

Right: The movement has tapered plates, four pillars and an anchor escapement. It has a five wheel train and uncrossed out motion wheels. This movement is typical of most made in the second half of the eighteenth century.

PLATE 30

Left: A shield dial tavern clock with the lower dial corners concaved in to meet the trunk; because of this the signature has been concentrated into two lines. The dial remains virtually unchanged from earlier clocks and is still decorated on the corners and has the same dial layout. The dial is seated on top of the concave top trunk moulding, and the trunk still retains the moulding around the door. Lacquering has by this time become just a shade less detailed with more background showing in the door and less gesso work. The base has changed to being deeply moulded and decorated with the usual flower and leaf scrolls. Circa 1775.
Maker: *Owen Jackson, Cranbrook and Tenterden 1767-1783.*

PLATE 31

A circular dial tavern clock. The black dial is conventionally written but has new hands, although conventional in style. The signature is now on the trunk itself, contained in two lines following the line of the surround. The 'w' in Daws is written like an 'n'. The trunk door style has altered with the top edge following the line of the dial surround; there is no moulding around its edge. The lacquer on the door shows more of the background than earlier clocks and there is very little raised work. Circa 1760.
Maker: *Thomas Daws, Northampton, 1745, died 1773.*

This shows the method of mounting the movement on a seatboard, hanging hole through the back of the case and the two side access doors. The pendulum hangs well below the level of the bottom of the trunk door. As with most tavern clocks the trunks are barely long enough to accommodate the pendulum.
Additional details: *Tapered plates, five wheel train with the second wheel on the left hand side, ten grooves on the barrel.*

Shield dial tavern clock by Matthew Worgan. See Plate 28 for details.

Below: Octagonal dial tavern clock by John Harrison. See Plate 29 for details.

Below: A black dial tavern clock by William Stevens. See Plate 32 for details.

*Above: Lacquered dial clock
by Thomas Lee. See Plate 33
for details.*

*Above: White dial tavern
clock by John Wright. See
Plate 34 for details.*

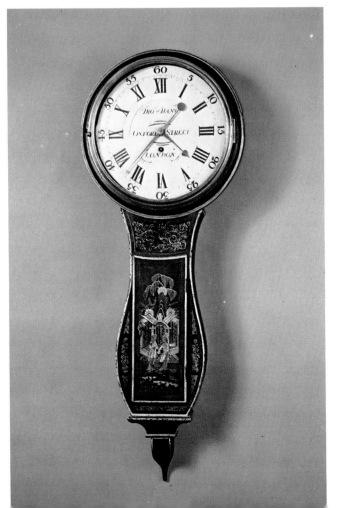

*Late teardrop tavern clock by
Thomas Dane. See Plate 35
for details.*

PLATE 32 (shown in colour on page 70)

A fine circular black dial tavern clock in original condition. The gilt numerals and outside minutes are now beginning to decrease in size although the minute divisions still have no difference between the five minute markings. The dial is made from three horizontal boards and has original brass hands except for the counterbalance on the end of the minute hand. The ear pieces have the original lacquering of leaf design, between which is the signature following the line of the dial and the top edge of the door. There is no moulding around the door, and in fact the only moulding on the entire trunk is at the top of the base to hide the end grain where it joins the trunk. Circa 1775.

Dimensions: Dial diameter 24in., surround diameter 28in., hour numerals height 2½in., minute numerals height 1¼in.

Maker: William Stevens of Gloucester and Cirencester was a member of the Clockmakers Company from 1775-1812.

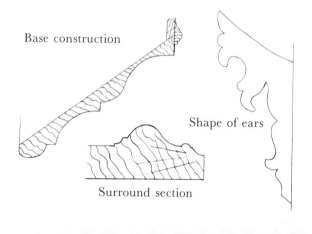

Base construction

Shape of ears

Surround section

Right: The movement has tapered plates with a four wheel train consisting of a very large diameter barrel wheel with 144 teeth gearing into the centre pinion with seven leaves. The barrel wheel also has six spokes as against four in the rest of the train and three on the motion wheels except for the hour. The holes in the bottom pillars are used for the seatboard screws securing the movement to the seatboard which is in turn nailed to the case.

This is a good example of a late lacquered tavern clock. The white dial has fairly small outside minute numerals with the minute divisions as strokes across a single circle. Three horizontal boards make up the slightly convex dial including the simply moulded surround. Hands, although crude, are undoubtedly original and there is a brass protection plate surrounding the hand centre and winding hole. The ear pieces are now much plainer in design and the lacquer, although quite well executed, has no raised gesso work at all. Circa 1790.

Dimensions: *Dial diameter 24in., surround diameter 27¼in., hour numerals height 2½in., minute numerals height 1⅛in., total length 57in.*

Maker: *Thomas Lee, Potton, Bedfordshire 1796. This clock was recently found only ten miles away from where it was made about 180 years ago.*

Private collection

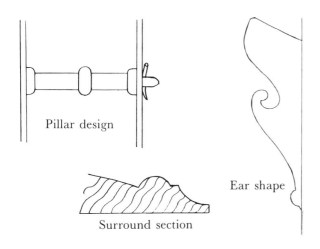

Pillar design

Surround section

Ear shape

Left: This movement has tapered plates with four pillars. It has a five wheel train and winds anti-clockwise. At the top of both front and back plates and also at the bottom is a small pin hole used for pinning the plates together when the clock was made. Also the centre line and the scribed circles are clearly visible on the front plate as also are many repairers dates.

73

PLATE 34 *(shown in colour on page 71)*

A superb example of a perfectly proportioned and decorated tavern clock. The white dial has mellowed down to a tobacco colour with outside minute numerals and dot minute divisions. Brass hands have heart shaped tips and the minute hand extends to the counterbalanced crescent moon shaped end; the winding hole is covered by a brass dust cover pivoting on a single pin. The surround is turned in one piece with the dial which is made up from three horizontal boards and is secured to the top of the trunk by four iron pegs, which are frequently used in tavern clocks as well as wood. The ears are of a very fancy design and the trunk door is decorated with a print. The trunk terminates with a deeply moulded base well decorated with gilt leaf scrolls. Circa 1785.

Dimensions: *Dial diameter 24½ in., surround diameter 28½ in., total height 58½ in., width of trunk 11¾ in.*

Maker: *John Wright, Dorking, is only recorded from 1791-1828.*

Below: The print in the trunk door is stuck onto the wood. At a table, on which stands a half empty bottle of wine and a bowl with wooden serving ladle, are seated a demurely, not to say, primly dressed lady and a gentleman in breeches, no doubt taking brief refreshment at an inn. His right arm encircles the lady while he toasts her with the glass raised in his left hand. She, while appearing to respond by fondling his neckerchief, has dexterously removed a substantial looking purse which she is in the act of passing to her maid servant who lurks in the half open door. The print is lacquered over its edge with a gilt line and at the top with three gilt leaves actually onto the print. The rest of the door is decorated at the top and bottom with close clusters of scroll design.

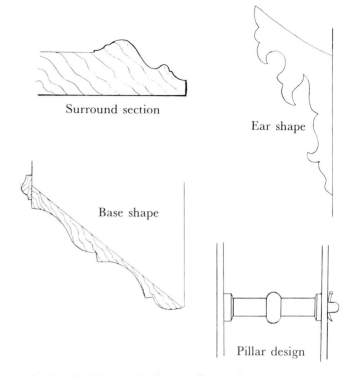

Surround section

Ear shape

Base shape

Pillar design

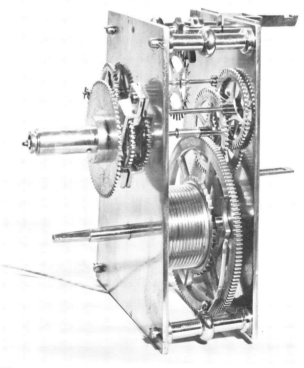

The movement has a large 4½ in. diameter barrel wheel with six spokes and 144 teeth gearing into the centre pinion of seven leaves. There is a twelve turn groove and the barrel wheel projects below the bottom edge of the plates and so the seatboard is cut out to accommodate this. The tapered plates are 7in. tall, 3¾ in. wide at the top and 4¾ in. at the bottom. The centre wheel with five crossings is mounted high up the plates due to the larger diameter of the barrel wheel.

A late teardrop tavern clock. Although the wooden dial has been heavily touched up, it has fairly small Roman numerals, minute divisions between two circles without difference at five minute intervals and outside minute numerals. The signature and town name are in conventional places but the 'Oxford Street' is written on the centre line of the dial, an uncommon practice, as is also the use of a bezel which has its lock set in the convex surround. The teardrop shape trunk has a long door which is straight sided and not teardrop shape as is normally the case. The trunk is lacquered with very little gesso on the door and the rest of the case including the sides are of flower and leaf scroll designs. At the very base of the clock is a separate bracket, screwed to the wall independently from the clock. Circa 1795.

Dimensions: *Dial diameter 16in., bezel diameter 17½in., surround diameter 20in., total height 52in.*

Maker: *Thomas Dane, Oxford Street, London recorded as 1790-1825.*

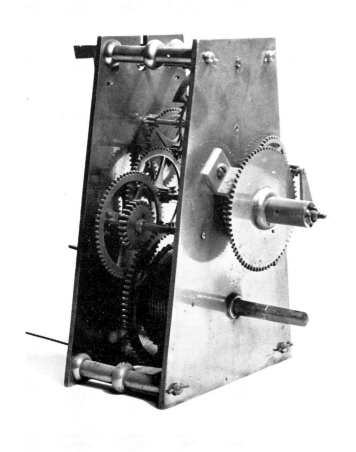

This movement has tapered plates of four pillar construction and a five wheel train. Clearly visible is the large brass pinion which meshes with the barrel to give extra duration, especially necessary on a clock with a comparatively short trunk.

PLATE 36
PLATE 37

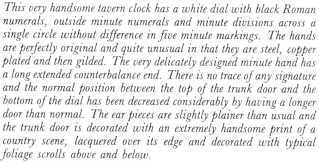

This very handsome tavern clock has a white dial with black Roman numerals, outside minute numerals and minute divisions across a single circle without difference in five minute markings. The hands are perfectly original and quite unusual in that they are steel, copper plated and then gilded. The very delicately designed minute hand has a long extended counterbalance end. There is no trace of any signature and the normal position between the top of the trunk door and the bottom of the dial has been decreased considerably by having a longer door than normal. The ear pieces are slightly plainer than usual and the trunk door is decorated with an extremely handsome print of a country scene, lacquered over its edge and decorated with typical foliage scrolls above and below.

A small tavern clock by William Clarke Junior, Lynn. The white dial has only a very narrow surround, small outside minute numerals and brass hands, neither of which are counterbalanced. The lacquering on the trunk door has virtually no raised work and is far less detailed than earlier clocks, also showing far more area of background. This clock is only about three quarters normal size, so despite the fact that it is quite late, it is quite unusual and therefore sought after.

PLATE 38

An 'East Anglian' wall clock or 'Norwich' clock as this type is most commonly called. Despite its rather deceiving name this typical example comes from the west of England. The case is constructed in oak and mahogany, veneered in mahogany and crossbanded with satinwood. It is further decorated with boxwood stringing and with a corner edge running the full length of the trunk, following through into the base. This particular example is unusual in not having a slide off hood but a top door and a lift up wooden bezel. The brass, silvered dial is very crudely engraved with ill proportioned Roman numerals and outside minute numerals with dot minute divisions. The blued steel hands have arrow head tips and the minute hand only has a counterbalanced end. Circa 1830.

Dimensions: *Diameter of dial 13½ in., diameter of bezel 16⅛ in., width of trunk 12½ in., total length 50in.*

Maker: *Robert Hall, Oswestry is recorded as 1828-1835.*

Normally Norwich clocks have only a four wheel going train; however this example has five wheels with slightly backtapered collets and the large brass pinion on the second arbor secured with two screws into a collet. The clock incorporates a passing strike, lifting the hammer directly from a pin on the motion work, and sounding a single blow at each hour on the bell above the rectangular plates. The bell in this case is new but all else appears original.

PLATE 39

Another example of a country scene print on a tavern clock trunk door. The decoration above and below the print appears extremely similar from one clock to another. Note that the decorated border around the door on the trunk itself only starts from the top corners of the door. The signature is not normally bordered at all except by the leaf scrolls on the ear pieces. The dial on this occasion is black with gilt numerals. Circa 1775.

Thomas Crofts Sen. Newbury   C. 1780
In Shaw

Thomas Crofts Jun: Newbury   1780 – 1795
In Northbrook Street
Free of Clockmakers Company 1790

Thomas Crofts & Sons   1795 – 1827
In North Brook Street

Supplied the Turrett Clock in Newbury Alms Houses in Market-Place Newbury June 7th 1795. Paid to Thomas Crofts & Sons £65. Receipt in Borough Record Office

In the Borough Record Office is a Licence issued to Mr Thomas Crofts "For use and Exercise the trade and Business of a Maker of, and dealer in Clocks, Watches or Time Keepers" dated 1797

Cleaned the Turret Clock, St Bartholomews Hospital, Newbury 15/- winding for 12 months 21/- (Voucher in Newbury Grammar School Archives, dated 1827.

Right: This paper was found inside the clock above and had possibly been there for some years. It is interesting to note that a licence issued to Mr. Thomas Crofts, due to the enforcement of the tax on clocks and watches in 1797, exists in the Borough Record Office.

Chapter 6

The English Dial Clock

The English dial clock had a fairly complex evolution, following no hard and fast rules, and with exceptions cropping up whenever any attempt was made to establish guide lines. One thing that is fairly certain is that dial clocks evolved from the English cartel clock with the black dial clock slotting more into the tavern clock structure. The black dial clock (Plate 40) has nevertheless a movement virtually identical to that of early dial clocks with tapered plates and a verge escapement. The case does not resemble any dial clock features in design or construction except that the backboard projects as with a salt box case.

English cartel clocks had flamboyant gilt wood cases decoratively carved with designs of leaf scrolls, flowers or shells. They were often asymmetric and usually surmounted by quite a large eagle (Plate 41). The silvered brass dial usually had outside minute numerals, false pendulum aperture, fancy pierced steel hands and was signed under the winding square. It seems as though the most usual dial size was between eight and nine inches, and that the dial and movement were put into the case from the back, unlike later dial clocks. Bezels were of concave section and very low in height with a flat glass. Movements had verge escapements and often narrow, straight sideplates with a straight line wheel train, small diameter barrel and a horizontal strap screwed across the backplates which secured the assembly into the case.

Cartel clocks began to appear around 1730 or thereabouts and must have been a direct plagiarism from the French cartel clocks which were popular at this time on the Continent. The main difference was that the French clocks were made of cast brass whereas the English ones had water gilded, wooden cases. The style did not, however, fit in with English taste very well and the clocks were never made in great numbers, appearing on the whole only in very upper class, lavishly decorated houses. There seems to have been little change in design or style and they gradually disappeared around the 1780s. Their importance was that they gave their dial and movement style intact to the first English dial clocks. A gradual change of case style did not occur except for one or two isolated examples of less flamboyant cartel clocks. The case of the English dial clock around 1770, was an entirely new venture probably aimed at a wider market wanting cheaper but still high quality clocks. It turned out that this new venture led to the most popular style of clock ever produced.

The first English dial clocks appeared with mahogany cases and salt box style backs. This was constructed with the two sides dovetailed onto the flat top and bottom, a large side door on the right hand side in a central position and a large bottom door to allow access to the pendulum bob for regulation. The back was then directly fixed onto the box and so the join was visible from the side. Both top and bottom of the backboard were extended and shaped. The top projection had a hole for hanging the clock and the bottom a hole for securing the clock. The surround was concave sectioned and had a similarly designed moulded mahogany bezel, hinged on the right hand side and with a lock set in the left side (Plate 42). The glass was generally flat, put in from the inside and puttied. The dial was about 9in. in diameter and was silvered brass, well engraved with large outside minute numerals and signed with the maker's name and town below the winding square. Above the hand centre was a false pendulum aperture and the hands were fancy blued steel. The movement had tapered plates, four pillars and a verge escapement. An exploded view of a movement with a verge escapement is shown opposite.

Changes quickly came with the size of the dial increasing to the most commonly used 12in. diameter, the false pendulum aperture was phased out which altered the signature position, the name going above the hand centre and the town below, and the mahogany bezel gave way to a similarly sectioned cast brass one (Plate 43). The minute divisions by the late 1790s were most usually single strokes crossing a single circle and without difference in five minute markings (Plate 44).

By 1800 the anchor escapement to dial clocks had been introduced, although it had been widely used on most other clocks throughout the preceding century. This necessitated a change in the style of the back box to a rounded bottom following the line of the surround in order to accommodate a longer pendulum. The construction of the box differed from the salt box case in that the sides were rebated to take the backboard; thus the sides went the full depth of the case and the joint of the back was not visible. The door in the bottom was also curved to the same shape as the base and the side door was raised up nearer the top of the case to give access when hooking the pendulum suspension spring onto the backcock. However, this change took another twenty years to become the standard design and so the verge escapement was still around when the wooden dial made its appearance around 1805. At first the dial was made independently from the surround and was usually convex (Plate 46). It was gessoed and painted with black Roman figures, outside minute numerals, minute divisions between two circles and with triangle or diamond shaped five minute markings. The hands had become plainer and were sometimes made of brass. As wooden dials appeared at around the same time as the change from verge to anchor escapement and the alteration in box style, it is fairly common to find them with the old salt box style cases but with anchor movements which sometimes had the bobs smaller than usual and the bottom doors chiselled out in an attempt to combine the up to date movement with an outdated case (Plate 45). By 1820 most dial clocks had wooden dials but were now made from the same piece of wood as the surround and commonly flat. The dial had lost the outside minute numerals, so the hour numerals increased in size and moved towards the outside. This left a larger space for the signature which often had the maker's name followed by the street name above the centre, with the town name remaining below (Plate 47). The surrounds of wooden dials had up until now been very narrow showing very little outside the brass bezel (Plate 48), but after 1820 they increased in width until they reverted back to a size similar to the first dial clocks of the 1770s.

With the establishment of the anchor escapement, trunk dial clocks with long extended boxes housing longer pendulums became popular. The front of the boxes were usually very well veneered with flame mahogany (Plate 49) and often inlaid, mostly with brass or boxwood stringing. They had a curved foot base gradually curving back to the wall from the front, or a flat chisel or a shaped base (Plate 50); either way both had a door for access to the rating nut. At the bottom of the trunk

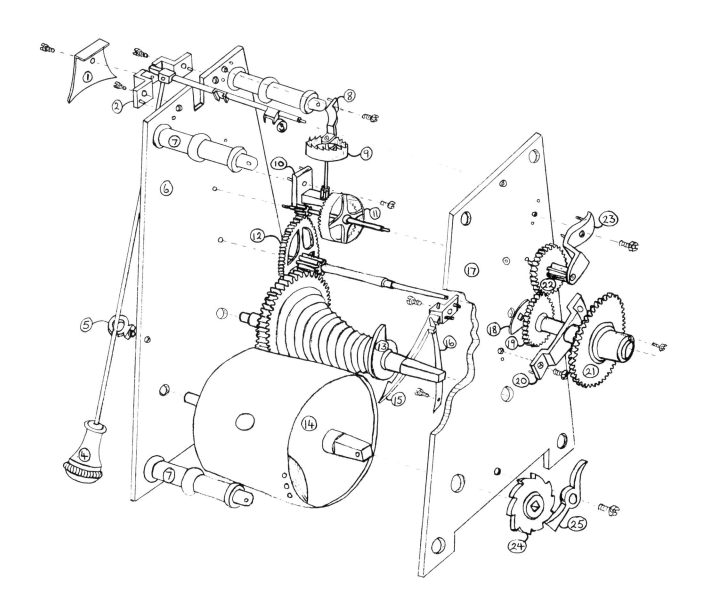

1 Apron	10 Potence	
2 Backcock	11 Contrate wheel	
3 Verge	12 Centre wheel	19 Minute wheel
4 Pendulum bob	13 Fusee	20 Minute wheel bridge
5 Pendulum hook	14 Barrel	21 Hour wheel
6 Backplate	15 Stopwork	22 Intermediate motion wheel
7 Pillars	16 Stopwork spring	23 Intermediate motion wheel bridge
8 Top verge cock	17 Front plate	24 Ratchet wheel
9 Verge wheel	18 Bowspring	25 Click

where the base started there was a simple moulding which was traditionally used to hide the join of the front and base panel. This was carried over from the earlier tavern clock era even though the veneers were generally carried through to the base in one sheet, hiding any join which would have been apparent. Usually the clocks had side ear pieces leading up from the trunk to the surround and these were either carved or simple fretcut designs (Plate 52). Although many clocks did not start life with ear pieces many more have since been removed, most accidentally.

By 1830 iron dials had made their mark, usually convex and painted with bold Roman figures. Brass dials had by now been well left behind but a few wooden dials appeared occasionally. With iron dials the surrounds were becoming plainer and often convex sectioned with brass bezels of a similar design. Movements became commonly rectangular plated often with shaped shoulders and a cutout at the bottom (Plate 51). The shape of the plates changed little over the following century except for losing the cutouts and the shaped shoulders over the next thirty or forty years. Pillars became simpler in design over the same period until they lost the bulge in the centre by 1880 (Plate 53).

Over the period bezels did change considerably in construction, with the convex sectioned cast bezel giving way to the similarly shaped cast bezel with a sight ring made in one piece which had a fitted bevel edged glass. Eventually by the 1860s the bezels began to be spun from thin sheet, first without sight rings with a plastered-in glass, and later with sight rings but still plastered in (Plate 54). The snap in sight rings which are often encountered today did not appear until well into this century and most are modern replacements. The glass, whether flat or convex, does not play any part in the evolution of dial clocks; both types were used throughout although flat glasses predominated after 1880.

Hands after 1830 became more often spade design with both hour and minute with spade tips, but the minute hand gradually lost this to become straight while the hour hand increased in boldness of design.

There were many other dial clock designs and adaptations, some were inset into walls or incorporated into a design or structure, but two of the most prominent designs were the octagonal dial and the drum dial.

The octagonal dial clock was made in three basic designs, all being made between 1830-1880. The first was octagonal from the front, with flat sides going the full depth of the case (Plate 55). Then there was the type with an octagonal surround which was pegged onto a rounded bottom back box. The third type was similar in design but fitted onto a trunk back box. All three styles had iron dials, usually convex sectioned bezels and were veneered with mahogany and generally inlaid with brass. The inlay was often a straight line and circle design or foliage scrolls and occasionally mother-of-pearl or pewter inlay was used as well.

The drum dial clock was popular over the same period but offered more scope in its size. It was made in varying sizes from 8in. diameter to 24in. diameter dials, possibly even larger, and, even at this late date, often appeared with a brass dial. The sides of the case went the full depth of the clock and were completely circular (Plate 56). The case was constructed by gluing together flat strips with chamfered sides to form a circle and then applying the solid back circle and the front surround. It was then veneered on the front and side, usually with well figured veneers, and with the grain running around the circle, not from back to front. Drum dials seem to have the doors in varying places, most commonly with a right hand side and bottom doors only, although a left hand side door is often found as well. Occasionally there is no door visible from the front and access is through a large back door.

Dial clocks with fusee movements were still being made well into the 1930s but, over the 160 or more years, only retained the basic circular shape — all other designs and features had changed. The dial clock now had a flat painted iron dial with bold Roman numerals, minute divisions between two circles and triangle five minute markings; it was often completely unsigned. The blued steel hands consisted of a large spade tipped hour hand and a straight sided minute hand. The bezel was in two designs, depending on the quality of the clock, either with a convex sectioned, cast brass bezel with a silvered sight ring cast in one piece and a flat bevelled glass, or a spun convex sectioned bezel with a separate sight ring and a flat glass. The case was made from oak or mahogany again depending on quality, with a convex sectioned, simple surround not made from one piece of wood but built up in sections. The rounded bottom back box had a flat, rebated door without side strips on the right hand side and a curved bottom door often with a gauged line around it to simulate a cockbead moulding. The movement had rectangular plates with four completely plain, straight sided pillars often being screwed to the backplate by means of a screw and washer and sometimes screwed through the front plate as well. The fusee either had chain or wire line and the setting up of the mainspring was effected by a steel plate squared onto the barrel arbor and screwed through the plate, thus dispensing with the ratchet wheel and click (Plate 57). Late movements also often had an adjustable eccentric bush for the front pallet arbor pivot and an adjustable crutch pin for setting the clock in beat.

Throughout their life dial clocks have been made in varying sizes with the smallest being about 6in. across the dial (Plate 58), the most common size being 12in. Early clocks were made in quite odd sizes, with no rhyme or reason to the diameter measurements. Large dial clocks were frequently made to specifications so their size depended on where they were to go, but 2ft. to 2ft. 6in. dials are not uncommon. One of the largest encountered is a weight driven trunk dial over 8ft. high and with a 3ft.6in. dial (Plate 59).

Two frequent uses to which dial clocks have been adapted are for inset dials and gallery clocks. Often a clock was secured into a wall without its back box but with the surround and bezel exactly as normal. It could then be wound from the front though regulation and starting the pendulum without removing the clock from the wall were problems. In such a case a rise and fall regulation was usually fitted, with a square arbor coming through the dial which could be turned by a key; a small hole was made around the figure VI through which a wire was poked to swing the pendulum. If the clock was to be placed in a gallery it was far easier to get to the back. Gallery dial clocks were therefore made with a back winding square and a set dial on the backplate which could be adjusted to the right time. This overcame the need to go down a couple of floors or so to check the time on the front of the clock when setting the hands. The movement of such a gallery clock was often enclosed in its own little cupboard within the structure of the gallery itself.

PLATE 40

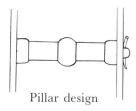

Pillar design

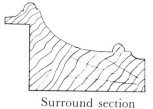

Surround section

This large black dial clock has a dial made from three horizontal boards, large gilt Roman numerals with minute divisions between two circles and triangle five·minute markings. The brass hands have heart shaped tips with the minute hand only counterbalanced. The pine surround is of concave section and is decorated with two gilt bands. It has a salt box style back with projections at both top and bottom and a tapered plated fusee movement with verge escapement.

Dimensions: *Dial diameter 22in., surround diameter 28¼in., hour numerals height 2¾in., length of salt box back 24½in.*

Right: A fine example of an English cartel clock. The carved, water gilt case is asymmetric, has a design of leaf scrolls and flowers and is surmounted by an eagle. It has a brass bezel of low concave section with a flat glass and a catch on the left hand side. The brass dial has an engraved circle within the large Roman figures and small outside minute numerals within triangle five minute divisions. Above the hand centre is the false pendulum aperture and below is the signature on either side of the winding square. The hands are later replacements. Circa 1745.

Dimensions: *Height 30in., width 18in., depth 5½in.*
Maker: *William Whitebread, London, was a member of the Clockmakers Company from 1728-1753.*

Biggs of Maidenhead

PLATE 41

PLATE 42

An early dial clock with an engraved, silvered brass dial which has small Roman hour numerals, outside minute numerals and minute divisions between two circles with triangle five minute markings. Above the hand centre is a false pendulum aperture. The signature is below the winding square. In common with all early dial clocks the dial is substantially smaller in diameter than the inside edge of the moulded mahogany bezel. The surround is of a similar design to the bezel and is quite wide. The back box is salt box style. The clock has a tapered plated movement with a verge escapement. Circa 1785.

PLATE 43

This silvered brass dial has the signature and street engraved above the hand centre with the town name underneath the winding square. The hour numerals still remain quite small and the minute divisions cross a single circle without difference in five minute markings. The cast brass bezel is of concave section and has the lock attached to the bezel on the left hand side. The mahogany surround is of similar section and is screwed through the front into the salt box case, so there are no pegs. It has one large door centrally on the right hand side and one on the bottom, both with the usual side strips. The movement is rectangular, with concave shouldered plates with four pillars, original anchor escapement (despite the salt box case), and is stamped F. HOLLAND on the inside of the barrel cap. Circa 1790.

Dimensions: *Dial diameter 12in., surround diameter 14⅛ in., hour numerals height 1in., minute numerals height ½ in.*

Maker: *Charles Puckridge, Goldsmith Street, London was apprenticed in 1763 and in the Clockmakers Company in 1776-1805.*

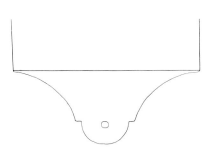

The projection at the bottom of a salt box case.

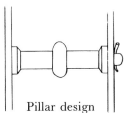

Pillar design

Concave shouldered plates

Bezel section

Surround section

PLATE 44

Private collection

An early silvered brass dial clock with small Roman numerals, outside minute numerals and minute divisions across a single circle. It has an offset winding hole at III and original blued steel hands. The concave sectioned bezel has a lock on the left hand side and is hinged on the right. The mahogany surround is screwed, not pegged, to the back box which is 'in between' style. The salt box back has a projection at the bottom but also has a rounded bottom base with a curved access door. Circa 1795.

Dimensions: *Dial diameter 12in., surround diameter 15⅛ in., long side door 6⅞ in. by 3in.*

Maker: *Recordon and Dupont, Tottenham Court Road, London, is recorded until 1796.*

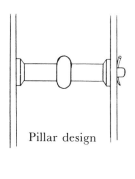

Pillar design

Bezel section

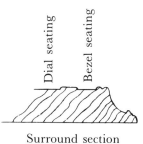

Dial seating

Bezel seating

Surround section

The movement has tapered plates with the initials R W cast into the backplate and the bottom edge cut out in an unusual design. It is of five pillar construction and has its original anchor escapement with a nicely shaped top edge to the backcock.

PLATE 45

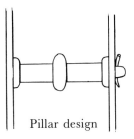
Pillar design

Bezel section

Dial

Surround section

An interesting dial clock with a convex wooden dial separate from the surround. The dial has its original background but has had the numerals repainted. The signature has been scratched out beyond recognition although 'Church St. Croydon' remains. Underneath 'Church St.' can be detected faint yellow figures of a previous number, 1593. There is a large gap between the outside edge of the dial and the outside of the minute ring, indicating either the repainted figures are too far in, or the dial originally had outside minute numerals. The cast brass bezel originally had a bezel lock on the left hand side but this has been removed and it is now kept shut by a turncatch. The surround is concave sectioned but as the bezel seating is completely flat without a moulding to keep it in place, the moulding may have been removed. The narrow surround is pegged onto the salt box back which has both top and bottom projections. The falseplate which is screwed to the back of the dial certainly appears always to have been there even though it is made from a matted dial centre from a longcase clock and bears the repair dates of 1841, 1845, 1851 and 1855. Circa 1810.

Dimensions: Dial diameter 10¾in., surround diameter 13¼in.

Right: The movement is just as interesting, with the tapered plates stamped W R 479 below the winding square, repair dates of 1818 and 1824 and the words 'T.M. KIRCHEL, CROYDON' — it could be that this is the missing signature. The backcock has been raised up to suspend the pendulum to enable it to clear the flat bottom of the case; again this appears always to have been like this.

PLATE 46

A very large early nineteenth century English dial clock with a wooden convex dial separate from the surround. It is painted with small Roman numerals, outside minute numerals and minute divisions crossing a single circle without difference in five minute markings. Above and below the signature it is unusually decorated with leaf scrolls.

The concave sectioned cast bezel matches the deeply moulded mahogany surround. The back box is square with a tapering off projection at the bottom to house the pendulum and a sound fret fitted to the top of the case.

The two train movement is of five pillar construction, has rectangular plates and an anchor escapement. It is rack striking, sounding hours only on a bell above the movement. Three brackets are provided to fix the movement to an oak seatboard. Circa 1810.

Dimensions: *Dial diameter 17¾ in., bezel diameter 19¾ in., surround diameter 21¼ in., hour numerals height 1½ in., minute numerals height ¾ in.*

Maker: *W.S. Ratcliffe, 40 New Road, Buckland. Unrecorded.*

PLATE 47

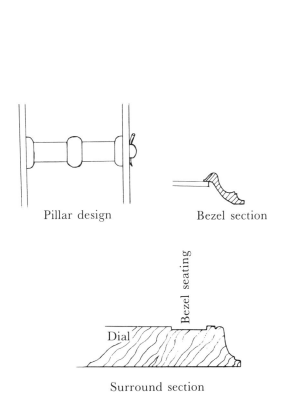

Pillar design

Bezel section

Bezel seating

Dial

Surround section

This dial clock has dial and surround made in one piece of wood. The flat painted dial has lost its outside minute numerals and the hour numerals have become larger. It is signed with both the name and street above the hand centre, with the town name below, written in typical style for this period.

The cast brass bezel is of concave section with the lock originally attached on the left hand side but now missing. The surround is slightly deeper than usual and is pegged to the rounded bottom case with iron pegs through shaped uprights. The movement is conventional but mounted on a seatboard secured through the sides of the case. Hands not original but a traditional pattern. Circa 1825.

Dimensions: *Dial diameter 12 ⅛ in., surround diameter 15 ½ in., hour numerals height 1 ½ in.*

Maker: *T. Combs, 109 Westminster Rd., London. Unrecorded.*

PLATE 48

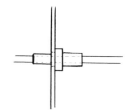

Extended wheel collet

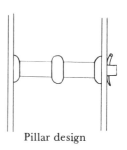

Pillar design

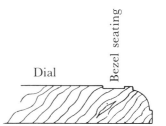

Bezel section

Surround section

A wooden dial with the surround and dial in one piece of wood. The flat dial has its original painting with no trace of ever having a signature. It has original blued steel hands, Roman numerals and triangle five minute divisions. The bezel is of convex section with a flat glass and originally had a bezel lock set inside the narrow convex mahogany surround. It has a rounded bottom back box with a large bottom door, 5 ¼ in. by 4 ⅛ in., the full depth of the case between the back and front boards of the box.

The movement has tapered plates, four pillars, long arbors going through the thick dial and extended wheel collets. It has a rectangular falseplate with three dial feet into the front plate. Circa 1830.

Dimensions: *Dial diameter 14 ⅛ in., surround diameter 16 ⅜ in., hour numerals height 1 ⅜ in.*

PLATE 49

This drop dial clock has a brass silvered dial with outside minute numerals and minute divisions crossing a single circle, without difference at the five minute markings. It is signed *JAGOE* in capitals above the centre and *London* below in flowing style. The mahogany bezel is of concave section with flat glass and a lock set in the left hand side. The trunk of the case has fine mahogany veneers with elaborate fretted ear pieces. The brass inlay and some of the base are possibly later alterations. The bottom door is moulded and is the full width of the trunk. *Circa 1805.*

Dimensions: *Dial diameter 11¾ in., bezel diameter 13¾ in., surround diameter 15in., hour numerals height $1^1/_6$ in., minute numerals height $^7/_{16}$ in.*

Maker: *John Jagoe of London is recorded 1809-11.*

Private collection

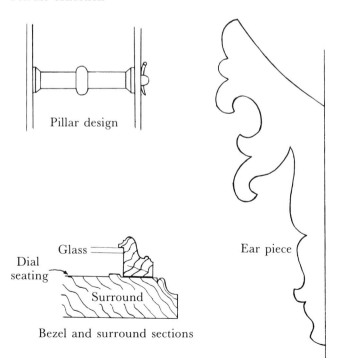

Pillar design

Glass

Dial seating

Surround

Bezel and surround sections

Ear piece

Private collection

Above: The movement has tapered plates with the dial feet permanently riveted to the frontplate, a tail to the click and a thicker centre to the ratchet wheel. It has a wheel train in a straight line including the barrel, which make it a fairly tall movement at 8⅛ in. high. It also has an anchor escapement and a shaped intermediate wheel bridge.

PLATE 50

A very fine quality drop dial clock with a silvered dial. The dial is engraved with small Roman numerals, outside minute numerals and minute divisions within two circles with triangle five minute markings. It is signed in full above the hand centre and has blued steel hands with heart shaped tips. There are no screws to secure the dial to the surround as the movement is seatboard mounted and secured by two screws into the lower pillars. The clock has a concave sectioned cast bezel with a convex glass and lock let into the concave surround itself from the back. The mahogany trunk has simple ears integral with the front panel and a moulding around the top of the chisel foot base which is actually a full opening bottom door. It has two side doors with decorative moulding instead of plain strips around the edges. Circa 1810.

Dimensions: Dial diameter 12in., bezel diameter 13¼in., surround diameter 15in., total height 21in., hour numerals height $1^1/_{16}$ in., minute numerals height $^7/_{16}$ in.

Maker: Thomas Harrison, London. There were several makers of the same name working in London at the beginning of the nineteenth century.

Right: The rectangular plated movement has a wide backcock for a turned suspension block, four pillars, very fine four spoke wheels and a half deadbeat escapement. Pivot cocks are provided for the front pallet arbor, back third wheel arbor and an end bearing cock for the back fusee arbor. The four dial feet are very short with only ½in. between the frontplate and the back of the dial.

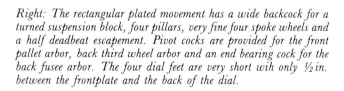

PLATE 51

A convex, iron dial clock. The dial, although repainted, has been well executed and probably follows the orignal lines with the signature in block letters and the town name leaning to the right with scrolls on the letter 'N'. The cast convex sectioned bezel has its convex glass, pinned and plastered, and has a latch through the narrow surround. The trunk is mahogany veneered through to the curved foot base with brass inlaid stringing and stars within circles. It is decorated with a moulding separating the trunk from the base and neat fantail ear pieces. Circa 1840.

Dimensions: Dial diameter 12in., surround diameter 13½in., length 21½in.

Maker: Joseph Thwaites, London, does not appear to have been any connection of the John and Aynsworth Thwaites family.

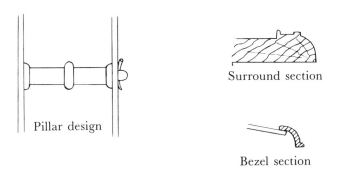

Pillar design

Surround section

Bezel section

Trunk moulding section

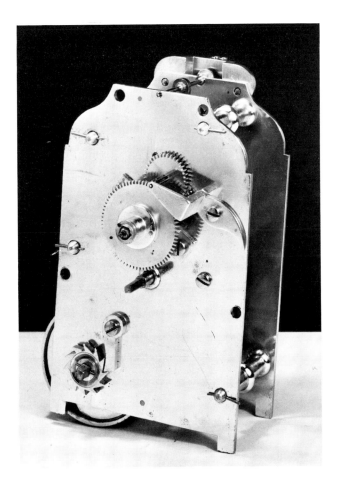

Right: The rectangular plates have shaped shoulders and are cut away at the bottom. There is a ratchet wheel of equal thickness and a click without a tail. At the back, the pallet cock is mounted very high up and overlaps the top edge of the plate considerably.

PLATE 52

Right: This handsome trunk dial clock has a convex, iron dial with large Roman figures and triangle five minute divisions but without minute numerals. The signature is all above the hand centre and there is a brass collet around the winding hole. It has a convex sectioned cast bezel which does not have a lock but is latched through the wide, convex sectioned mahogany surround. It is conventional with convex iron dials to have a separate falseplate attached to the dial by short dial feet to eliminate the curve of the dial. The longer pillars are then attached to the falseplate for the movement, so that the movement dial feet project from the falseplate at ninety degrees. In this particular clock the dial has four dial feet into the falseplate and three into the movement.

The trunk of the clock is mahogany veneered, with brass inlaid circles and stringing around the glass aperture, through which the pendulum bob is visible. Carved ear pieces are attached to the sides for decoration. Circa 1845.

Dimensions: *Dial diameter 12in., surround diameter 15½in.*
Maker: *J. Beeland, Newcastle. Unrecorded.*

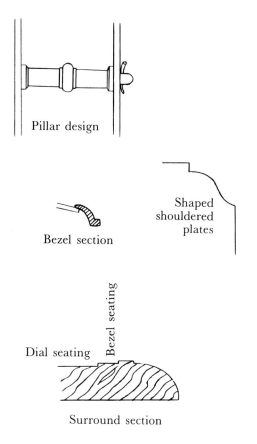

Pillar design

Bezel section

Shaped shouldered plates

Bezel seating

Dial seating

Surround section

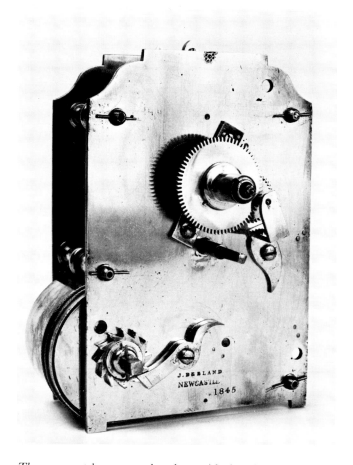

The movement has rectangular plates with shaped shoulders and a low cut out at the bottom. It has an anchor escapement and the third wheel is unusually mounted on the pinion itself at the centre wheel end of the plates. It is stamped with the maker's name and date at the bottom edge of the front plate.

The holes at the very top edge are for the pallet arbor pivot indicating that the clock has been badly repaired in the past. The central hole has been punched all the way round to close up a worn hole, instead of rebushing by means of a brass insert. This wicked method of repair is virtually impossible to remove and is unfortunately very common on all clocks.

Dial clock by John Brydnt.
See Plate 65 for details.

PLATE 53

This flat iron, painted dial has conventional minute divisions between two circles, triangle five minute marks and an uncommon design of club shaped hour hand. The convex sectioned, brass bezel has its sight ring cast in one piece and a fitted glass.

The mahogany case has a convex sectioned surround made from one piece, a rounded bottom and doors with side strips. As it is a striking clock the top of the case is fitted with a silk backed sound fret. Circa 1870.

Dimensions: *Dial diameter 11⅞ in., bezel diameter 12½ in., surround diameter 14½ in.*

Right: The two train movement has rectangular plates, four plain pillars and an anchor escapement. It is rack striking and sounds the hours only on a bell mounted above the movement. The unconventional coiled hammer spring is original and attached to a lower pillar. Note the fly fan blades which are neatly fretted out on the inside edges.

PLATE 54

This late nineteenth century dial clock has a flat, painted iron dial with bold Roman numerals, triangle five minute divisions and large spade hands.

The convex sectioned cast bezel has a separate sight ring which is plastered in to hold the flat glass. It has a mahogany convex sectioned surround made from one piece of wood and a rounded bottom box. The side door does not have side strips but is solid with rebated sides and the bottom door is without a cockbead edge. Circa 1890.
Dimensions: *Dial diameter 14in., surround diameter 17½in.*
Maker: *W.R. Bullen, 47 London Street, Norwich. The firm of W.R. Bullen started in 1885, was succeeded by W.S. Bullen and D.H. Bullen in 1954. The company still exists and is now known as W.R. Bullen Ltd., Jewellers, 29, London Street, Norwich.*

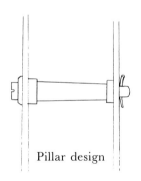

Pillar design

3786

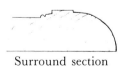

Surround section

Bezel section

The rectangular plated movement has four plain pillars which are screwed into the backplate and conventionally pinned at the front. It has an anchor escapement and the barrel projects below the plate edge. It is stamped near the bottom of the frontplate with a trade mark and the number 3786.

PLATE 55

An early octagonal dial clock. The convex iron dial has large Roman numerals, triangle five minute divisions and is unconventionally signed in having the road name below the hand centre, a space usually reserved for the town name. The case is mahogany veneered to all sides and the front which is also inlaid with brass in leaf scroll design. The front edge of the case does not have a moulding around it but, as with most early octagonal clocks, has dark wood stringing. Apart from the doors on the right hand side and the bottom it also has a large back door for easy access to the pendulum. Circa 1830.
Dimensions: *Dial diameter 12in., bezel diameter 12½in., case diameter across the flats 14½ in.*
Maker: *Harris, Wandsworth Road. Unrecorded.*

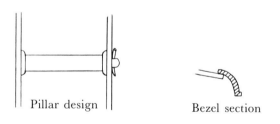

Pillar design   Bezel section

Right: A rectangular plated movement with deeply cut shaped shoulders and a large cut out at the bottom. The ratchet wheel is thicker in the centre and the click has a tail. It has four pillars which are straight sided, without a raised part in the centre, an anchor escapement and the hand centre situated high up the plate.

PLATE 56

This large drum dial clock has a flat, painted iron dial with large Roman numerals, triangle five minute divisions and fine blued steel hands. It is screwed into the case by four dial screws which screw into tapped brass inserts. The cast brass convex sectioned bezel has the silvered sight ring cast in one piece and a bevelled glass. Circa 1840.
Dimensions: *Dial diameter 14in., case diameter 17in.*
Maker: *William Connell of 22 Myddelton Street, London is recorded as 1839 and later succeeded Ganthony at 83 Cheapside in 1845. He died in 1862 and his son William George died in 1902.*
The case is built up with flat strips glued together to form a circle. The whole of the case is then veneered over to cover the joins. This clock has two access doors, one on the right hand side and one at the bottom. Both have the conventional strips of wood to the edge of the door which are rounded off to form a cockbead. Locks are included which are both bolt type, whereas the bezel lock, set in the case, is the spring loaded type.

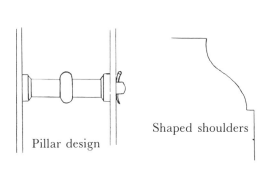

Pillar design   Shaped shoulders

Glass

Bezel section

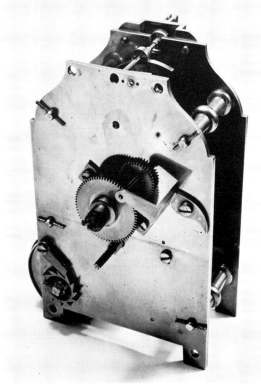

Right: The movement is on conventional lines with shaped shouldered plates cut away at the bottom, pallets secured to their collet by two screws, shaped intermediate motion wheel bridge and four pillar construction.

PLATE 57

A twentieth century 14in. trunk dial clock with a flat, painted iron dial with bold hands and hour numerals. Originally the clock had a spun bezel but has been 'upgraded' by substituting a cast bezel with sight ring. The oak surround is made up from four sections glued together, usual in most twentieth century dial clocks, and is a late style of convex/concave section. The trunk, also of oak, has very simple ear pieces, and the rounded bottom does not follow the curvature of the surround, also common in this century.

Private collection

Left: The front view of the movement shows the coarse manufacture with all brasswork heavily grained. It has squared cocks and brackets, friction on the hour hand, not on the hour wheel, and a brass plate substituting the barrel ratchet wheel and click.

Right: The back view shows the straight pillars screwed into the backplate and the stamped letters, below the back fusee pivot, T.A & B.

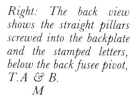

M

PLATE 58

A fine small English dial clock. The flat iron dial has Roman numerals, diamond five minute divisions and original spade hands. With many small dial clocks the winding hole is offset, usually on the right of the centre; this winding hole is unusual, being offset at IX. The bezel is a type not often encountered and only apparent in the smaller clock. It has a sprung-in convex glass but the cast bezel does not have a sight ring. The mahogany surround is screwed direct onto the rounded bottom box and so does not have any pegs.

A newspaper cutting pasted inside the bottom door reads: 'The death is announced of Mr Henry Perigal, of the Admiralty, in his hundredth year. He belonged to a celebrated family of Watchmakers in Bond Street, London, the firm, however, no longer existing. October 1867. WW'. Circa 1835.

Dimensions: *Dial diameter 7in., surround diameter 9¼in.*

Maker: *Perigal & Duterrau, 62 New Bond Street, London, are recorded as being watchmakers to the King. 1803-1840.*

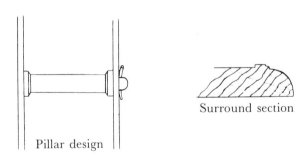

Pillar design

Surround section

Bezel section

Right: The movement has shaped shouldered plates with chamfered bottom corners to allow clearance through the surround. It is signed in flowing style on the backplate. The four pillars do not have any raised portion in the centre but are straight sided.

The wheel train is laid out in a peculiar manner with fusee high up and the barrel set slightly off centre underneath the centre wheel.

PLATE 59

Probably one of the largest traditionally styled drop dials in existence. The conventional central dial is 2ft. across but, including outer seconds, the complete dial diameter is 3ft. 6in. The seconds hand, painted red, has a very necessary counterbalance and is suitably strong to avoid excessive vibration of the tip. The enormous and very heavy, polished, cast brass bezel with solid sight ring is unusually hinged on the side. Normally large bezels are hinged from the top to decrease the strain on the hinge.

The mahogany case has a long trunk door and a chisel shaped base making the total height around 8ft. 3in.

The weight driven movement is of excellent quality construction with counterbalances for the hands, long seconds pendulum, maintaining power and a deadbeat escapement.

This clock orignally came from a demolished swimming pool in the E.C.1 area of London. Circa 1920.

PLATE 60

An early nineteenth century dial clock with a brass, silvered dial. It has small Roman numerals with outside minute numerals, triangle five minute divisions and original hands. The concave sectioned cast brass bezel has the lock attached to the left hand side and a flat glass. The concave sectioned surround is quite narrow and is fixed directly to the back salt box without use of pegs. The salt box projection is unusually veneered, but this could have been added at a later date. The construction of the box is itself unconventional as well, with the sides attached to the back as in rounded bottom boxes. Circa 1805.

Dimensions: *Dial diameter 14in., bezel diameter 15½in., surround diameter 16⅞in., hour numerals height 1¼in., minute numerals height ¾in.*

Maker: *John Caldecott, Huntingdon is recorded as 1795.*

Private collection

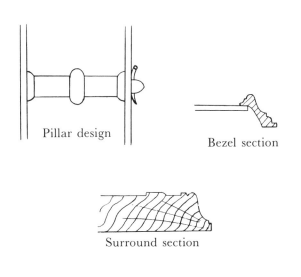

Pillar design

Bezel section

Surround section

Right: Although rectangular plates were not standard for early clocks, they do occasionally appear. These plates are quite robust with a size of 6¾in. by 4⅝in. and five pillar construction. The style of the intermediate motion wheel pinion, with a short pinion forming an arbor with the wheel, collet mounted, indicates an early clock. Later, all dial clocks had the wheel riveted onto the pinion itself. The pendulum hook securing the verge bob pendulum is obviously not original but does use the correct hole.

PLATE 61

This style of dial clock was produced in large numbers with 12in. convex iron dials with bold hour numerals and spade hands. This particular example is unsigned and has an offset winding hole. The convex sectioned bezel has a convex glass, plastered in without a sight ring. The mahogany, convex surround is pegged onto a rounded bottom box and has one side and one bottom door. Circa 1870.

Right: The movement has shaped shouldered plates, anchor escapement and the fusee winding square offset on the right. It has four movement pillars but only three dial feet.

Chapter 7

Styles

Tavern Clocks

The main features of the tavern clock which give indications for assessing or dating, together with the case, are the dial and surround shape, trunk shape, ears and base. (Drawings of these features are on pages 112-123.)

Drawing 1 shows the five major surround shapes; the square shield dial, which did not have a signature on the dial itself, was the earliest type, probably from 1720-1735; the rectangular shield dial which was constructed of vertical boards and had the signature along the lower edge in a single line and dates 1730-1750; the shield had concaved bottom corners which concentrated the signature into two lines — this shape was also constructed of vertical boards and dates 1745-1775; the octagonal dial was never over-popular, but is found over the period 1750-1800 in lacquer or walnut; finally the circular dial, the most common shape from 1750 onwards, which was constructed with horizontal boards.

Although surround sections (Drawing 2) vary widely in actual design, a few facts can be obtained from them. Number 1 shows a squared shield dial surround with the dial put in from the back, like a picture in a picture frame; it has simple mouldings and is very wide. Number 3 is a later shield dial surround with slightly more detailed mouldings. The dial in 6 has been put in the same way but since this is a circular dial the surround is therefore not so wide. In 5 and 7 these circular dial surrounds have had the mouldings built up onto the dial before turning to the shape required, which was normal practice with early circular dials. As 2 is dated 1750, it is most likely that the top moulding has been removed. Numbers 8 and 9 show circular surround sections which have had the mouldings turned in the same thickness of wood, the latter with a convex dial. Both of these date around 1790. Number 4 is an octagonal surround.

Drawing 3 shows the three basic designs of trunk door. Number 1, with a moulding around its edge, is used with all the shield dials and with the octagonal dial and is generally shorter than the other two designs. Number 2 is used exclusively with the circular dial with the semi circular concave top matching the line of the dial, while 3 is used exclusively on teardrop shaped trunks which exactly match the door shape. Both 2 and 3 generally have rebated edges rather than mouldings.

The early tavern clock bases were cushion shaped, but from the shield dial onwards the bases were of very similar designs (Drawing 4), the most common shape being that seen in 2 with occasional slight variations. With both these bases the bottom was attached to the sides showing the end grain of the wood. No attempt was made to disguise them except at the front where a moulding was added across the join and this followed around the sides.

With ear pieces (Drawing 5), 1 shows a simple design from a 1760 walnut tavern clock; such a design was not used on lacquer of the same period and only

A fine trunk dial clock and movement by
Brockbank and Atkins. See Plate 67 for details.

reappeared in similar simple designs on the later mahogany tavern clocks. Lacquer clocks with circular dials tended to start with flamboyant designs as in 2, becoming more simple as the years went by until 3 and 4 in the 1790s.

Movements of tavern clocks are remarkably similar in style and construction, wherever their origin. The plates on pre-1750 clocks were, occasionally, slightly different in shape, with either one or two projecting shoulders half way down the plates or, alternatively, slightly bulbous in the middle. Otherwise all the plates were tapered until the end of the eighteenth century when some became rectangular. The layout of the trains varied slightly but this was due entirely to the maker's preference rather than any date guide. With a four wheel train the barrel was mounted directly under the centre wheel and often all the wheels were planted in a straight vertical line. With a five wheel train, the extra wheel was mounted on either side of the barrel, though not in a set position, and the barrel wound anti-clockwise. The motion wheels usually had three spokes to the minute and intermediate wheels, with the hour wheel uncrossed. The intermediate wheel shifted its position according to the manufacturer's fancy, but virtually all are stud mounted unless they have counterbalances on the backplate.

The pillars varied little from one clock to another and were virtually all the design shown in Drawing 6.

Providing they can be established as original, hands are a fairly good date guide. In Drawing 7 it can be seen that the hands started with simple designs with arrow headed tips as in 1 for the early squared shield dial, changing to heart shaped for the rectangular shield dial in 2. By 1765 the hands were becoming more elaborate as in 5, 6 and 7 but later tended to revert back to simple lines as in 8, 9 and 10 with occasional exceptions like 11. Number 12 is from an early Norwich clock. It can be seen that three-quarters of all tavern clocks had counterbalanced minute hands and with most of the earlier ones the hour hands were also balanced. There was no great need to balance hour hands, but it was virtually essential for the minute hand, and clocks which did not have counterbalances on the hands themselves were, almost without exception, balanced inside the clock.

English dial clocks

The earliest style of case had its surround screwed directly to a salt box back, as shown in Drawing 8. The box was virtually square with dovetailed joints at the corners, a large side door, with side strips, usually in a central position and another door on the flat bottom. The backboard was extended below and often above as well, and cut to a shaped design. This board was attached to the back, showing the joint, whereas with later rounded bottom boxes the back was let into the sides and showed no joint from the side as in Drawing 9. With this type of box the side door became smaller and moved up, but retained the side strips. The bottom door was curved to fit the base and had thin wooden strips attached to the sides to form a cockbead. The surround was attached onto the box by means of four wooden pegs pushed through the surround uprights. The back box did not change much until about 1900 when the side doors were made solid with rebated edges and the bottom door lost the side strips which were often simulated by a gauged line.

Most early dial clock surrounds tend to be well moulded, concave section designs, developing into convex/concave section and later to complete convex section. The dates given in Drawing 10 are from actual examples found but such examples can be found before and after the given dates, sometimes up to several decades. Number 1 is exceptionally early and from one of the first true dial clocks made. It has a wooden bezel, hence the long, flat section to take the wide bezel, and an elaborate moulded surround. Numbers 2, 9 and 12 are also surrounds with wooden bezels. As can be seen, the intrusion of the convex shape into the moulding came very early as in 7 and 11, around 1790-1795, and was very apparent by 1805 as in 14, although concave surrounds continued up until about 1840. Numbers 18 and 19 were very common in early convex sectioned surrounds but 23 predominated throughout the later years of the dial clock.

Bezel sections started in the same way with concave sections. In Drawing 11, numbers 1 and 2 are brass bezels from cartel clocks; a very low bezel was possible because the dial was put into the case from the back with ½ in. of wood between the dial and the bezel, thus leaving plenty of room for hand clearance. Numbers 3-7 are wooden bezels, all with concave sections as also were the first brass bezels, 8-18. All these were much higher than the earlier cartel clock bezels, as the dials were put in from the front and so hand clearance was required. If the bezel was at all low, it had to have a convex glass. The concave bezel was not necessarily used only with concave surrounds; convex surrounds were also used. The earlier convex bezels were not a true arc but were often almost straight sided, curving at the top and then dipping back down to the glass as in 19-21. Number 22 was a type of bezel, used almost exclusively with small dial clocks with less than 10in. dials, and had a fitted glass, sprung into the recess. Number 23 was the very common low convex bezel which had a convex glass plastered in. The first spun bezels were used without a sight ring, but it was not long before the silvered sight ring was applied and plastered in to hold the flat glass as in 24 and 25. Cast bezels were still used in the better quality clocks but now they had a sight ring cast in one piece, with thick, flat, bevelled glasses as in 26 and 27. Number 28 shows the very last type of spun bezel to be used, first in American dial clocks, and now the only modern replacement available with snapped in sight rings.

With the movements themselves the main points are plate and pillar styles. Drawing 12 shows the main plate shapes, with 1 and 2 being used only for English cartel clocks. However, examples of these have been found in very early dial clocks though in each case it has been found that the movements were originally in a cartel clock and later recased into a dial clock. Number 3 shows the tapered plate which was used in most dial clocks and trunk dials in the late eighteenth and early nineteenth centuries up until about 1870. Other shaped plates were also in use at this time especially rectangular shouldered plates, as in 5, which were virtually always used for striking clocks. Numbers 6 and 7 were most commonly used in clocks with less than a 10in. dial.

Several designs were used in the shaping of the corners of the plates as in Drawing 13. Number 1 was used solely on cartel clocks with the shaped shoulder about a third of the way up the plate and on one side only. Number 2 is the concave shouldered plate which was quite early but not used to a great extent. Number 5 is generally termed a convex shoulder with 4, 6, 7 and 8 termed as shaped shoulders, the most common of which was 6.

In Drawing 14 different pillar styles are shown with number 1 from a cartel clock. Number 2 was fairly common in very early dial clocks and had very little projection in the centre as against the slightly later one shown in 4. Different forms of this design occurred throughout the dial clock period, as in 5-10, 13, 14 and 16. Around 1830 the central design on the pillar was occasionally left out and the pillar was then either straight sided, tapered or curved as in 11, 12, 15, 17-19. By 1900, the pillars were often completely straight sided with no shaping at all as in 20. The earlier pillars were riveted into the backplate as normal, then later screwed into the frontplate. Very late examples were often screwed through both front and backplates.

Hands of dial clocks are very useful in assessing age, providing it can be ascertained that they are original to that particular clock, for they are fairly interchangeable. Hands have been split into three different sections, heart and spade, fancy and moon hands.

In Drawing 15, numbers 1 and 2 emerge from the tavern clock style of hands. Number 3 shows an early spade hand which is shaped over its length whereas 4 and 5 have areas fretcut out and have both minute and hour hands with spade shaped tips. Number 6 shows a large pair of hands with the minute hand counterbalanced, and although the hands of 7 are just as long, this minute hand shows no counterbalance on the hand, which would normally be balanced inside the movement. Over the years these spade hands became more simple in design and this is shown in 8-12, 16-18. In 16 the hour hand gradually leads into a point and the minute hand is slightly tapered between the base and the tip. Such hands were used very widely on standard 12in. convex and flat iron painted dials before 1900 but were replaced, after 1900, for 'run of the mill' clocks by 18. The main differences were that the tip of the hour hand was now broad and the minute hand was an even width throughout its length. Around 1840-1850 a similar type of hand was in occasional use as in 13, with a variation on this in 14 and 15 which were used by Frodsham, Gracechurch Street, London in both brass and steel.

Fancy hands were generally similar in design to those used on longcase clocks and early ones were extremely well made and finished. Drawing 16 numbers 1-5, show hands typical of the eighteenth century dial clocks, gradually becoming less intricate over a period of thirty years. Numbers 6-11 show diamond shaped tips to the hands, some of which were also very apparent on painted dial longcase clocks of a similar period. Numbers 11-14 are hands very typical of those used by Thwaites on wooden dial wall clocks between 1800-1825 all made in brass with the exception of number 11 which was steel used also on enamel and iron dials. Number 15 shows a fleur-de-lys hand used in the latter half of the nineteenth century but not common on English clocks.

Moon hands were widely used throughout the nineteenth century and varied little in design as shown in Drawing 17. Numbers 1 and 2 are early moon hands with the open circle cut up into the tip of the hand, whereas 3 and 5 show that this later disappeared. Number 4 is from a clock of German origin around 1840 but basically similar in design.

Drawing 1. Surround shapes.

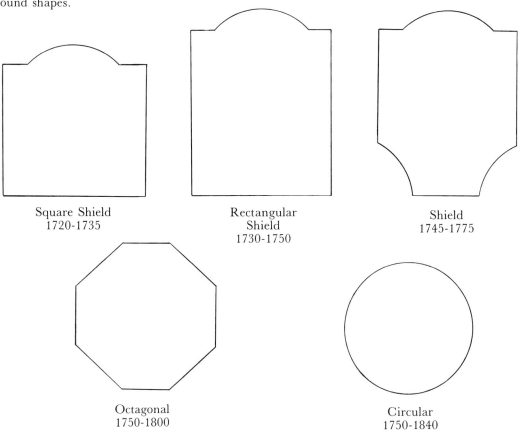

Square Shield
1720-1735

Rectangular
Shield
1730-1750

Shield
1745-1775

Octagonal
1750-1800

Circular
1750-1840

Drawing 2. Tavern clock surround sections. Dates are from actual clocks.

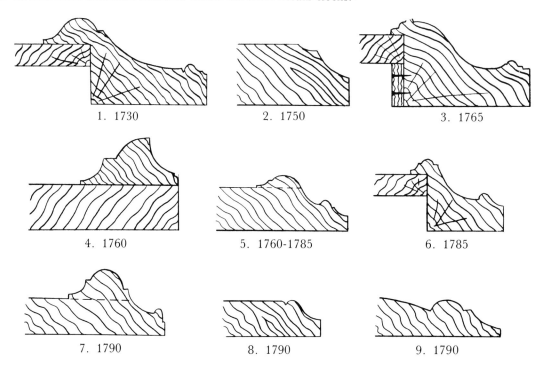

1. 1730

2. 1750

3. 1765

4. 1760

5. 1760-1785

6. 1785

7. 1790

8. 1790

9. 1790

Drawing 3. Door shapes

1. Used with
   shield and
   octagonal dials

2. Used exclusively
   with
   circular dials

3. Used exclusively
   with teardrop
   trunks

Drawing 4. Tavern Bases.

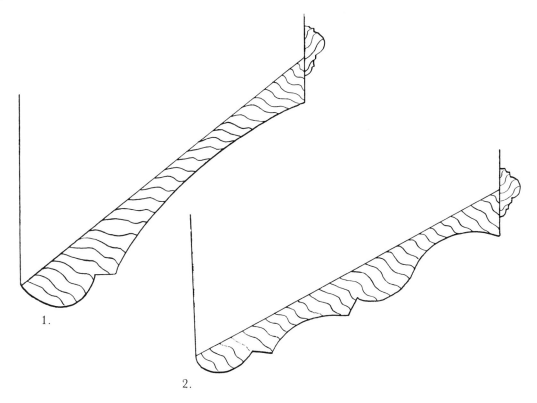

1.

2.

Drawing 5. Ear designs. Dates from actual clocks.

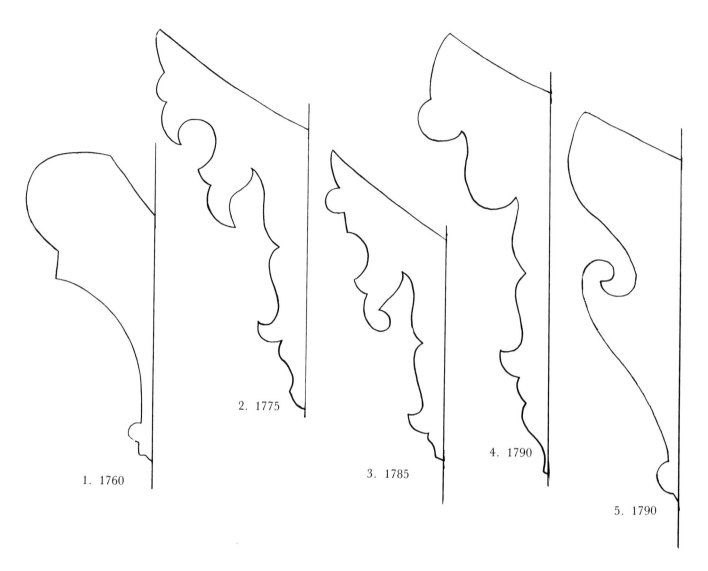

1. 1760

2. 1775

3. 1785

4. 1790

5. 1790

Drawing 6. Tavern clock pillar.

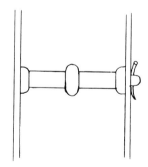

Drawing 7. Tavern clock hands. Dates from actual clocks.

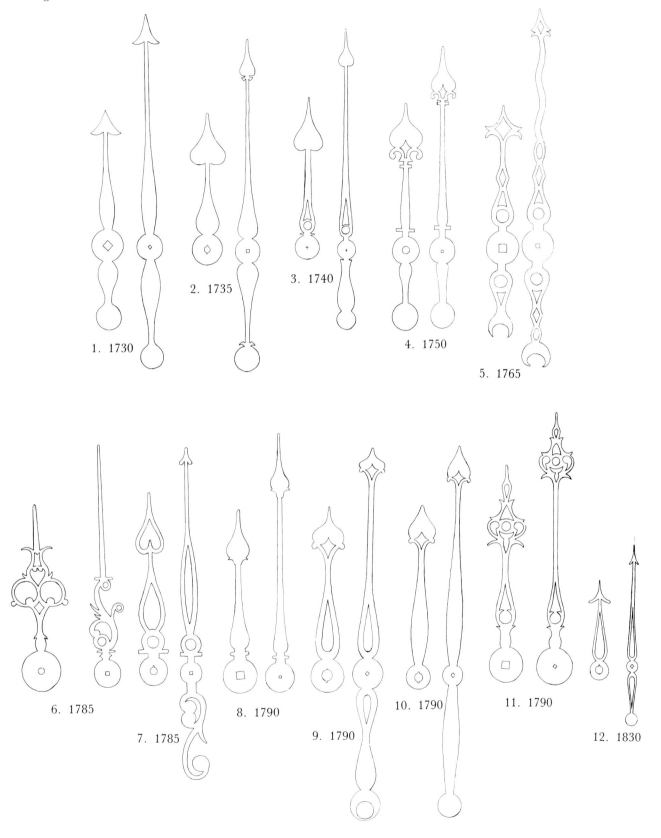

1. 1730

2. 1735

3. 1740

4. 1750

5. 1765

6. 1785

7. 1785

8. 1790

9. 1790

10. 1790

11. 1790

12. 1830

Drawing 8. Salt box back.

Drawing 9.
Normal construction
of a rounded bottom box.

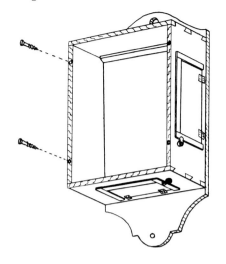

Drawing 10. Dial clock surround sections. Dates from actual clocks.

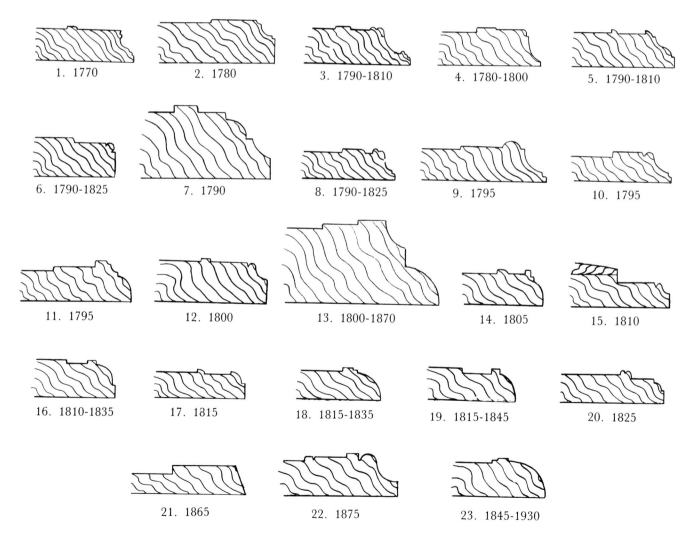

1. 1770

2. 1780

3. 1790-1810

4. 1780-1800

5. 1790-1810

6. 1790-1825

7. 1790

8. 1790-1825

9. 1795

10. 1795

11. 1795

12. 1800

13. 1800-1870

14. 1805

15. 1810

16. 1810-1835

17. 1815

18. 1815-1835

19. 1815-1845

20. 1825

21. 1865

22. 1875

23. 1845-1930

Drawing 11. Bezel sections. Dates from actual clocks.

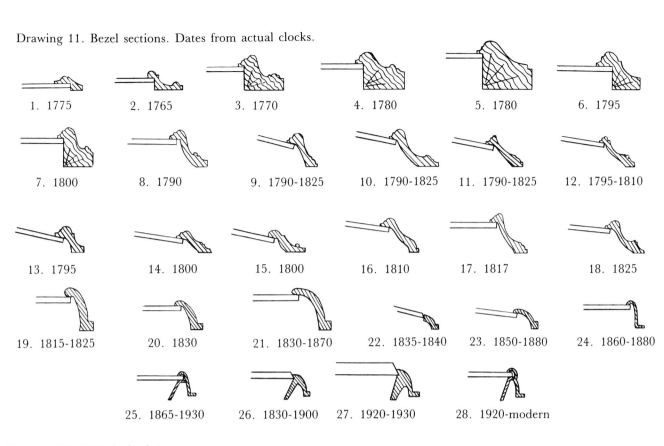

1. 1775   2. 1765   3. 1770   4. 1780   5. 1780   6. 1795

7. 1800   8. 1790   9. 1790-1825   10. 1790-1825   11. 1790-1825   12. 1795-1810

13. 1795   14. 1800   15. 1800   16. 1810   17. 1817   18. 1825

19. 1815-1825   20. 1830   21. 1830-1870   22. 1835-1840   23. 1850-1880   24. 1860-1880

25. 1865-1930   26. 1830-1900   27. 1920-1930   28. 1920-modern

Drawing 12. Dial clock plates.

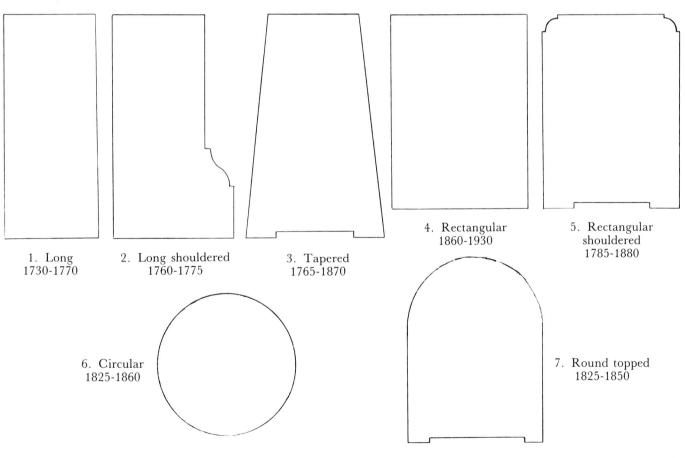

1. Long
1730-1770

2. Long shouldered
1760-1775

3. Tapered
1765-1870

4. Rectangular
1860-1930

5. Rectangular
shouldered
1785-1880

6. Circular
1825-1860

7. Round topped
1825-1850

117

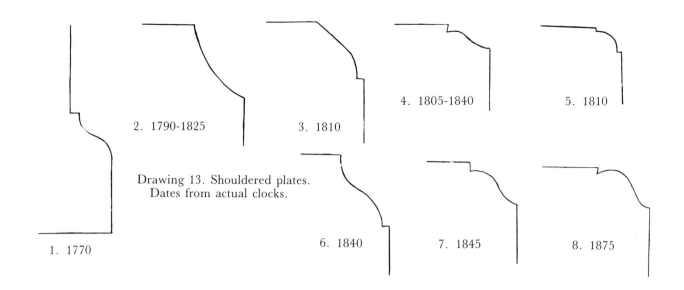

2. 1790-1825

3. 1810

4. 1805-1840

5. 1810

Drawing 13. Shouldered plates.
Dates from actual clocks.

6. 1840

7. 1845

8. 1875

1. 1770

Drawing 14. Pillar designs. Dates from actual clocks.

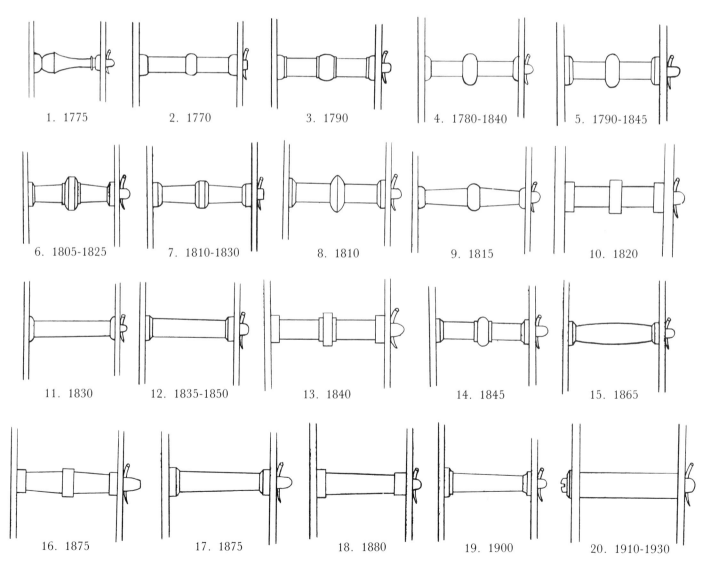

1. 1775

2. 1770

3. 1790

4. 1780-1840

5. 1790-1845

6. 1805-1825

7. 1810-1830

8. 1810

9. 1815

10. 1820

11. 1830

12. 1835-1850

13. 1840

14. 1845

15. 1865

16. 1875

17. 1875

18. 1880

19. 1900

20. 1910-1930

Drawing 15. Heart and spade hands. Dates from actual clocks.

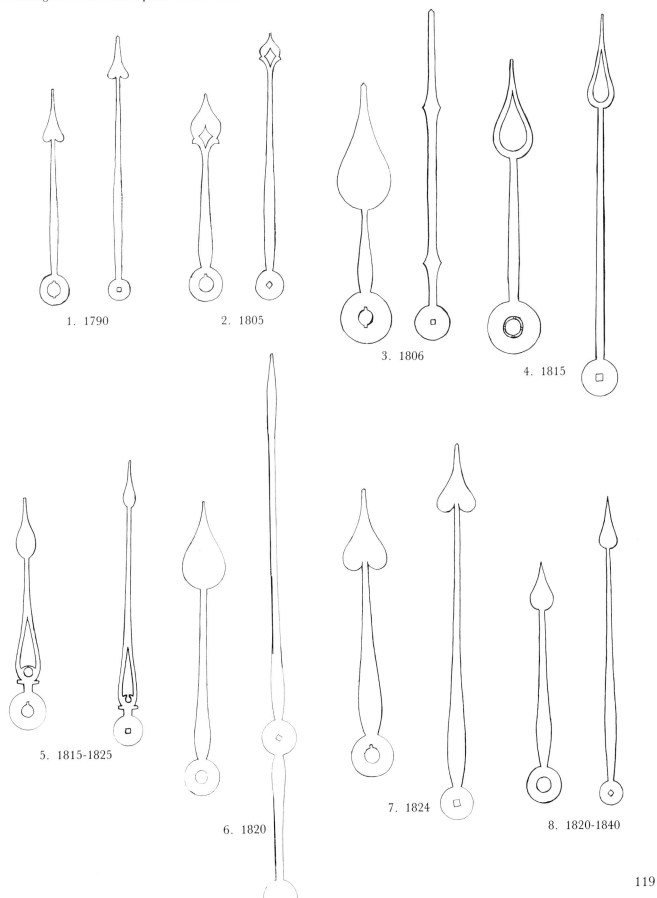

1. 1790

2. 1805

3. 1806

4. 1815

5. 1815-1825

6. 1820

7. 1824

8. 1820-1840

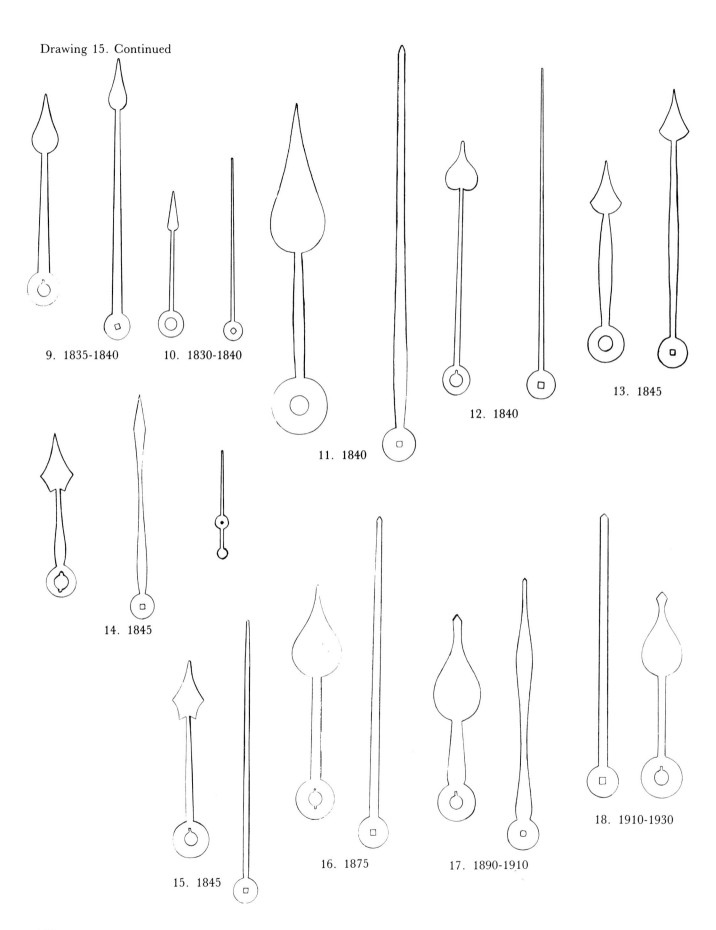

9. 1835-1840

10. 1830-1840

11. 1840

12. 1840

13. 1845

14. 1845

15. 1845

16. 1875

17. 1890-1910

18. 1910-1930

Drawing 16. Fancy hands.

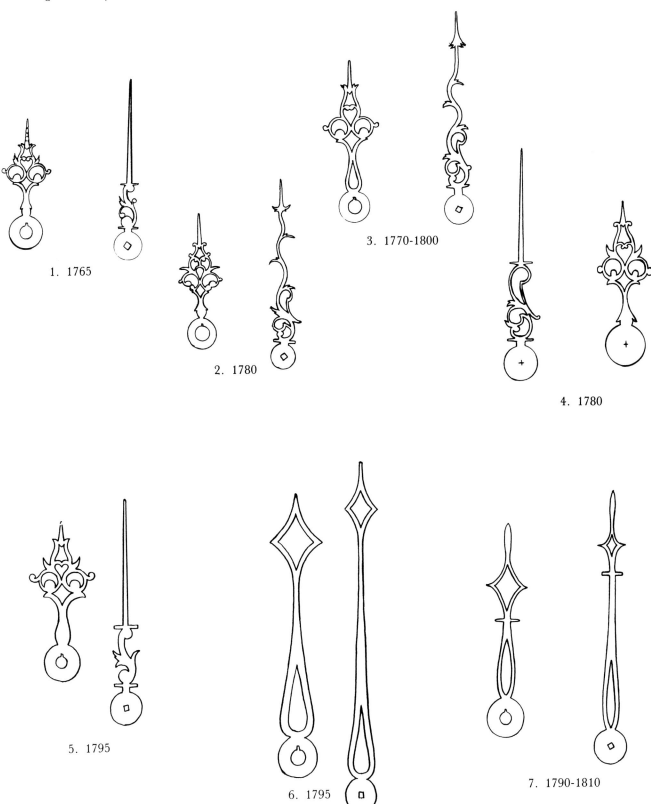

1. 1765

2. 1780

3. 1770-1800

4. 1780

5. 1795

6. 1795

7. 1790-1810

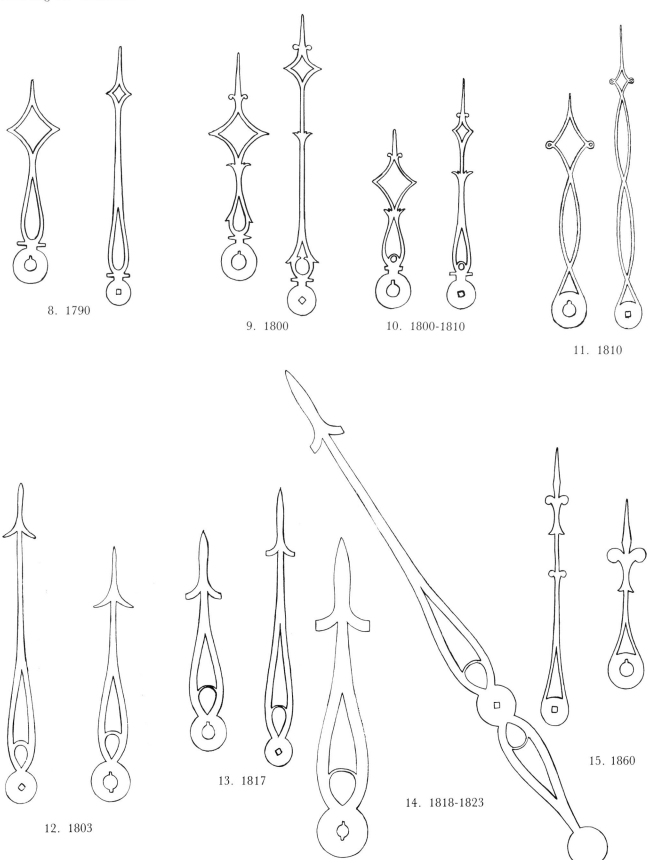

8. 1790

9. 1800

10. 1800-1810

11. 1810

12. 1803

13. 1817

14. 1818-1823

15. 1860

Drawing 17. Moon hands.

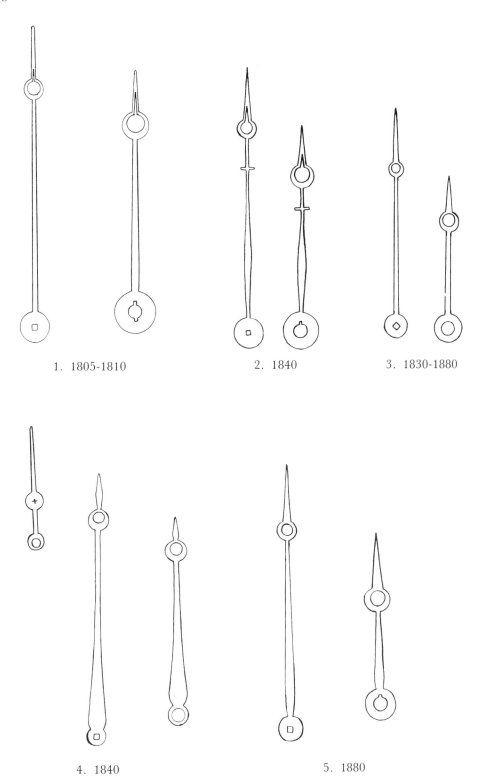

1. 1805-1810   2. 1840   3. 1830-1880

4. 1840   5. 1880

PLATE 62

A typical railway clock with a flat iron painted dial with numerals 13-24 written within the normal Roman hour figures, and signed 'B.R.(S). John Walker, 1, South Molton St; London' and numbered '1540S.E.' It has large blued steel spade hands, with the minute hand counterbalanced within the movement on the backplate. The oak case is of very sturdy construction with a slide off hood supported by carved scrolls. The hood door opens through the complete width and has a silver painted sight ring attached. The trunk has a long panelled door with a chisel shaped base. Circa 1920.

Dimensions: *Dial diameter 18in., total height 77in.*
Maker: *John Walker supplied most of the railway clocks and the firm is still flourishing at the same address. These clocks were, however, normally made and supplied by Gillett & Johnston, Union Road, Croydon. Type number 215.*

Right: The good quality movement has large rectangular plates 7⅛ in. by 8⅛ in., four pillars and is weight driven. It has a deadbeat escapement, maintaining power and a wooden rod pendulum.

PLATE 63

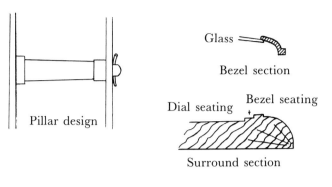

Glass

Bezel section

Dial seating

Bezel seating

Surround section

Pillar design

Right: A late nineteenth century dial clock of a type very common around this period. It has a convex, painted, iron dial with Roman hour numerals, triangle five minute markings and is unsigned. The bezel is of the low convex type, cast brass and used with convex glasses. The makogany case has a convex sectioned surround, rounded bottom box and conventional doors.

The movement has rectangular plates, shaped intermediate and back cocks, anchor escapement and is without a minute wheel bridge. Circa 1880.

Dimensions: *Dial diameter 12in., surround diameter 14¼in.*

PLATE 64

Private collection

This small drum dial clock has a brass silvered dial with fine engraving, moon hands and winds at III. The cast bezel has a sight ring cast in one piece and a fitted, bevelled glass. The mahogany case has only a bottom and a back door and is rosewood veneered to the front and sides. Circa 1830.

Dimensions: *Dial diameter 10in., bezel diameter 10½in., diameter of case 11½in.*

Maker: *James Whitelaw, Edinburgh was at 15 Register Street between 1820-1828 and West Register Street in 1846. He died at 6 South Saint Andrews Street on 9 April 1846, aged 70.*

This movement has round top plates with a keyhole shape cut in the backplate, to pass the pallets through, and a flush fitting backcock. The lower left two holes show that at some stage it had a pendulum fixing block, with the fixing nut screwed in the larger hole on the right hand edge of the backplate when not in use. The small hole underneath the fixing nut hole and the matching hole on the opposite side were used when the clock was made with the plates pinned together for marking out. Four pillars, anchor escapement.

PLATE 65 *(shown in colour on page 97)*

A late eighteenth century, early English dial clock with a silvered brass dial and fancy blued steel hands. It has outside minute numerals and minute divisions crossing a single circle without difference in five minute markings.

The movement has tapered plates, four pillars and a verge escapement. Circa 1795.

Dimensions: *Dial diameter 11⅞in., bezel diameter 14¾in., surround diameter 16⅜in., hour numerals height 1in., minute numerals height ⁷/₁₆ in.*

Maker: *John Brydnt, London. Unrecorded.*

This very attractive and extremely unusual bezel is concave sectioned with two bands of beaded decoration. The concave surround is mahogany as is the salt box back with projections at both top and bottom. Both doors have side strips and turncatches with a lock also on the bottom door.

PLATE 66

Private collection

This silvered brass dial wall clock has outside minute numerals, triangle five minute divisions, fancy pierced hands and a fine scroll signature. The cast brass bezel is of concave section, as is the mahogany surround. The back salt box case is made of oak with conventional doors and the whole of the case is ebonised. *Circa 1795.*
Dimensions: *Dial diameter 10in., bezel diameter 11¼ in., surround diameter 12⅝ in., hour numerals height 1¼ in., minute numerals height ⁹/₁₆ in.*
Maker: *Thomas Applewhite, London. Unrecorded.*

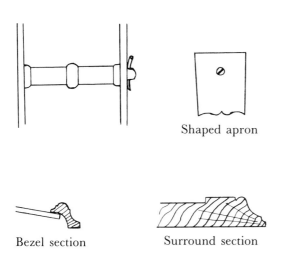

Shaped apron

Bezel section   Surround section

Right: The verge movement has tapered plates with four pillars and a nice shaped apron to the backcock. It has a straight line wheel train with the centre wheel at the front of the plates and a very short verge pinion. The fusee has 19 turns to the groove and since it has 84 teeth, meshing with a centre pinion with 7 leaves, it has, in fact, a duration of nine and a half days. It also has a squared stopwork fixing and a stud mounted intermediate motion wheel, both early signs.

PLATE 67 (shown in colour on page 108)

Right: This beautiful movement has plates 6⅜in. by 8in. with a depth of 2½in. and is signed on the backplate 'Brockbank & Atkins LONDON. 2140.' The hammer spring is on the backplate, as is the cock supporting the extended hammer arbor. The large bell mounted above the movement is 5⅛in. in diameter. To the side is shown the ebony rod, pendulum with brass fittings and a rating nut dovetailed into the massive bob, 4in. in diameter, 1⅛in. thick and weighing 3¾lb.

A very fine quality English trunk dial with a flat, painted iron dial with large Roman numerals, triangle five minute divisions and spade hands. The convex sectioned brass bezel has a sight ring cast in one piece and a flat fitted, bevelled glass. The mahogany surround is concave sectioned and has the bezel lock set in the left hand side. Circa 1875.

Dimensions: Dial diameter 14in., bezel diameter 15½in., surround diameter 19in., total height 23½in.

Maker: Brockbank and Atkins, London 1863-1881 (perhaps the son of the first Atkins, 1815-1839).

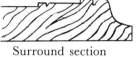

Surround section

Bezel section

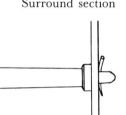

Pillar design

The trunk of the case, also mahogany, has a veneered front and concave base and is decorated with applied carvings on the front. It can be seen that the movement is seatboard mounted and the top of the case is rounded to house the bell. On either side is a door which has pierced wooden sound frets.

Design of side door sound frets

The side view shows the chain fusees and maintaining power. It also has rack striking, five pillars and a half deadbeat escapement.

PLATE 68

This large clock has a convex wooden dial, separate to the surround, with small hour numerals, diamond five minute markings and fine moon hands. The bezel is of an unusual section and has the lock attached to the bezel on the left hand side. The mahogany surround is convex sectioned and is pegged onto the curved foot trunk which does not have any ear pieces. On the back of the dial is a falseplate made from a longcase painted iron dial plate. Circa 1810.
Dimensions: *Dial diameter 14in., surround diameter 16½in., hour numerals height 1¼in.*
Maker: *William Randall, Newbury, 1795-1812.*

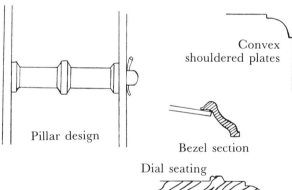

Convex
shouldered plates

Pillar design

Bezel section

Dial seating

Surround section

Right: This very large movement has slightly tapered plates, is convex shouldered and measures 5¼in. across the flat bottom edge of the plate, tapering up to 4⅛in. over a height of 7⅛in., and has a thickness of ⁵/₃₂in. The centre arbor and winding square are very long in order to go through the thick convex dial. It has four pillars, a deadbeat escapement, large fusee wheel 2⅝in. diameter, a barrel height of 2in. and diameter of 3in. The steel rod pendulum is also large with a bob diameter of 4⅜in.

PLATE 69

Right: An interesting anonymous miniature verge dial. It has a convex iron painted dial with small Roman numerals, diamond five minute divisions, spade hands and winds just below III. The bezel is of the type only normally used for small clocks, has a fitted convex glass, and is unusually hinged from the left hand side. The convex sectioned surround is mahogany with a bolt type lock let in from the back. Circa 1830.

Dimensions: *Dial diameter 8in., surround diameter 9½in.*

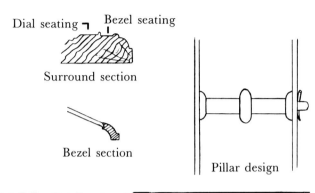

Dial seating ⌐   Bezel seating

Surround section

Bezel section

Pillar design

The back box has chamfered corners so that they do not project beyond the surround and a central door on the bottom and right hand side. From the back can be seen the peculiar method of dial fixing. The dial is attached to a falseplate by two pillars; the falseplate is then secured to the case by two further pillars, at the nine and three positions, which project through the surround on the outside of the box, and are then pinned through. With this method there are no screws visible on the edge of the dial. The movement is mounted onto four dial feet riveted onto the falseplate.

The movement, with round topped plates cut out at the base, has an extension for the front verge pivot and a knife edge suspension in the round topped backcock which has a small apron.

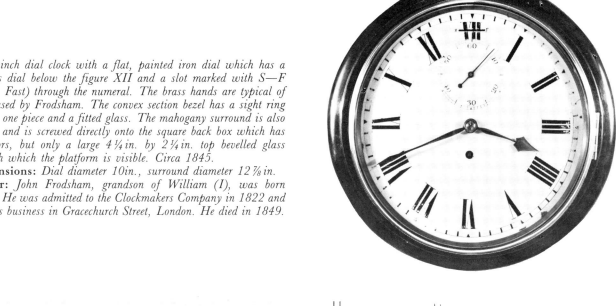

A ten inch dial clock with a flat, painted iron dial which has a seconds dial below the figure XII and a slot marked with S—F (Slow, Fast) through the numeral. The brass hands are typical of those used by Frodsham. The convex section bezel has a sight ring cast in one piece and a fitted glass. The mahogany surround is also convex and is screwed directly onto the square back box which has no doors, but only a large 4¼ in. by 2¼ in. top bevelled glass through which the platform is visible. Circa 1845.

Dimensions: *Dial diameter 10in., surround diameter 12⅞ in.*

Maker: *John Frodsham, grandson of William (I), was born 1785. He was admitted to the Clockmakers Company in 1822 and had his business in Gracechurch Street, London. He died in 1849.*

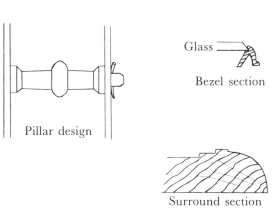

Glass

Bezel section

Pillar design

Surround section

The rectangular plated mvoement, cut away on the bottom edge, has a large ratchet toothed lever escapement with escape wheel and pallets mounted underneath the platform which is 1⅞ in. by 1¼ in. The diameter of the uncompensated balance is 1¼ in. Maintaining power is clearly visible on the right hand side and would be expected in a lever escapement clock. The backplate is stamped in three lines, 'FRODSHAM, GRACECHURCH STREET, LONDON.'

PLATE 71

Left: A large trunk dial with a flat wooden dial, which has been repainted, in one piece with the surround. It has a concave sectioned bezel and mahogany surround. The simple ears on the trunk are made in one piece with the front panel and blocked, for support, from behind. The chisel foot base has a full size bottom door with a ¼ in. convex moulding around it. Circa 1820.

Dimensions: *Dial diameter 17¼ in., bezel diameter 18¼ in., surround diameter 19⅝ in., total length 25½ in.*

Maker: *Probably Dwerrihouse, Carter & Co., Davies Street, London, around 1825.*

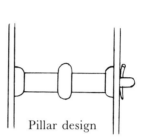

Pillar design

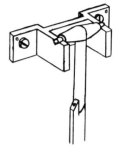

Suspension block

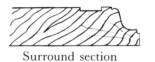

Surround section

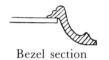

Bezel section

This movement has an anchor escapement with a backcock to take a regulator type suspension block. The threaded hole in the lower pillar is to take the screw, securing the movement to the seatboard.

Left: As can be seen, the clock is hung by a hole in the top of the backboard and has two side doors. The movement is seatboard mounted, and has a very low centre arbor and is stamped on the bottom edge of the front plate 'DM'.

PLATE 72

The trunk, viewed from the back, shows the method of constructing a curve. The base is made in the same way as the round top, by gluing together flat strips of wood with chamfered edges and then veneering over the front surface. The trunk slides onto the main case by well fitting dovetail joints visible on the top edges of the photograph.

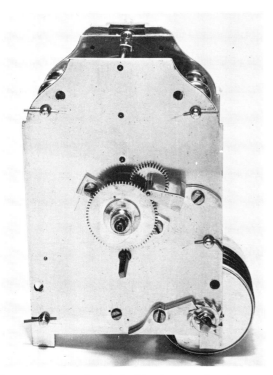

The movement has shaped shouldered rectangular plates, cut away at the bottom edge. It has four pillars, an anchor escapement and the barrel projecting below the bottom edge of the plates.

An extremely elegant trunk dial clock, with a round topped case and straight sides leading down to the ear pieces and terminating in a curved foot base. It is decorated with brass edging and inlaid flower sprays on the ebonised, veneered mahogany structure. The convex iron dial has triangle five minute markings, moon hands and a fine signature. The bezel is convex sectioned, without a sight ring, and has a convex glass. Circa 1840.

Dimensions: *Dial diameter 12in., width 14½in., depth 5⅝in., total height 30in.*

Maker: *Santiago James Moore French was at 15 Sweetings Alley from 1808-1838 and at 18 Cornhill (Royal Exchange) from 1839-1842.*

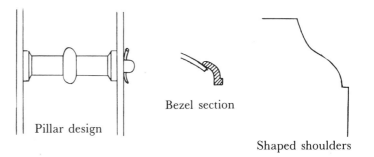

Pillar design

Bezel section

Shaped shoulders

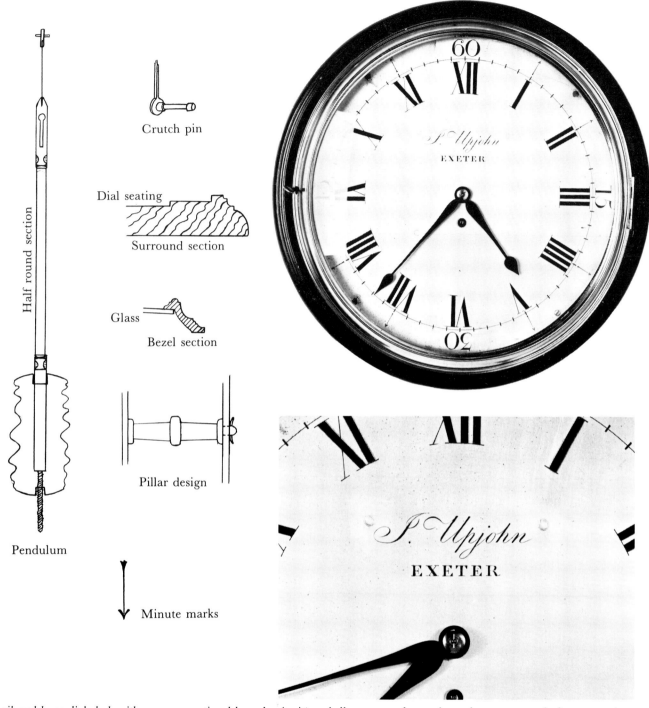

PLATE 73

Crutch pin

Half round section

Dial seating

Surround section

Glass

Bezel section

Pillar design

Pendulum

Minute marks

A silvered brass dial clock with a concave sectioned brass bezel with a shallow convex glass and a mahogany surround of convex section. The back box has two side access doors and a rounded bottom base. The dial has outside minute numerals only at the quarters and arrow markings at the other five minute positions, but the actual minute ring has single strokes throughout, crossing a single circle. It has a rectangular plated movement with an anchor escapement, four pillars and a well designed pendulum rod with a keyhole slot for the crutch pin to prevent it falling out of engagement.

The signature has the J. Upjohn engraved normally and EXETER in capitals, but unusually both are engraved above the hand centre. Circa 1795.

Dimensions: *Dial diameter 14in., surround diameter 17½in., minute numerals height ¾in., plates 6¼in. by 4⅝in.*

Maker: *Although several Upjohns are recorded in and around Exeter during the eighteenth century, this particular J. Upjohn appears to be unrecorded.*

PLATE 74

Left: This silvered brass dial clock has a concave section bezel and concave mahogany surround screwed direct onto the back salt box and so has no pegs. The dial has small Roman figures, does not have any outside minute markings, and winds at VII. It is signed 'Thos. Watkins, Stratford, Essex' and is unusual in naming the county. Circa 1810.
Maker: *Thomas Watkins, Stratford, Essex, 1809-1828.*

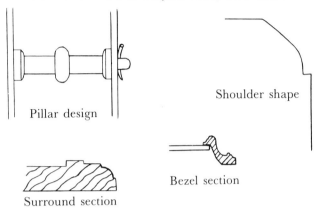

Shoulder shape

Pillar design

Bezel section

Surround section

Above: The view from underneath the clock shows clearly the size and form of a normal bottom door of a salt box case and the absence of pegs on the sides. Unusually the salt box projection is the only part to be veneered.

Left: The movement has shaped shouldered rectangular plates, cut away on the bottom edge and a verge escapement with large shaped apron.

PLATE 75

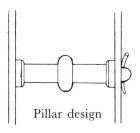

Pillar design

Surround section

Bezel section

Private collection

Left: An interesting silvered dial clock with a case style in between the changeover from salt box to rounded bottom. It has a brass dial with minute divisions across a single circle, without difference in five minute markings, and outside minute numerals. It also has fine spade hands and the full signature all above the hand centre. The bezel is concave sectioned with a bezel lock on the left side and the surround is convex sectioned. The movement has rectangular plates and an anchor escapement. Circa 1800.

Right: This shows an unusual method of securing the surround to the back box. The sides of the box are cut away so that they enter into the surround and are located by a single peg on either side.

Dimensions: *Dial diameter 12 ⅜ in., bezel diameter 13 ½ in. surround diameter 15 ⅛ in., hour numerals height 1 ⅛ in., minute numerals height ⅝ in.*
Maker: *Charles Goodal(l), 26 Bridge Street, Covent Garden, 1793-1824.*

PLATE 76

This miniature wall clock in a brass case has a painted iron dial, recently repainted, and brass spade hands. The case is turned and ringed and has a cast sight ring with a flat bevelled glass. The iron back has a circular door with a brass turncatch to allow access to the rectangular plated movement. The small thirty hour movement has a going barrel, four finely turned and ringed brass pillars and similarly designed blued steel dial feet. The ratchet tooth lever esapement has horizontal staffs with separate cocks on the back but front pivots located in the main front plate. Both plates are numbered at the base 3080.

Although this clock is not, strictly speaking, a dial clock, two points indicate that it is not a ship's clock as there is no flange for securing it and, more importantly, it is backwinding and handsetting. Circa 1860.
Dimensions: *Diameter of case 6 ⅝ in., depth 1 ⅝ in.*
Maker: *Carter, Cornhill, London.*

Private collection

Chapter 8

Alterations and Marriages

Whenever a clock is assessed several questions should be asked; do the styles of the case, dial and movement look right together? Are there any spare holes? Is there any conflict between the expected dates of any of the components? If there are any doubts at all the clock should not be dismissed out of hand, but investigated for evidence and explanations.

It is extremely difficult to attach an exact date to any of the parts of an English dial clock, but the starting point must be to decide if the dial, movement and case appear to be of a similar date. If the dial is painted iron, the case is a trunk dial and the movement a verge escapement, one would immediately be suspicious. However, examples of a verge movement combined with an iron dial do exist, and so do long verge pendulums in trunk dials. The dial should be removed from the case and the surround checked for extra wood screw holes, which might once, perhaps, have secured a different dial into the case. Then the dial feet should be checked against the movement to see if any spare (previous) dial feet holes exist in the frontplate. Similarly there should be no trace of any alteration of the dial feet themselves and the winding hole should line up exactly with the winding square. If a marriage has taken place between the dial and movement it usually involves filing over the winding hole in the dial, and drilling a new set of holes for the dial feet in the frontplate, at very least perhaps only one extra hole, and filing over the others to suit.

Often there is a logical reason for what, at first glance, seems radically wrong. Take the example of a dial clock which, when the surround is unpegged, reveals an extra set of peg holes. It is easy to say that the surround has been married to a back box, but a spare set of holes is not proof enough. Extra holes can appear when, unusually, the bezel is hinged on the left hand side, with the catch which passes through the surround replaced the wrong way up after a repair. The repairer may not have realised his mistake until he attempts to fit the surround onto the box and, being most reluctant to undo the work he has just done, he decides to drill the peg holes in a new position and fit the dial in the wrong way up as well. This can be established by reversing the surround to check if the holes line up the other way.

The bezel may have been replaced fairly often, so it should be checked to see if it fits the recess properly, but don't reject it too hastily if the hinge or bezel lock appear incorrect. The hinge may have been replaced by one which is too small, leaving a gap on either side in the surround. Whether or not this has happened can be checked by seeing if the hinge is dovetailed into the bezel in its original position. Locks are frequently replaced by catches passing through the surround. A large hole in the surround where the lock would have been seated will be quite noticeable, though the keyhole in the bezel may have been expertly filled and difficult to detect.

Dials have, unfortunately, been subjected to frequent repainting, with different names added sometimes. An original painted dial would have a slightly crazed or discoloured background and the figures and name would be neatly written, although they may have faded considerably. By holding the dial to the light a virtually worn out signature can usually be detected when the black has worn off, since the original signature shows up yellow. A common signature mistake on repainted dials is where the end of the name terminated in a scroll, which is mistaken, when repainting, for an 'e'. Do not be put off by a dial where the figures look blotchy, as the corners and straight lines often wear first, leaving a black mass in the centre.

The reasons for alterations in the past have usually been legitimate for the period. It would be quite natural that a repairer in the last century would have said to his customer, ''The clock is worn out, would you like a new movement fitted?' Or, 'A verge escapement will not keep good time so shall we convert it to anchor?' Although the clock was a piece of furniture, the inside was simply the mechanism which moved the hands, and no value attached to its authenticity.

Nowadays, however, the situation has changed and many recently performed marriages come to light, carried out for financial gain, and aimed to deceive.

The most difficult point to account for is when spare holes are found in the movement. Plate 77 shows a very good and perfectly legitimate clock with just one extra hole on the left hand side of the backplate. This was the original position of the pendulum hook which is now missing. It has been substituted by a piece of bent brass wire, soft soldered onto the plate on the opposite side. This is not serious and can easily be rectified. The main point being that no alteration to the plate has been made in any way.

Plate 78 shows a conversion from verge escapement to anchor. The holes in the backplate have been left unfilled and so are very prominent. All the loose holes can be accounted for; the top two small ones underneath the replacement backcock are the steady pin holes for the verge top cock. The other two small ones are the steady pin holes for the verge wheel potence, and, in between these two, the one that is filled and now takes the escape wheel pivot, the original screw hole for the potence. On the left hand side nearer the bottom is the original hole for the pendulum hook.

Plate 78 also shows the movement with an unusual conversion from line to chain and with added maintaining power. This conversion was probably carried out at the same time as the anchor escapement was put in, and one wonders why, in this case, the complete movement was not changed, as this would probably have been easier. The hole for the original line can be seen in the fusee and the barrel has the three holes for the tie off of the line. Now the fusee has been regrooved to take the square section of the chain and an extra wheel added between the fusee itself and the fusee wheel for the maintaining power lever. This lever is clearly visible on the nearside between the pillars. Note that its collet is the same in style to the replaced third wheel and escape wheel collets.

Plate 79 shows a movement with two aspects of change; one is the substitution of parts from another clock, the other the bringing together of an earlier movement with a later case and dial. The fusee and barrel are both from another movement and because the arbors were too short they have been packed out at the front. By extending the shoulder of the barrel arbor it has shortened the square projecting through the plate, so the ratchet wheel only just fits on and there is no room for a pin. The fusee has been originally chain but is now line and the winding square is some way back from the dial.

The backplate of this movement has eight large spare holes, one of which is a pendulum hook hole. The others are due to the several different methods of fixing in a cartel clock with a strap secured across the back. The fact that the dial is a perfect fit to the holes in the frontplate leads us to suspect that the dial was made up originally for this movement and so is not a direct marriage. The dial appears to be of similar date to the case and would be expected to be about 1805 whereas the movement was probably made about forty years earlier.

Most marriages and alterations can be discovered easily enough with a bit of thought and detective work. However, a difficult marriage to detect is when a trunk dial and movement have been put into an ordinary rounded bottom case or vice versa. Evidence of a change of movement and dial would be apparent by the extra wood screw holes in the surround underneath the dial, but as the marriage may appear with contemporary components, the length of the pendulum may not be suspect unless a wheel count is done. If the pendulum is with the clock there is still no reason why it should be the correct one, it may even have been put there to deceive. Obviously it is not always possible to take the clock apart and do a wheel count, especially if the clock is in an auction, but it may be possible to set the clock going for five or ten minutes, checking its accuracy, just to make sure. The only other rough check that can be made is to count a quarter of the wheel teeth and multiply by four in an attempt to establish the wheel count without taking the movement down. However, if a mistake is made it may well give an entirely false picture; for a rough check one or two teeth out may not matter too much, though a wrong count on the pinions will.

Gallery clocks and insert dial clocks have often been suspected of being marriages because of their cases, but this is often a totally wrong impression. It must be remembered that if a building housing such clocks is demolished, or either of this type of clock is removed from a building, it is difficult to use them again for practical purposes unless components are added. The complete insert dial usually consists of the movement, dial, bezel and sometimes surround, and a back box has to be fitted in order to display it, but it is still a complete and perfectly legitimate clock however out of keeping the back box may appear. The points to look for on an insert dial are rise and fall regulation from the front of the dial and a small hole near the bottom of the dial for starting the pendulum with a piece of wire.

Gallery clocks are often back winding with the back box often part of the gallery itself, and so obviously the box cannot be kept with the clock when this is removed. Either a new back box has to be fitted or the existing back box modified. If a gallery clock is to be hung on a wall it is troublesome to have the take the clock, which is often large, off the wall every week to wind it from the back; the best solution is to make up a further backboard. This is hinged to the back of the original box, which can swing out every week for winding without removing the clock from the wall. In this way the original box and back door can be kept intact (Plate 80).

Gallery clocks and insert dials are by no means common as many have been scrapped in the past as being quite impractical to reuse. Since these clocks are usually of top quality and often remain as complete as they ever were, they should not be underrated, as they have been in the past.

Tavern clocks have suffered very little by marriages but to a great extent by bad or ignorant renovations and Plate 81 shows an example of each. The dial has been repainted in basically the correct style but very badly executed with the Roman numerals of the V and X badly spaced and the addition of triangles on the inner circle. The hands, also basically correct, are not wide enough near the centre to be in proportion. The trunk and door remain very original but the ear pieces at the sides have been lost. The replacement base indicates a common fault, being a flat chisel shape instead of deeply moulded.

An alteration sometimes encountered on tavern clocks is a new dial. Originally dials were usually constructed of three boards glued together and, with shrinking over a long period, the joints are often quite apparent. New dials, however, do not have these joints showing and the painting of the dial is often an immediate giveaway. It must be remembered that tavern clocks seem to have stuck fairly rigidly to style and form and any great deviation from these should be queried. Circular dials have sometimes replaced original shield dials but, because of the difference in shape, the gap between the dial and trunk door has been boarded over and the trunk appears exceptionally long.

Plate 82 shows an interesting alteration. Originally the clock ran for about five and a half days and the alteration was carried out to increase this length of time, as shown in figures (a., b. and c.). Figure (a.) shows the board, between the dial and the top of the original trunk, used to fill in the gap. Figure (b.) shows the back of the trunk moved down the uprights to raise the dial. Figure (c.) shows the movement supported at the very top of the case for maximum drop, and it can be seen that an intermediate position was also tried out. With the position of the movement as shown in this photograph, it would only have been possible to attach the pendulum by removing the dial as the side door is below the seatboard. As no major structural alterations were made it was possible to return the movement and dial back to their original positions and the original five and a half day duration. As has been said before, tavern clocks did not have a standard duration and ranged between five and fourteen days.

Recently it has come to light that two very distasteful practices have been taking place, in separate London workshops. In one instance correct clocks have had their iron dials discarded and replaced by badly styled brass dials with semi-famous names engraved on them — for example, 'Dutton, London'. Apart from the styles being incompatible and the absence of outside minute numerals, the easiest way to recognise such a clock is by inspecting the back of the dial which is 'clean' and painted matt black.

The other practice concerns original anchor escapement clocks; in this case all types are being converted to verge. Again, the give away is in the style.

Both these practices are carried out purely for financial gain, but ruin otherwise authentic clocks, and it is hoped that those who are involved will reconsider the damage they are doing.

PLATE 77

Private collection

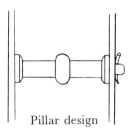

Pillar design

Bezel section

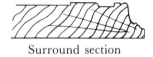

Surround section

*A late eighteenth century brass dial clock. **The** silvered dial engraved with small Roman figures, outside minute numerals and minute divisions crossing a single circle. The concave sectioned, cast brass bezel has a convex glass and matches the section of the mahogany surround. At the back is a conventional salt box case with a projection on the bottom only. Circa 1790.*
Dimensions: *Dial diameter 12in., bezel diameter 13⅞in., surround diameter 15¼in., hour numerals height 1⅛in., minute numerals height ⅝in.*
Maker: *Samuel Hardy, son of John, worked in Somerset Street, Aldgate and was a member of the Clockmakers Company between 1778-1805.*

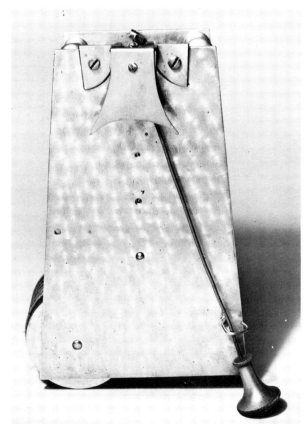

Right: An eight day fusee movement with tapered plates, original verge escapement and a well shaped backcock and apron. The pendulum hook has been soft soldered onto the plate on the wrong side. The original would have been screwed in on the left where the hole remains. The snailing — or spotting — of the plates is decorative and has been put on by a past repairer; the movement would not have been finished originally in this way.

PLATE 78

Private collection

This clock has a silvered brass dial with outside minute numerals only at the quarters, minute divisions crossing a single circle and unusual small diamond five minute divisions. Outside the minute numerals is an engraved circle, with the four screw holes securing the dial beyond this. It has a brass, concave bezel and a concave mahogany surround screwed direct onto the salt box case. On the back of the dial is a repair date 'T. Clark Octr 1812'. Circa 1805.
Maker: *Joshua Gibbins (Gibbons) is recorded between 1809-1824 at 45 White Street, Borough, London.*

Bezel section

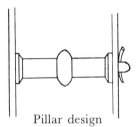

Pillar design

Surround section

Left: The tapered plated movement has been converted from verge escapement to anchor. The backcock, pallets, escape wheel and pinion, and third wheel and pinion have been put in. The holes for the original backcock and the top verge cock are underneath the present backcock and so are not visible from the back. The frontplate has been built up at the top edge to take the pallet arbor pivot.

Right: The side view shows the large, plain collets of the replacement parts; escape wheel, third wheel, pallets and maintaining power detent. The maintaining power is an addition, probably made at the same time it was converted from verge and from line to chain.

PLATE 79

Private collection

This brass dial has outside minute numerals, dot minute divisions and fancy blued steel hands, although the tip of the minute hand has been replaced with the wrong design. It has a low concave sectioned bezel and a concave mahogany surround. The surround is screwed directly onto the salt box back. Circa 1805.
Dimensions: *Dial diameter 9⅛ in., bezel diameter 10⅞ in., surround diameter 11¾ in., hour numerals height ¹⁵/₁₆ in., minute numerals height ⅜ in.*
Maker: *Martin, London. Could be one of many.*

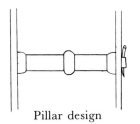

Pillar design

Bezel section

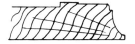

Surround section

This early movement probably dates from around 1765 and has several holes in the backplate, where it has been used for strap fixing in a cartel clock. As the dial feet match the frontplate holes perfectly it can be assumed that the dial, with the case, was originally made up for this movement which may then have been about forty years old. The long, shouldered plates have the barrel mounted in the projection and it has an original verge escapement and five pillars. The barrel and fusee are replacements from another clock. Both arbors have been packed out at the shoulders as they were too short for these plates. Hence the winding square is set a long way back from the dial and the ratchet wheel, with a larger square, barely fits onto the barrel arbor and leaves no room to be pinned on.

143

*Above: An early dial clock and
movement by Theodore Morison.
See Plate 86 for details.*

*Right: A rare dial clock by
Thomas Read. See Plate 87 for
details.*

PLATE 80

PLATE 81

A fine example of an early gallery clock modified for normal use.

The large wooden dial has Roman numerals and triangle five minute markings to the minute ring. It is signed in a semi-circular arc just below the figures 'Payne, 163 New Bond Street.' The blued steel hands are of an unusual design similar to moon hands but without the centre hole.

It has a very deep but narrow bezel with a flat, plastered in glass and does not open. It is secured to the surround by four threaded studs screwed into the bezel, with nuts on the back of the surround. The surround is also extremely narrow as to be almost invisible from the front. Circa 1830.

Maker; *William Payne was working at 62 South Molton St., 1816; 39 High St., Bloomsbury, 1825; 163 New Bond St., 1830-1850.*

Private
collection

A mid eighteenth century tavern clock which has suffered in several respects. The dial has been repainted with poorly proportioned X and V numerals as well as inside triangle divisions which were almost certainly not there originally. It has lost its ear pieces at the top of the trunk. The hands are new and not of a well proportioned design. The base has been renewed wrongly: the flat chisel shape should be deeply moulded. However, the front of the trunk itself appears to have escaped and bears very fine original lacquer work and the signature of Francis Perigal, London. The movement has five pillars, tapered plates and a five wheel train. Circa 1750.

Dimensions: *Surround diameter 29in., total height 58in.*

The view from the back shows two of the four bezel securing nuts and the original back box with two side doors and a rear door. The backboard from which the clock hangs, is new but is a perfect way to retain a gallery clock in its original state, without alterations. It enables the clock to be swung out on the hinges for winding and hand setting.

The rectangular plated movement is of fine quality with an anchor escapement, backwind and back handsetting by means of the small blued steel hand read against the engraved minute ring on the backplate.

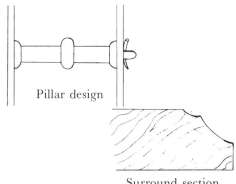

Pillar design

Surround section

PLATE 82

a.

Private collection

d.

This shows the dial moved back to its original position by removing the centre board.

Left: This shield dial tavern clock has a repainted dial, only part of the original hands left and no lacquer work. It underwent alterations which altered its appearance for the sake of increasing the duration. The movement only ran for five and a half days so the case was stretched to give the weight extra drop.

This photograph shows the dial raised above the original line of the trunk and the gap boarded over.

b.

The back has been lowered to raise the dial and a wooden crosspiece put in between the uprights. The peg holes were redrilled in the new position.

e.

The added crosspiece at the back has been removed and the trunk pegged back onto the dial using the original peg holes.

c.

The seatboard of the movement has been raised up through an intermediate position, but this would have made it impossible to fit on the pendulum without removing the dial, as the side door is below the seatboard.

f.

The movement seatboard has been returned to its starting position and the added blocks removed. The door is now in the right position in relation to the movement.

Chapter 9

The Rarer Clocks

Dial Clocks

The design of English dial clocks has tended to follow certain guidelines. The vast majority were only timepieces and apart from the appearance of striking clocks after 1820, any additional feature can be classified as rare.

Some clocks are rare simply by virtue of their age, others because of certain characteristics; any wooden bezel, brass dial, verge clock is rare. The age factor is shown in Plate 83, a black dial clock by Webster with a tic-tac escapement dating around 1760. Another early dial clock is shown in Plate 84 which is a large 14in. convex vitreous enamel dial in a circular water gilded case.

The change from cartel to dial clock was very quick and clean cut and an example made at an appropriate date during the changeover is exceedingly unusual. Plate 85 shows just such a clock, carved in mahogany and decorated with restrained gilding. The 8½in. silvered dial does not have a false pendulum aperture and its design is similar to dial clock lines. Another early example is shown in Plate 86; this particular dial and movement were probably in a cartel clock case, prior to being placed in an early dial clock case, which was undoubtedly made for them. The movement and dial would probably date from about 1760 and the case from about 1775. An exceptionally early clock, it very closely resembles the clock in Plate 87, which is another early dial clock with an 8¼in. dial and a false pendulum aperture. This clock, however, has an extremely rare feature — apart from its age — and that is the use of datework. In this case the date is shown against a pointer, central in the segmented aperture and the right hand square on the dial is for date adjustment.

With most other types of clock datework was usual, but with dial clocks it is undoubtedly rare. Plate 88 shows the use of datework on a 12in. silvered dial clock, this time showing through a square aperture. The ultimate for this type of clock, however, has to be Plate 89 where not only the date is shown but also the day of the week, lunar phase and lunar date. A later example of extreme importance is seen in Plate 90 which shows date, day of week, month and how many days in the month.

With escapements the most common was, of course, the anchor escapement, with deadbeat and half deadbeat being used occasionally. Verge escapements were used for the earlier clocks. Lever escapements are not common and other platform escapements such as cylinder, duplex, chronometer, etc., would be classed as rare. Plate 91 shows a rare dial clock with a silent verge escapement, a type usually only found in bracket clocks and even then not very often. The pallet face is a piece of taut gut line which, although it can be heard, is a vast improvement on the ordinary, very noisy verge escapement. Plate 92 shows another silent verge with very wide gut pallets and an unusual style of case. Plate 93 shows another rare form of escapement, the pin wheel, seldom used in any domestic clocks.

Another uncommon feature is the weight driven dial clock, not to be confused with the tavern or Norwich clock. As the trunk is quite short, it is difficult to obtain sufficient drop for a weight, so the barrel has to be of a very small diameter. Plate 94 shows this small barrel with a large diameter wheel attached to it driving directly to the centre pinion.

The duration of all dial clocks is generally eight days, with occasional variations of a day either side usually due to manufacturing miscalculations. Thirty hour English dial clocks do not seem to exist but month dial clocks do, and these rate as exceptionally rare, however late. A dial clock with a month movement is shown in Plate 95 and, although it was made this century, it must be considered as one of the most unusual aspects of any dial clock. Another late dial clock of rarity is that shown in Plate 96, which has centre seconds, beating half seconds, maintaining power and an engraved iron dial. The engraving of the dial is likely to be a prototype in an effort to mass produce dials by blacking in the numerals and adding the white with a roller.

Two other types of dial clocks not often encountered are alarms and passing strikes. Alarms usually have the setting hand on the dial centre, extending to the minute divisions, and a pull cord winding operation as in Plate 97. Alarms cannot be switched off before they run down except by turning the setting hand, and are usually only found in clocks later than 1850. Passing strikes were used throughout the period on all types of dial clocks and sound a single blow on a bell at each hour. Plate 98 shows a passing strike incorporated in a circular plated, miniature trunk dial.

Full striking dial clocks are not uncommon on clocks of the nineteenth century, but eighteenth century striking dial clocks are very rare. Plate 99 shows a very fine and rare late eighteenth century verge, with silvered dial and salt box case, which has a strike. The reason why early dial clocks did not strike is uncertain but it is possible that, since the original object of the dial clock was to be cheaper and to appeal to a wider market, adding a strike defeated this objective.

Ting-tang and quarter chiming English dial clocks have always been uncommon, mainly due to the size of the movement which limited their use to large clocks. Ting-tangs, on two trains, were used occasionally on English clocks but more frequently on German clocks as shown in Plate 100. Most English ting-tangs, however, were on three trains and so basically of quarter chiming construction. Quarter chiming clocks seem to have been mostly used in large bank clocks or drum cases as in Plate 101.

Rare features on dial clocks continue to arise and recent examples brought to light include a world time clock and a watchman's dial clock. There are probably many more unusual clocks yet to be recognised.

Tavern Clocks

Tavern clocks are, of course, quite uncommon at any time but an early example, especially the square or rectangular shield dial, is rare. Plate 102 shows such a clock.

These clocks were virtually all timepieces with weight driven movements and very similar in design to one another. Occasionally an example with a passing strike may appear, with the bell mounted above the movement and the hammer sounding on it once at each hour. The hammer was lifted direct from the motion work, so it still operated from a single train.

Full strikes are very rare indeed, although an occasional marriage of a Norwich clock or even a longcase clock movement does appear. The genuine movement, however, has no pillar holes in the front plate and is not as deep as a longcase movement. Plate 103 shows a striking movement with a long centre arbor to pass through the thick wooden dial and a few turns in the groove of the barrel due to the limited depth of tavern clock cases. Plate 104 shows a similar movement, but in this case one which drives the motion work from an off centre wheel, rotating once in two hours.

Another rare feature on a tavern clock is date work, as shown in Plate 105. The date is shown against a pointer in a segmental aperture and is operated by a pin on the hour wheel. The date wheel and jumper spring are both recessed into the back of the dial, and the wheel is attached to a stud into a brass plate on the dial face itself.

Plate 106 shows a later Norwich type clock which has very unusual world time incorporated.

PLATE 83 (shown in colour on page 157)

A large wooden dial clock with a black dial and black lacquered case. The dial has been repainted but was probably originally black judging by the wide surround normally associated with black dial clocks. White dial clocks without a bezel generally have narrow surrounds and are considerably later in date. This clock has its original heart shaped brass hands with the minute hand counterbalanced. The name of Webster is not conclusive, as although he made several clocks with tic-tac escapements, as this one has, the few examples seen of dial clocks with this escapement have all been either by obscure or totally anonymous makers. Circa 1760.

Dimensions: *Dial diameter 13 ⅜ in. Surround diameter 16 ½ in.*

Private Collection

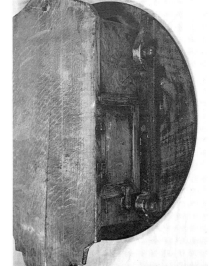

The oak back box has projections of the salt box at both top and bottom and as can be seen a pegged on surround, conventional with black dial clocks but not with later silvered dial verge wall clocks. The box has an access door on both sides but none at the bottom.

The long rectangular plated movement with four pillars, a verge type pendulum hanging down below the bottom edge of the plate and the early type of pendulum fixing hook.

This escapement is rare on dial clocks with the tic-tac pallets embracing 2 ½ teeth and pivoted from the backcock screwed on one side only which is general for these escapements.

An early nineteenth century wall clock with an unusual 14in. enamel convex dial, regulation dial below the figure 12 and a hole just above the figure 6 for starting the pendulum. It is signed Geo. Yonge, London. The actual maker is Thwaites numbered 4380, with this type of blued steel hands being typical of him. It has a concave section brass bezel and a deeply moulded water gilded surround retaining most of its original gilding. Circa 1809.

Dimensions: *Dial diameter 14in. Total case diameter 24in.*

Maker: *George Yonge, 131, Strand, London 1776-1815. Actually John Thwaites numbered 4380.*

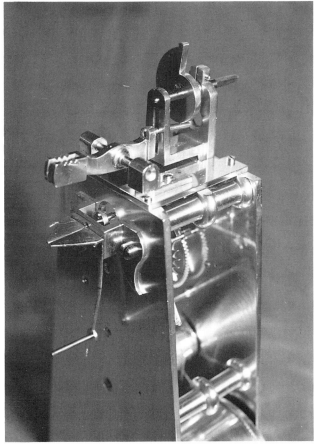

The tapered plated movement of five pillar construction has typical Thwaites rise and fall regulation from the front of the dial. A hand fits on the front square which carries a cam on its arbor, and upon its edge rests a steel stud attached to the brass support for the pendulum suspension. This support rocks on its arbor pivoted between two brackets screwed to the top plate. The suspension passes between two cheeks on the back cock which control the pendulum's effective length.

PLATE 85

This unusual wall clock has a silvered dial with outside minute numerals and minute divisions without difference on five minute markings. The dial does not have a false pendulum aperture, which is unusual in cartel clocks, and has later hands. The bezel is low, concave section, with a flat glass and a lift up catch on the left hand side.

The case is carved extremely well from a single piece of mahogany and is finished in a very dark colour and decorated with restrained gold leaf. Circa 1765.

Dimensions: *Dial diameter 8½in., height 15in., width 13in., depth 5¼in.*
Maker: *Heeley, Deptford. Could be Joseph.*

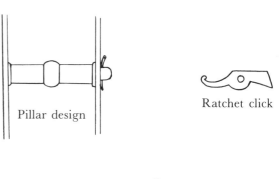

Pillar design

Ratchet click

Glass

Bezel section

Left: The movement with tapered plates, fits into the case from the back, and has a bracket for fixing at the bottom instead of the more usual strap fixing across the back. It has early style pillars with a very little raised middle section. The clock has been reconverted back to verge; the poor design of the backcock and the pendulum bob are readily noticeable.

Left: A small early dial clock with movement and dial originally from a cartel clock, but housed in a dial clock case made for them, probably about fifteen years later. The dial has a single engraved circle within the hour numerals, outside minute numbers and minute divisions without difference on the five minute markings. It has a false pendulum aperture and original fancy blued steel hands. The mahogany bezel is concave sectioned as is also the surround which is unusually pegged onto an original oak salt box which has projections at both top and bottom. Circa: case 1775, movement and dial 1760.

Dimensions: *Dial diameter 8in., surround diameter 11in.*

Maker: *Theodore Morison, London; worked in Saint Swithins Lane, died in 1766.*

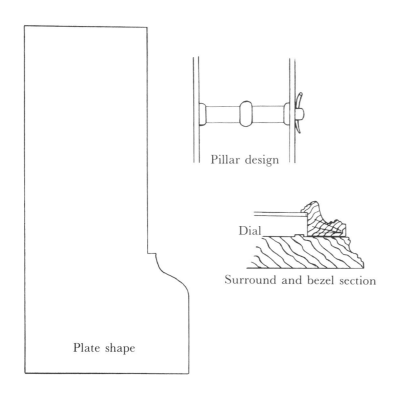

Pillar design

Dial

Surround and bezel section

Plate shape

Right: The fine movement has long shouldered plates, five pillars and original verge escapement with a small apron at the back. It has two spare holes on the backplate which were originally used for strap fixing into a cartel clock case. The intermediate motion wheel is stud mounted and the stopwork has a square fixing into the plate.

PLATE 87 (shown in colour on page 144)

A very rare, small English dial clock. The brass, silvered dial has a single circle engraved within the hour numerals, outside minute numerals and triangle five minute divisions. It has an engraved false pendulum aperture, original hands and an engraved dial centre. Below the hand centre is a segmental date sector with a central pointer. The right hand square is for correcting the date. It should be noticed that there are no screws to secure the dial, as this is attached to the movement which is seatboard mounted. The mahogany bezel has a flat glass and is concave sectioned as is also the surround which is not pegged but screwed onto the back salt box. Circa 1780.

Dimensions: Dial diameter 8¼ in., bezel diameter 10⅝ in., surround diameter 11⅜ in., hour numerals height ¹⁵/₁₆ in., minute numerals height ⁵/₁₆ in.

Maker: Thomas Read, Ipswich, born 1733, died 1817.

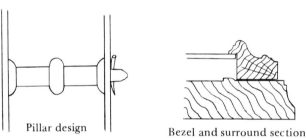

Pillar design   Bezel and surround section

To prevent them showing from the front the corners of the case back have been chamfered. The hole at the top was cut when the movement was converted from verge to anchor when it became necessary in order to get to the top of the pendulum, since the case was not made to take a detachable pendulum. It was also necessary to hinge the side door at the front though it was originally hinged at the back.

The tapered plates are of five pillar construction and the movement has been converted from verge to anchor. The original centre arbor has been retained but has a groove turned in it to clear the third wheel. It has also had a flush fitting backcock fitted. The date is turned by a pin on the hour wheel and can be corrected by the ratchet toothed wheel, stud mounted, to the right of the hour wheel.

PLATE 88

This brass dial wall clock also has datework, but this is shown in an aperture below the winding square. The dial has the signature and town above the hand centre, outside minute numerals and minute divisions crossing a single circle with small diamond five minute markings. The hands are replacements. The brass bezel is concave section with a flat glass and is fitted onto an unusual sectioned surround. The salt box case has projections at both top and bottom. Circa 1790.

Dimensions: *Dial diameter 12in., hour numerals height 1³/₁₆ in., minute numerals height ½ in.*

Maker: *Richard Ward of Winchester is recorded between 1770-1795.*

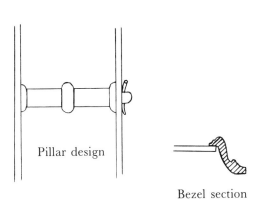

Pillar design

Bezel section

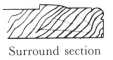

Surround section

Left: The verge movement has tapered plates, four pillars and date work. The date wheel is mounted above the centre and meshes at a 2:1 ratio with a pinion attached to the hour wheel. The date circle is, in turn, moved by a pin on the date wheel once in twenty-four hours.

155

PLATE 89

The silvered dial has outside minute numerals, triangle five minute divisions and three segmental apertures. The top one shows lunar phase and lunar date, the left shows the day of the week and the other the date of the month. The hands are a later replacement.

Private Collection

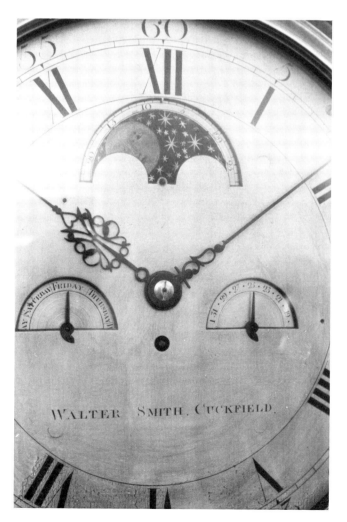

A superb example of a late eighteenth century verge dial clock. The case has a concave section surround of mahogany with a salt box back. The movement has large rectangular plates 5⅜in. x 7¼in. and original verge with shaped apron. It has two date wheels meshing with the hour wheel, one for driving the day of the week and the other for driving both date and lunar date. Circa 1795.
Dimensions: *Dial diameter 12in. Surround diameter 15⅜in.*
Maker: *Walter Smith, Cuckfield, was baptised in 1754 and was the son of William and Ann Smith. He is mentioned in the* Sussex Weekly Advertiser *on 1st November 1773. The advert headed* RUN AWAY *reads: 'From Walter Smith, of Cuckfield, in this county, Clock and Watch-maker, the 6th of July, last, RICHARD POTTER, his APPRENTICE, aged about 18 years, lisps in his speech, strong made, black complexion, wears his own dark hair, about five feet, six inches high, and stoops in the shoulders: Had on when he went away, a light-blue cloth coat, a buff lappelled Waistcoat, and Leather Breeches. This is to caution all Masters of the said Business, and others, not to harbour or employ him on any Pretence whatever, as they will be prosecuted as the Law directs. But if any Person will give Information of the Said Apprentice, or apprehend him, so that he be returned to his Said Master, they shall be rewarded for their Trouble.' On March 15th 1780 he also advertised with his advertisement reading as follows: 'WALTER SMITH, Clock and Watch-Maker, Makes and sells all sorts of WATCHES, Weight and Spring Dials, Repeating and Plain clocks, on the most approved Principles; Begs Leave to acquaint his Friends and Customers, That he continues selling all sorts of IRON-MONGERY and CUTLERY Goods, on the lowest Terms. Having laid in a fresh Assortment of the above Articles, humbly requests the Continuation of their Favours, the Public's in general; which will be gratefully acknowledged, by Their humble Servant, WALTER SMITH. N.B. Likewise buys and sells al sorts of GOLD and SILVER, CREST of ARMS, & C. neatly engraved.'*
He apparently died in the workhouse on 4th September 1817.

An early nineteenth century wall clock. See Plate 84 for details.

Large dial clock with black lacquered case. See Plate 83 for details.

PLATE 90 (shown in colour on page 160)

A large octagonal trunk dial calendar clock. The mahogany case has a curved foot to the base and some ornamental carving to the trunk. The white painted dial has a conventional time dial above the centre, sweep date hand and two subsidiary dials, the left hand dial showing the month and how many days in that month and the right hand dial showing the day of the week. It is signed John S. Fisher, Maker, Walsall. The movement is wound through the centre of the date hand. Circa 1870.

Dimensions: Dial diameter 14in. Bezel diameter 15in. Surround diameter 19½ in. Total length 31½ in.

Maker: John S. Fisher, Walsall. Born 1809. At 60 Park Street 1861-1892.

This interesting movement has the mainspring barrel at the bottom left driving the fusee at the very centre, which in turn drives the would-be centre arbor (at about the 2 o'clock position) which carries a 40 tooth wheel. It is from here that the power to drive everything is taken. The train up to the time hands is a simple set of 40 toothed wheels to conventional motion work. The wheel on the would-be centre arbor drives down to the calendar through another 40 tooth wheel carrying a pinion of 6 meshing with a wheel of 72 which is fixed to a 40 toothed wheel at the front meshing with a wheel of 80 teeth. This wheel has a finger for actuating the day of week star wheel and a pin to actuate the centre date wheel. The centre date wheel carries a pin to turn the 12 pointed star wheel on the left which is fixed to a wheel of 64 gearing with another of 64 to give the month a clockwise direction.

Mr. R.J. Street

PLATE 91

A fine dial clock with a brass dial, small Roman hour numerals, outside minute numerals and minute divisions across a single circle. It is signed in flowing style and has its original hands. The brass, concave sectioned bezel has a convex glass and a bezel lock on the left hand side. The dial is secured to the mahogany surround by three screws with polished heads which locate into brass screwplates let into the surround. The back box has a rounded bottom with a large bottom door, without side strips, overlapping at the edges. Circa 1790.

Dimensions: *Dial diameter 12in., surround diameter 14½in., hour numerals height $^{15}/_{16}$ in., minute numerals height ½in.*
Maker: *John Gudgeon, Bury St. Edmunds, 1785-1801.*

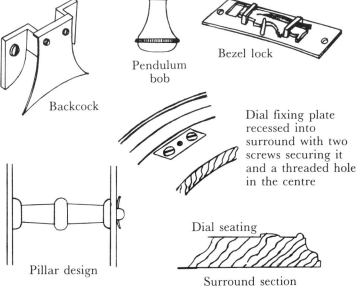

Backcock

Pendulum bob

Bezel lock

Dial fixing plate recessed into surround with two screws securing it and a threaded hole in the centre

Pillar design

Dial seating

Surround section

Bezel section

Gut pallets

The movement has tapered plates, four pillars and a straight line wheel train. The barrel ratchet wheel is thicker in the centre and the click has a tail, both signs of an early clock.

The silent verge escapement can be clearly seen with the gut stretched taut over two steel projections and pinned into the arbor. The front verge pivot is raised up by a projection on the frontplate and the back pivot is a knife edge.

Trunk dial calendar clock by John Fisher. See Plate 90 for details.

Rare trunk dial clock by John Berryhill Cross. See Plate 97 for details.

Right: Movement of a carved German wall clock. See Plate 100 for details.

Below: Views of the movement of a drum clock by John Barwise. See Plate 101 for details.

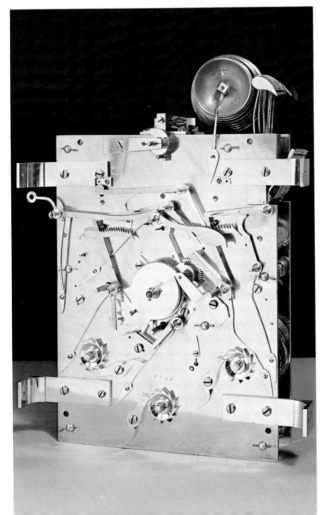

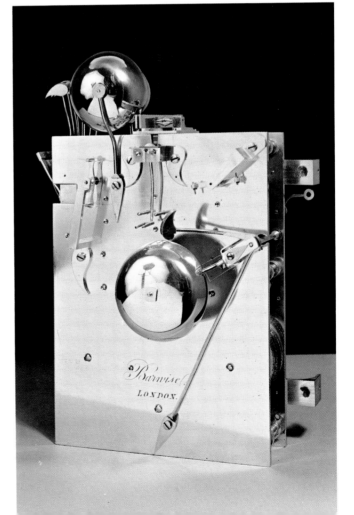

PLATE 92

A fine early nineteenth century circular wall clock, turned from a single piece of mahogany with a circular back door, which has steady plates on both sides without any access doors and so has a hole just to the left of the figure 6 for pendulum starting, a concave section cast brass bezel and original brass heart shaped hands. The dial is painted on a flat brass sheet and signed John Jardin, London. Circa 1805.

Dimensions: Dial diameter 8in. Bezel diameter 9¼in. Case diameter 12½in. Total depth including glass 5¾in.
Maker: John Jardin 1740-1811. Movement by William Robson, Red Cross Street, and Bridgewater Square, 1771-1823.

The front plate with round top and separate bridge for the front pallet pivot. The clock has a straight line wheel train and the motion work and intermediate wheel cock is also on the centre line. Plates size 6½ x 4¾ in. with 1⅞ in. between plates. The stamp of WR 246 above and below the winding square is the mark of William Robson.

This shows the unusual silent verge escapement with a back knife edge suspension. The gut pallets being as long as possible is another unusual feature with the reasoning perhaps that the longer the gut the quieter it was.

Robson also marked the inside of his barrel caps and numbered them as did Thwaites.

Martyn Pettifer

PLATE 93

This extremely rare movement for an English dial clock has a pin wheel escapement. The four spoked escape wheel has its teeth cut on one side from a solid blank and the deadbeat style pallets embrace 7½ tooth spaces. On most pin wheel escapement clocks, mainly turret clocks, the pallet faces are together, one underneath the other, and so embrace only half a tooth space.

It has rectangular plates with four pillars and squared stopwork fixing. The motion work is geared for the twenty-four hour dial so that the minute hand still makes one revolution per hour but the hour hand only makes one revolution per day. The wheel count of the motion work is:

> *Minute wheel 30 teeth*
> *Intermediate wheel 60 teeth*
> *Intermediate pinion 6 leaves*
> *Hour wheel 72 teeth*

The clock bears several early repair dates including one of 1821 on the frontplate. It is, of course, possible to change any clock to twenty-four hour time simply by changing two motion work wheels and repainting the dial accordingly. It is very likely that this clock may have been altered in this way but if so it would have been done a long time ago. Circa 1815.

Tavern clock by William Warin.
See Plate 103 for details.

World time wall clock.
See Plate 106 for details.

PLATE 94

A large, weight driven, trunk dial clock. It has a convex wooden dial, which is separate from the surround, with small Roman numerals, diamond quarter divisons and triangle five minute markings. There is a brass insert in the dial for the winding hole and the original blued steel hands are of an open spade design. The concave section cast brass bezel has a convex glass and a lock attached to the bezel on the left hand side. The case has a convex section surround, nicely shaped ear pieces, a trunk veneered in one sheet running through the base and the door, and inlaid boxwood stringing. Circa 1815.

Dimensions: *Dial diameter 16½ in., surround diameter 19½ in.*
Maker: *Samuel Allport, Birmingham, is recorded between 1790-1836.*

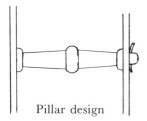

Pillar design

Moulding shape around trunk

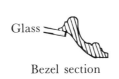

Glass

Bezel section

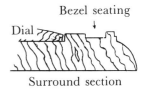

Bezel seating

Dial

Surround section

Left: This rare movement is attached to a falseplate, screwed to the back of the dial, which is signed 'OWEN, BIRM.' The falseplate maker being Edward Owen, Birmingham 1803-1820. The chamfered shouldered plates are of four pillar construction with long centre arbor and winding square 1⅛ in. from the plate. It has the minute hand counterbalanced from the intermediate motion wheel arbor, pivoting between the plates, with the counterbalance on the back made from a cast wheel blank. The barrel wheel is 3½ in. diameter with a ratchet wheel of 2⅛ in. diameter and ten turns of the ¾ in. diameter barrel itself. It has a deadbeat escapement with well shaped pallets and is driven by a rectangular 8lb. weight.

PLATE 95

This late 12in. dial clock has a flat painted iron dial with triangle five minute divisions and spade hands. The convex section bezel has a thick bevelled glass and matches the surround. This is made up in sections as can be seen by the joints at II, IIII, VIII and X — the normal way of making up surrounds this century. The rounded bottom box is deeper than usual, for a larger movement, measuring 5 ⅜ in. and constructed from ⅝ in. thick mahogany. Normal boxes are about 4 ¾ in. deep, made from ½ in. material. The doors, in conventional positions, are also larger than usual with the bottom one 4 ⅝ in. by 4 ⅜ in. with side strips, and the side door made solid with rebated edges. Circa 1920.

Dimensions: Dial diameter 12in., surround diameter 15in.

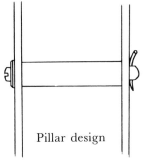

Pillar design

Bezel section

Surround section

Left: This large, rare month movement has large plates, 7 ¼ in. by 5 ⅜ in. by ³/₁₆ in. thick with a distance of 2 ⅛ in. between the plates. The month duration wheel train has the fusee wheel at the front, the stopwork fixed on the backplate and an extra wheel and pinion between the fusee and the centre wheel. It has plain straight sided pillars screwed into the backplate, a large barrel 2 ⅞ in. by 2in. high, and an anchor escapement. It is numbered 1747 on the backplate. Because of the extra train wheel it is anti-clockwise wind.

Wheel count

Fusee 88	
Second wheel 80	Second wheel pinion 12
Centre wheel 84	Centre pinion 12
Third wheel 78	Third pinion 7
Escape wheel 33	Escape pinion 7

166

PLATE 96

An exceptionally rare twentieth century trunk dial clock with centre seconds. The mahogany case has a convex section surround with a very plain rounded bottom box. The front panel, as often as this date, is screwed on with visible brass screws; no attempt was made to hide them as they were intended for decoration. The side access door is solid and rebated, the bottom door has no cockbead but a scored line around its edge to simulate one. The clock has a good quality convex section cast bezel with integral sight ring and flat bevelled edge glass. The dial is most unusual with the figures machine engraved on the iron plate; it can only be speculation that this was an attempt to mass produce dials by blacking in the figures and rollering the dial over in white. It is noticeable that the first figure of the 11 is engraved on the wrong side making it too close to the figure 10. The hands are blued steel spade, with a red painted aluminium seconds hand. Circa 1920.

Dimensions: *Dial diameter 12in. Bezel diameter 12½in. Surround diameter 14⅝in. Total length 19¾in.*

The rectangular plated movement has four plain pillars screwed through the back plate and both plates numbered 10832 on the bottom edges. The would-be centre arbor drives through an extra wheel to the motion work with wheels of 44 teeth, pinion of 7 to the hour wheel of 84. The main wheel train is fusee 96, second wheel (centre wheel equivalent) 64 with pinion of 8, third wheel 60 with pinion of 8, centre seconds wheel 60 with pinion of 8 and escape wheel 30 with pinion of 30. The clock also has maintaining power and a half dead beat escapement.

R.E. Rose

167

PLATE 97 *(shown in colour on page 160)*

Rare trunk dial clock with strike and alarm. The mahogany case has an ebonised convex surround with a mahogany veneered rounded bottom trunk. There are doors in the base and a full length one at the back but imitation doors on both sides with silk backed wooden frets. The cord for the pull wind alarm hangs down on the right hand side. It has a convex section cast bezel with integral sight ring. The dial has long Roman numerals with outer minute divisions, triangle five minute marks and an inner circle marked out in quarter hour divisions for alarm setting. Signed Jn° B. Cross, 70 Cornhill, London. Circa 1850.

Dimensions: *Dial diameter 12¼ in. Surround diameter 14½ in. Total length 19¼ in. Depth of box 5½ in.*
Maker: *John Berryhill Cross, 70 Cornhill, London, 1839-1863.*

The rectangular plated movement shows the pulley containing the alarm mainspring on the top left and the transit block and nut at the bottom for securing the pendulum. When not in use the transit nut lives in the hole in the plate just below the hammer arbor bridge. The backplate is also fully signed.

The two wheel alarm train is visible and shows the hammer verge coming up vertically to the horizontal brass hammer which strikes the bell internally on both sides.

PLATE 98

An exceptionally small English trunk dial. The 7in. convex iron dial has triangle five minute divisions, moon hands and the winding hole at IIII. The low convex section bezel has a plastered in convex glass and a bezel lock let into the back of the convex section surround. The brass inlaid trunk has simple ear pieces and appears slightly wide in order to house the width of the movement. Circa 1850.
Dimensions: *Dial diameter 7in., surround diameter 9in.*
Maker: *H. Read, London. Unrecorded.*

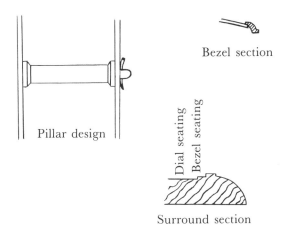

Bezel section

Pillar design

Dial seating

Bezel seating

Surround section

This unusual movement, with 5in. diameter circular plates, is of four pillar construction, has an anchor escapement and a passing strike sounding a single blow at each hour on a bell at the back of the movement (not attached in the photograph).

PLATE 99

An exceptionally fine and rare striking, verge dial clock. The brass silvered dial has outside minute numerals, dot minute divisions and fancy blued steel hands. The concave section cast brass bezel has a flat glass, a dovetailed and pinned hinge and a bezel lock on the left hand side. Its mahogany surround is well moulded, concave section and screwed direct into the back salt box case which has both top and bottom projections. There is a side door on either side and a door on the flat base. The movement has rectangular plates, verge escapement with a small apron and is rack striking. Verge dial clocks are rarely made with a striking train. Circa 1795.

Dimensions: Dial diameter 12in., surround diameter 14½in., hour numerals height 1¼in., minute numerals height ½in.

Maker: Benjamin Ward was at London Road, Southwark from 1780 and at 45 Upper Moorfields between 1790-1808.

PLATE 100

An unusual carved wall clock probably of German origin. The convex iron dial has a seconds dial, actually making one revolution in thirty seconds despite being marked out in sixty divisons, and moon hands. The carved pine case is finished in mahogany colour and has a backboard which is slightly smaller than the front surround, but carved and finished in a similar design. Circa 1840.
Dimensions: *Dial diameter 12in., surround height 29½in., width 21½in., depth 6½in.*

(movement shown in colour on page 161)

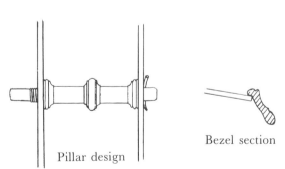

Pillar design   Bezel section

This beautiful ting-tang striking movement has all the lever collets, wheel collets and pillars well shaped and ringed as also are the centre and hammer arbors. The deep domed bells are also ringed. The chain driven movement has an anchor escapement, fine regulation from the top of the backcock, stopwork irons both attached to the same block and blued steel levers and screws. The pin wheel pivots both run, in holes, in adjustable screws in the plates.

PLATE 101

A large three train drum dial clock. The brass silvered dial has a semi-circular scale, engraved under the XII, for rise and fall regulation, and below this, a seconds dial beating half seconds. The minute hand is counterbalanced on its end and the hour hand is counterbalanced on the hour wheel. The bezel is convex sectioned with a separate gilt sight ring with leaf design. The mahogany veneered case has two side doors with fish scale sound frets, a bottom door and a large back door. Circa 1820.

Dimensions: *Dial diameter 18in., bezel diameter 19¾in., case diameter 21¼in., case depth 8in.*

Maker: *John Barwise, 29 St. Martins Lane, London, 1790, died in 1842. He was chairman of the British Watch Company.*

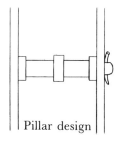

Pillar design

Private Collection

Left: The flirt action, eight bell, chiming mechanism is of eight pillar construction, has chain fusees, maintaining power and a deadbeat escapement. The going train has a five wheel train, all with six spoke wheels, although the other trains have four spoke wheels. It is numbered on the frontplate 9905.

Right: The outside fly fans and the hour bell mounted on the hammer bracket can be seen from the back. It is signed on the backplate Barwise, London. The massive pendulum has a circular steel rod and a bob made from two blanks screwed together.

Dimensions: *Plates size 12in. by 9in. by ⁷/₃₂in. thick. Chiming barrel 3in. across and 2in. deep. Pendulum bob 3⅞in. diameter and 1 ⁷/₁₆ in. thick. Weight of pendulum 5lb., weight of movement 36lb.*

(Movement shown in colour on page 161)

PLATE 102

A very large and early tavern clock with a rectangular shield dial decorated on the corners with leaves and long Roman numerals to the dial with outside minute numerals and minute divisions without difference for five minute marks. Original counterbalanced arrow head brass hands and a script on the lower part of the dial 'The Gift of Severall masters of Vessels. Jos: Jackeman on London Bridge'. The trunk and base are of very unusual design with a small trunk door, a bulbous base with lenticle terminating in a moulded taper all decorated with raised chinoiserie. The clock was presented to the Poole Unitarian Church, by Master Mariners using the Port of Poole, in recognition of the services provided to them during the time they stayed in Poole. Circa 1725.
Maker: *Joseph Jackeman, London Bridge, is listed by Baillie as 1682-1716, but it is unlikely that the clock is this old, and possible that the date of 1716 is not the final working date.*

Poole Museums

PLATE 103 (shown in colour on page 164)

*An eighteenth century tavern clock with a full striking movement.
The black dial has a gilt circle within the Roman hour numerals,
outside minute numerals and minute markings between the two
circles without difference in five minute divisions. Both winding
holes have cover plates and the hands, although correct in style, are
later replacements. The trunk has elaborate ear pieces, a signature
above the door and a deeply moulded base. Circa 1760.*
Dimensions: *Dial diameter 24½in., surround diameter 28in.,
hour numerals height 2½in., minute numerals height 1¼in., total
height 57½in.*
Maker: *William Warin, Thirsk, is recorded between 1760-1770.*

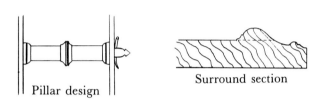

Pillar design   Surround section

*Left, The rectangular plated movement has four well designed
pillars, only nine turns on the barrel groove and an hour wheel
crossed out on one side only. The locking off of the striking train is
done by a lever within the plates, which contacts a pin on the
gathering pallet wheel. The arbor of this lever projects into a square,
upon which is fitted the rack hook. When the rack hook drops into
the last and deepest tooth of the rack the locking lever contacts the pin.*

PLATE 104

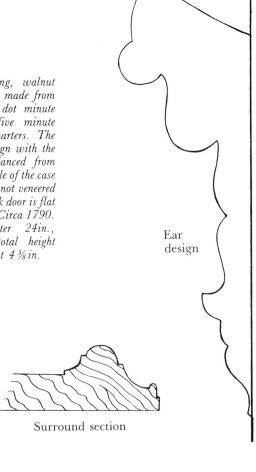

Left: A very unusual striking, walnut tavern clock. The white dial, made from three horizontal boards, has dot minute divisions with strokes at five minute intervals, and stars at the quarters. The hands are of an elaborate design with the minute hand only counterbalanced from within the movement. The whole of the case is constructed of solid walnut, not veneered unusual in any clock. The trunk door is flat topped, again unconventional. Circa 1790.
Dimensions: *Dial diameter 24in., surround diameter 28in., total height 58¼ in., hour numerals height 4⅜ in.*

Ear design

Surround section

Left: This rare movement has conventional rack striking, four pillars and ten turns on the barrel groove. It has a peculiar going train with centre wheel mounted off centre and above the winding square and rotates once in two hours. Onto the extended arbor is fitted a wheel which gears into the intermediate motion wheel at a ratio of 2:1. This in turn gears with the minute wheel fixed onto an extended arbor pivoting between the plates. This arbor is extended at the back as well, onto which fits the minute hand counterbalance.

Right: The back view shows the counterbalance passing underneath the crutch of the anchor escapement.

PLATE 105

A fine circular dial tavern clock. The white dial has outside minute numerals and dot minute divisions. The brass hands are of an ornate design, with the minute hand counterbalanced on its end. The winding hole has a brass cover plate and above the hand centre is a date aperture. The trunk has fine shaped ear pieces with the signature between them above the trunk door with raised gesso work. Circa 1785.
Dimensions: Dial diameter 25in. surround diameter 28¾in., hour numerals height 2¾in., minute numerals height 1⅜in., total height 58in.
Maker: Wraight & Woolley, Tenterden, Kent, recorded as before 1803.

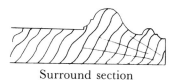

Surround section

The segmental date aperture has a central pointer and dot date divisions. The chamfered edge is gilt lined and below is a brass plate to take the stud of the date wheel.

The back of the dial is recessed to take the 62 toothed date wheel and jumper spring mounted on top. The wheel is turned one tooth per twelve hours which is equivalent to half a day on the dial itself.

The tapered plated movement has four pillars, a five wheel train and an anchor escapement. The pin which turns the date dial can be seen projecting horizontally from the top of the hour wheel.

PLATE 106 (shown in colour on page 164)

This nineteenth century world time wall clock has a case of pine throughout, a long narrow trunk with reeded corners, concave base and a lift off bezel. A narrow door in the trunk provides access for winding and regulating. The decoration is of gilt lines and scrolls on a stained ground of near black. The circular brass dial consists of a revolving inner zone, a revolving concentric zone and a fixed outer zone.

The inner zone has a silvered centre engraved with the moon's age which is read aginst a brass pointer, the tail of which is fixed to the intermediate zone. The outer half of the inner zone contains a penny moon aperture, showing in a blue ground with gilt stars. The intermediate zone is silvered and engraved with twenty-four place names around the world, each name contained within an engraved triangle, the point of which reads off against the outer zone the time at that place. Unfortunately the engraving of the place names is in reverse order probably due to an engraver's error, with the result that, with the exception of New Zealand and Great Britain, they do not in fact show the correct time in relation to each other.

The outer zone, also silvered, is engraved for twenty-four hours, I-XII twice, with dot minute divisions, diamond and star at the five minutes, and single stars at the quarters. The reading of the hour is facilitated by the fixed tail of the moon pointer being extended as an hour pointer. Minutes are indicated by a blued steel counterbalanced central hand.

The clock is anonymous but has much in common with East Anglian wall clocks or Norwich clocks. Circa 1840.

Dimensions: *Dial diameter 14¼ in., bezel diameter 17½ in., width of trunk 11¾ in., total height 58in.*

Left: The movement has tapered plates, four pillars and an anchor escapement. Power to the four wheel train is provided by a brass covered oval weight, wound by means of an endless chain from within the trunk, due to the impossibility of winding through the revolving dial centre.

Chapter 10

Unusual Dial Clocks

Many dial clocks which have been made for different reasons can be classified as unusual due to the small quantity manufactured, sometimes as single items. Although these one off clocks may be quite late, they are often unique and yet may not have any great horological interest. Their rarity could be due to size, shape or the use to which they were put. Others may be of exceptional horological interest due to their function or the ingenuity incorporated in the mechanism and yet have little to offer in the way of appearance.

The basic fusee movement was reliable, flexible and often practical to use in clocks which were required for special purposes such as advertising. These clocks were quite popular as in Plate 107 which advertised Thornley's Ale by placing the letters where the numerals usually were; the brass silvered dial had the engraved letters of Thornleys filled in black wax and the letters of Ale filled in red. Advertising could be used not only for the product name but for other purposes as well, as in Plate 108, where the advertisement is for the Mohawk Minstrels playing at the Royal Agricultural Hall.

Some clocks have unusual case designs either for a special order or as an exercise in creativity; Plate 109 shows such a clock which is probably unique, in the shape of a diamond. It has a 10in. wooden dial and was made around 1825 to the usual fine standard associated with clocks of this early date. Several problems due to unusual design have been overcome such as regulation; it is not possible to have a bottom door as the arc of the pendulum would foul the sides of the case, therefore the pendulum bob has been chamfered off on the corners and the rating thread is on the rod itself, as in some bracket clocks, where access is from the back door. The bezel catch is at figure 8 and not by the figure 9 as a lock could not be incorporated here.

Another case design is shown in Plate 110 where the quality of casework is excellent and the maker has demonstrated his creativeness by the unusual shape of the surround. Plate 111 shows a clock specially made to show 24 hour time; this was fairly simply achieved by altering the motion work of the hour wheel to 24:1 instead of 12:1 but the reading of normal 12 hour time was extremely difficult to work out. For this reason few of these clocks were made and organisations which required 24 hour time used the method employed by the railways of a conventional dial with additional inner numerals 13-24 written in red. (A railway clock of different interest is known to exist, which has a 12in. convex dial with a Thwaites and Reed movement numbered 10029 and dates as 1838, and started off life on the London and Croydon railway (the first line opened out of London), only nine years after Stevenson's Rocket making it one of the earliest clocks in existence.)

A special dial layout is shown in the R.A.F. Operations Room clock in Plate 112. These clocks were used throughout the Second World War to plot fighter plane activity; every Operations Room had one but many have since been repainted with a conventional dial. In the Operations Room was a large map table with counters coloured red for enemy and black for friendly, with information on height and strength. Every counter had with it a direction arrow corresponding to the colour of the triangle on the clock at the time it was placed on the table. Each time a report was sent from the Filter Room to the Operations Room the direction arrow was moved and changed to the new colour on the clock dial. Providing the reports kept on coming the arrows should all have been the same colour. An odd arrow showing a different colour was immediately noticeable and showed a lost or neglected raid. (Although most clocks commissioned for the R.A.F. displayed the emblem (shown here), it has been omitted from the clock illustrated in Plate 112.)

Some clocks are unusual simply by virtue of human error which has not been corrected. Several have been found which repeat the same figure twice, or have a stroke missing on Roman figures thereby repeating the number. Engravers often misspelt names as well but the clock in Plate 113 has both mistakes on the same dial, with the figure 10 blatantly back to front and the name William Bucknell without the N.

PLATE 107

An advertising clock made for Thornley's Ale with an engraved brass dial. The word Thornleys has letters filled in black wax and the word Ale filled in red wax. The case style is identical to those of German manufacture, very shallow with an access door in the rounded bottom and a full size removable back. The clock has a spun brass bezel with a sight ring plastered in, and simple spade hands. Circa 1940.

Dimensions: *Dial diameter 10in., bezel diameter 10½in., surround diameter 12¾in., depth including bezel 5in.*

Private Collection

The movement is a common Coventry Astral numbered 39426, which has a going barrel, anchor escapement and straight pillars screwed through the backplate. The trade mark with the word Coventry within a winding key is always on the backplate in this position.

180

A very interesting 12in. dial which is not advertising a product but a music group. The unusual combination of white letters on black advertises The Mohawk Minstrels playing at the Royal Agricultural Hall. To avoid confusion a small white diamond appears on either side of the word 'THE'. The manufacturer's name is also on the dial centre. The clock has a convex sectioned cast bezel with integral sight ring and a mahogany case with rounded bottom.
Maker: *Kendal and Dent, 106 Cheapside, London 1881-1884.*

Private Collection

The minute and hour hands are substituted by a pointing finger and a banjo.

181

*An advertising clock by
Kendal and Dent. See Plate
108 for details.*

*An early diamond shaped
dial clock by Thomas
Dolyer. See Plate 109 for
details.*

*A trunk dial clock by
Samuel Elliott Atkins. See
Plate 110 for details.*

An unusual 24 hour dial clock.
See Plate 111 for details.

R.A.F. Operations Room clock.
See Plate 112 for details.

PLATE 109 (shown in colour on page 182)

A unique early dial clock in a diamond shaped case, which is not square hung by the corner as it may at first appear but is a true diamond shape. The convex painted wooden dial is signed Thos. Dolyer, Bath, and has a convex section cast bezel with a plastered in glass. The mahogany case has mahogany veneers and is inlaid with ebony decoration. At the right side is an access door with an imitation one on the left where there is also the key hole for the bezel lock; a full size door is also incorporated at the back enabling easy access to the pendulum for regulation. The four pillar movement has shaped shoulders to the plates, an anchor escapement and pendulum regulation above the bob as in many bracket clocks. Circa 1825.
Dimensions: *Dial diameter 9¾in., bezel diameter 10⅝in., height 17in., width 16in.*
Maker: *Unrecorded.*

R.E. Rose

unusual shaped
shoulders

A trunk dial clock with an unusually shaped octagonal surround inlaid with brass on mahogany veneers. The curved foot trunk has a brass bordered pendulum aperture and large carved earpieces; the convex painted iron dial, signed S.E. Atkins, London, has fine spade hands with very long tips and a bezel of convex section. The movement has offset winding and unusual shaped shoulders to the plates. Circa 1840.
Dimensions: *Dial diameter 12in., bezel diameter 12¼ in., surround diameter 16in., total length 26in.*
Maker: *Samuel Elliott Atkins, London, apprenticed 1821, Clockmakers Company 1831, Master 1881 and 1889. Died 1898.*

Private Collection

PLATE 111 (shown in colour on page 183)

An unusual 24 hour dial clock with the figures written alternately in black and red. This form of dial was not favoured due to the difficulty of reading conventional time from it. The more popular 24 hour dial was conventional with extra figures of 13-24 added inside the existing numerals. The clock has a spun bezel with a sight ring plastered in and a convex mahogany surround. Originally the clock probably seated on top of a framework as the flat bottom has never been finished off and it has a back door for backwinding. The movement has rectangular plates with riveted pillars and motion work geared to turn the hour wheel at a 24:1 ratio. Circa 1900.

Dimensions: Dial diameter 14in., bezel diameter 14⅞in., surround diameter 17⅜in.

Private Collection

An R.A.F. Operations Room clock with a slave movement and ribbed aluminium spade hands. The mahogany case which fits close to the wall has a convex surround and its original green painted spun brass bezel screwed on to the surround as a fixture; its dial has outside minute divisions and coloured triangles of red, yellow and blue covering a 2½ minute period. The hour numerals are within the triangle points with the numbering 13-24 inside. The purpose of the Operations Room clock is described in the text. Circa 1940.
Dimensions: *Dial diameter 18in., bezel diameter 19¼in., surround diameter 22in.*

Headquarters No. 1 Group, Royal Observer Corps, Maidstone

PLATE 113

A convex silvered brass dial with arabic numerals, dot minute divisions and a well engraved signature. The maker is almost certainly William Bucknell of London and not William Buckell as engraved, and the figure 10 is back to front. This type of mistake is not unusual, but that it should not only be accepted but also escape later correction is rare. The clock has a concave section bezel with convex glass, a concave surround and a salt box back. The movement is smaller than normal with tapered plates and an anchor escapement. Circa 1820.

Dimensions: *Dial diameter 11 ⅞ in., bezel diameter 13 ⅜ in., surround diameter 14 ⅝ in.*
Maker: *William Bucknell, Westminster, London, 1816-1828.*

A.A. Moore

Chapter 11

The Later Years

As the nineteenth century progressed the quality of dial clocks was sustained but the amount of decoration was cut down (Plate 114) and the type of decoration changed (Plate 115). The application of brass inlay to trunk dials decreased, until by 1880 it was seldom used and was replaced by small amounts of carving. By 1900 trunk dial clocks were seldom decorated at all and did not incorporate earpieces which had been traditional since they began. It is not unusual to see the front panels screwed on with brass wood screws from the front and sometimes the sides as well as in Plate 116. Surrounds were either the usual convex section which persisted until dial clocks finished, or a new type which had not been used before 1870, as in Plate 117. The use of natural colour oak became far more common and was increasingly utilised as the twentieth century progressed as in Plate 118. Dials were now virtually always flat and increasingly used arabic numbers although Roman figures were always the more popular design. Several new designs appeared such as the square case in Plate 119 and the style known as the Bank clock which usually sits on top of a bracket.

English fusee movements became cheaper as inflation did not exist to any degree and methods of manufacture improved, with short cuts taken which did not affect the quality only the finish. Pillars were perfectly plain, plates were unshaped and decoration dispensed with. Few strikes were made after 1900 (Plate 120) by the English manufacturers. Imports of foreign dial clocks increased enormously and it must have been obvious that home produced striking dial clocks could not compete, especially when the German striking clocks were of such good quality as in Plate 121. By 1910 the German movements were made even cheaper by changing from the fusee movement to a going barrel and were imported into this country in vast numbers (Plate 122). Official statistics relating to the import and export of all types of clocks show the degree to which the British market was flooded.

	NUMBERS			VALUES		
	1911	1912	1913	1911	1912	1913
From Germany	2,434,152	2,451,555	2,043,866	310,779	335,077	335,902
From U.S.A.	250,456	422,633	229,470	57,775	74,549	46,672
From other countries	96,348	95,377	140,590	40,043	52,206	59,437
Exported from U.K.				33,273	35,650	36,587

It can be seen that German imports averaging under 3/-. each and American under 5/-. each would not have much competition from the home market when the price of the lowest grade dial clock was 32/6d. in 1912. An import duty of 33⅓%

was applied in 1915 which did help to stimulate British trade for a short time.

By 1920 British made clocks were being manufactured along German principles but not by the long established clock companies, whose clocks were made more to engineering practices such as the Coventry Astral clock (Plate 123) made in both lever and pendulum, Rotherham's and later the Smith's Empire (Plate 124). By this time dial clocks did not simply depend on mechanical hand wound movements, as electric impulse clocks had now been on the scene for many years in the form of electrical correction and slave clocks. Electrical correction was used on all types of clocks but mainly dial clocks, especially those of a large size in important places. From 1880 until around the 1930 period a time signal was transmitted automatically every hour from the mean solar clock at Greenwich Observatory to the Post Office. From there, time signals were distributed to subscribers in the form of electrical currents which forcibly corrected the hands. One method used was a scissors arrangement where two levers came together clamping the minute hand to the hour. The more common method was to make the clock gain slightly but prevent the minute hand from passing the hour by a stop activated by electro magnets precisely at the hour, allowing the hand to pass.

Slave clocks receiving electrical impulses from a master clock were in use before 1910 (Plate 125) and were very popular in large buildings where many of these slaves could be positioned with only one master clock. The Post Office commissioned thousands to be made as in Plate 126 which had the dials marked with the letters G.P.O. Often with government contract clocks the dials were also marked with the emblem of the reigning monarch as in Plate 127.

Although slave clocks were made by the electrical industry and going barrel movements by the engineering industry it did not mean that fusee movements ceased to be manufactured, but were made in decreasing numbers by the original clock making factories; Plate 128 shows an example of a quality fusee dial clock by J.J. Stockhall of around 1920 and another in Plate 129 of around 1930. Probably the last fusee dial clocks made by a clockmaking factory were by the firm of F.W. Elliott (Plate 130) who last made a batch as late as 1968 but then donated their fusee engine to the Horological Institute.

During the late nineteenth and early twentieth centuries one of the most important clock manufacturing companies was that of Gillett & Johnston. The business started with William Gillett who began work as a maker of small clocks in the village of Hadlow in Kent, from where he migrated to Clerkenwell, and finally established his business at Union Road, Croydon. Charles Bland became a partner in the mid-1850s when the firm became known as Gillett & Bland, during which period the firm also started making turret clocks. In 1877 Arthur Johnston bought a partnership in the firm which continued to operate under the title of Gillett, Bland and Co. until 1884 which was presumably the date of Charles Bland's death. The business which had been confined to the manufacture of clocks was further extended to include a bell foundry.

Sometime during the late 1800s Johnston took full charge of the foundry (Gillett is reputed to have emigrated to America and was joined by his son in 1902) and Cyril Johnston succeeded upon his father's death in 1916. In 1925 the firm became a limited company known as The Croydon Bell Foundry Ltd., but in 1930 the name was changed to Gillett & Johnston Ltd. Gillett & Johnston's order books are extremely similar to those by Thwaites on pages 31 and 32 where comparisons can be made from the following random extracts.

1874 MARTIN & SON, Cheltenham

5	14in. Round Dial (light oak) 52/6d		Chains 5/-
3	16in. ditto	65/-	ditto 5/-
1	18in. ditto	120/-	ditto 10/-
1	20in. ditto	130/-	ditto 10/-

APR 29 1875 MR. TREE

1	16in. Mahogany Round Dial to strike one at the hour on a gong chain 5/-, ½ dead beat 5/-	£4/5/-
	maintaining power 10/-	£1/-/-
		————
		£5/5/-
		————

1878

12in. Mahogany, best case, plate glass, chain	£2/15/6
14in. Mahogany, best case, plate glass, chain	£3/ 3/-
8in. Lever Marine timepiece	£8/10/-

Apr. 5th 1878

WESTLAKE J. 32, King Street, Southwark.
Description of a weight driven pavilion clock
Name on dial WESTLAKE, LONDON.

May 9th 1901 Hitchin P.O.

1	12in. Mahogany short drop, chain, E R	£2/15/-

Oct. 22 1912 India Office

18	12in. Timepiece clocks, round, chains, Dials named I.S.R. 1912 £2/17/6d each.

Nov 5th 1912

2	12in. Common Mahogany round, 8 day Timepieces, gut line, spun bezels, named PAGE, KEEN & PAGE, PLYMOUTH.	32/-

1874

November 23rd

Parkinson & Frodsham
4 Change Alley

An 8 day Spring Timepiece with
Chain, Maint^e power. 1/2 dead
Escapt—, 18 inch Black & White Dial
in Oak Case to pattern, plate
Glass, Lacquered bezel   Sheet—

Length of Bracket— 30 inch
Depth of Drum Head 6 inch
depth of body 7 inch diamet 2 ft
depth of Bracket 8 inch

The ditto in Mahogany
        deduct— Cost of plate Glass—

The ditto in Mahogany long trunk
Case, Sheet— glass (thin)

    22 in Pend

1. 12 inch Best Lacq^d Ring

Prici of blue & Gold Dial

	£	s	d
door at side & bottom, Hinges of Bezels at top	8	10	"
	8	10	"
	£7	0	0
	2	5	"

PARKINSON
4 Change Alley
and London
FRODSHAM

It can be seen from this short list that the clocks were getting considerably cheaper, by comparing the entry of 1878 for a best quality 12in. dial at £2/15/6d and the entry of November 5th 1912 for a bottom quality 12in. dial at £1/12/-. This could be achieved by the use of gut line and spun bezel as specified. The actual comparison of the same quality can be done by the preceding entry of October 22nd 1912 where the clocks are £2/17/6d, an increase of 2/- in 34 years. It is also interesting to see the reappearance of Mr Westlake on April 5th 1878 saying precisely what he wanted written on his dial as he did with Thwaites back in 1866 (see page 22).

These order books were of course hand written as the example shown opposite.

In case of difficulty in reading or deciphering the abbreviations it says:

1874
November 23rd.
Parkinson & Frodsham
4 Change Alley

An 8 day Spring Timepiece with chain,
maintaining power, ½ dead (beat) escapement,
18 inch Black and White dial in Oak case to
pattern, sheet glass, lacquered bezel.
length of bracket 30 inch

Depth of Drum Head 6 inch	door at side	
depth of body 7 inch,	& bottom	
diameter 2 ft	Hinge of	
depth of bracket 8 inch	bezel at top	£8.10.0

One ditto in Mahogany
deduct — cost of plate glass   £8.10.0

One ditto in Mahogany, long trunk
case. Sheet glass (thick)
22 inch. Pendulum £7.0.0

1 12 inch Best lacquered ring [bezel]
Price of blue & gold Dial.   £2. 5.0.

Gillett and Bland, later Gillett and Johnston, worked for many well-known clockmakers with names such as Dent & Co., James McCabe, Negretti and Zambra, Parkinson and Frodsham, Payne & Co., to name but a few. From their 1906 catalogue (Plate 131) several interesting points can be observed. Page 3 mentions their opinions on piece work which was typical of all the major clockmaking companies, that quality must persist, regardless of the fact that orders may decline. The photograph on page 4 shows a selection of dial clocks on test with the most interesting item being the E.R. on some of the dials. This signified the reign of Edward VII for the government contract clocks but because of the brevity of his reign, surviving examples with E.R. on the dial are now quite rare.

Page 28 shows the prices with comparisons for gut line or chain fusee but would not be complete without the condemnation of 'the cheap foreign made article on the market' which of course refers to the German and American imports. Page 29 shows a few of the styles produced; Nos. 140 and 215 can be referred back to Plates 59 and 62 respectively.

In 1923 all the manufacturing of dial clocks and domestic clocks was taken over by the company of F.W. Elliott Ltd. with whom they shared premises. Gillett and Johnston later moved to Sanderstead Road, Croydon where they continue to flourish as one of the world's leading makers of turret clocks.

The firm of Elliott's started in 1886 with James Jones Elliott, having served his apprenticeship with Bateman of Smithfield, naming the company J.J. Elliott Ltd., at Percival Street, Clerkenwell. In 1901 the firm moved to larger premises in Rosebery Avenue, Clerkenwell, where James's son, Frank Westcombe Elliott took over in 1904 when his father died aged fifty-five. In 1909 an amalgamation took place between J.J. Elliott Ltd. and Grimshaw Baxter and the firm moved to Gray's Inn Lane in 1911 and to St. Anne's Road, Tottenham in 1917. The amalgamation did not survive and in 1921 Frank Elliott sold the name of J.J. Elliott to Grimshaw Baxter. Shortly afterwards Frank joined Gillett & Johnston Ltd. at Union Road and in 1923 formed the present company F.W. Elliott Ltd., taking over all the domestic clock production from Gillett's.

Frank's three sons all joined the company, Horace in 1919, Ronald in 1929 and Leonard in 1946. At the outbreak of war in 1939 the production of clocks was temporarily reduced and the factory made test gear and apparatus for Rolls-Royce Merlin engines used in the Spitfires. (Frank Westcombe Elliott died in 1944 aged sixty-nine.) The company still make quality reproduction clocks and are based in Hastings. Plate 132 shows four generations of Elliotts. Plate 133 shows the F.W. Elliott works staff in 1926 of around 100 employees and Plate 134 the large wheel and pinion making department in Union Road, Croydon.

F.W. Elliott numbered most of their movements throughout, but they were not dated except for those made for government contract. The backplates of the fusee dial clocks were numbered — 2770 F.W. ELLIOTT 1937, or a later number of 20344 F.W. ELLIOTT 1942, and after the war as ELLIOTT. LONDON 5 EFW 55/6 25788 which represents June 1955, but all Elliott's cases are dated from 1952. The last batch of fusee dial clocks was made in 1968.

Not all the Elliott clocks have fusee movements, in fact the vast majority in the mid-twentieth century did not. Plate 135 shows the 14 day pendulum timepiece generally used in the dial clocks taken from a catalogue of 1950. Plate 136 shows the type of case being used at this time with these movements. Plate 137 shows the dial clocks produced with lever or pendulum movements. The price of an 8in., 10in., or 12in. 14 day pendulum timepiece was £8/17/6d and with an 8 day lever movement £12/-/-, both including purchase tax.

Although Elliott's were probably the last to make fusee dial clocks in any great numbers the story is unlikely to finish there as individual clocks are still being made and enthusiasts are assembling them from the 'How to make' series that are so popular nowadays. It is only a matter of time before the reproduction dial clock reappears with the traditional fusee movement.

(shown in colour on page 201) PLATE 114

A flat painted iron dial clock with spade hands and a convex section bezel without sight ring. The mahogany case with convex surround has a veneered trunk with a brass bordered pendulum aperture, edged with satinwood, inlaid brass and foliage earpieces. It has a rounded bottom box with an access door without a lock and a solid rebated side door. This is a late example of brass inlay work. Circa 1870.
Maker: *C.A. Woodward, 1a Park Side, Knightsbridge. Unrecorded.*

R.E. Rose

PLATE 115 (shown in colour on page 201)

An octagonal drop dial clock with rosewood veneer decorated with carved earpieces and carved border to the pendulum aperture. The trunk has a curved foot with an access door and two side doors. Circa 1870.
Dimensions: *Dial diameter 12in., surround diameter 18in., total length 29in.*
Maker: *Bennet Dufner, Coventry, 1850-1880.*

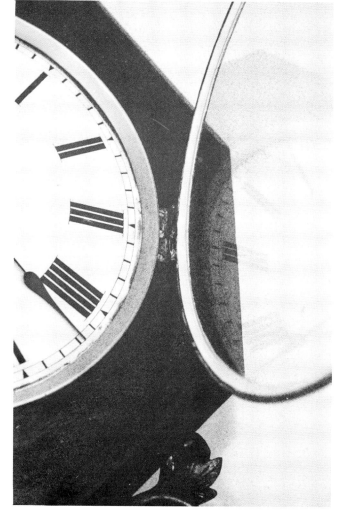

A type of bezel not often encountered and usually found only on good quality dial clocks. The silvered sight ring is a permanent fixture on top of the dial, secured by four studs passing through the edge of the dial and through the surround with square nuts on the back. The convex section bezel opens as normal.

Private Collection

PLATE 116

This shows the construction which is quite common in early twentieth century trunk dial clocks. The front panel is not veneered and is screwed with brass screws directly through the front and sides leaving the screw hands visible for decoration.

A typical good quality early twentieth century trunk dial clock, which has a flat iron dial, spade hands and a convex section bezel with integral sight ring and bevelled glass. The case, with convex surround, has a simple rounded bottom box without earpieces. Circa 1910.

Dimensions: *Dial diameter 12in., bezel diameter 12½in., surround diameter 14½in., length 19½in.*

Maker: *J.W. Benson, Ludgate Hill, London.*

The rectangular plated movement has a cylindrical lead bob pendulum with a wooden rod, a snailed decoration to both plates and is engraved on the backplate J.W. BENSON, LUDGATE HILL, LONDON and numbered 78-39.

Private Collection

PLATE 117 (shown in colour on page 204)

surround section

shaped shouldered
plates

A light oak trunk dial clock with flat iron dial, spade hands and a spun brass bezel with a plastered in sight ring. The wide surround is quite common around this date. The rounded bottom box is decorated with elaborate carved earpieces and carved border to the pendulum aperture. The rectangular plated movement has straight shoulders and a wire line fusee. Circa 1880.
Dimensions: *Dial diameter 12in., bezel diameter 12½in., surround diameter 15½in., length 22in.*
Maker: *H. Bright, Leamington. Recorded as 1860-1868, but this clock is certainly of a later date.*

Private Collection

A twentieth century round dial clock in a light oak case with a rounded bottom box. None of the wood is veneered and it has a solid rebated side door and a surround made up with tongued and grooved sections. The flat iron dial has arabic hour numerals, steel spade hands and a convex bezel with integral sight ring. The rectangular plated movement has pillars screwed through the backplate, chain fusee, anchor escapement and brass screws are used throughout. Circa 1930.
Dimensions: *Dial diameter 12in., bezel diameter 12¼in., surround diameter 15¾in.*

Private Collection

PLATE 119

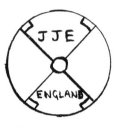

Trade mark for
James Jones Elliott

This style of square case was used in the early part of the century; mahogany cases with two side doors were often made in this style in the larger sizes but rarely for small clocks as in this example. It has an unsigned flat iron dial and a convex bezel with integral sight ring. The movement has straight pillars screwed into the backplate which is marked JJE ENGLAND in a trade mark and made in England 69617. Circa 1915.
Dimensions: *Dial diameter 12in., bezel diameter 12¼in., width 16¾in., height 22in.*
Maker: *James Jones Elliott (see text).*

Private Collection

Iron dial clock by C.A. Woodward.
See Plate 114 for details.

Octagonal drop dial clock by Bennet Dufner.
See Plate 115 for details.

PLATE 120 *(shown in colour on page 208)*

An example of a late striking English dial clock, which has a flat painted iron dial, spade hands, convex section bezel with integral sight ring and a rounded bottom box with access door. Circa 1875.
Dimensions: *Dial diameter 12in., surround diameter 14½in.*
Maker: *Edward White, 20 Cockspur Street, London 1863-1881.*

The rounded top back box normally used with striking dial clocks to house the bell; also normal for strikes is the two side doors with brass sound frets backed by silk.

The typical heavy quality double fusee movement used in English clocks towards the end of the nineteenth century with top mounted bell.

PLATE 121

A typical late nineteenth century German dial clock. The mahogany case has a convex section surround and a conventional rounded bottom back box with access doors on both sides with sound frets. The depth of the box is similar to normal timepiece English boxes even though the gong is mounted on the back of the case; this would not be possible with the deeper English movements where the bell is mounted on the top of the movement. The clock has a flat iron dial with spade hands and a spun bezel with the sight ring plastered in to hold the glass. On the back of the dial is the retailer's name of GAY, LAMAILLE & CO. who are listed in Loomes as LONDON 1881 French clocks wholesale. Circa 1890.

Dimensions: *Dial diameter 12in., bezel diameter 12⅜in., surround diameter 14¾in.*

Maker: *Winterhalder & Hofmeier.*

German movements can be identified by the narrower distance between front and back plates, circular hammer head and fixing to the arbor, screwed pillars and pins in the pin wheel projecting backwards. This clock has chain fusees, dead-beat escapement and a double leaf suspension spring, and is marked W & H Sch 2 on the backplate.

Private Collection

Trunk dial clock by H. Bright. See Plate 117 for details.

Twentieth century dial clock. See Plate 118 for details.

PLATE 122

A German timepiece dial clock typical of those made around the early twentieth century. The oak case has a convex surround made up in four pieces, a shallow back box without side doors and a bottom door with a cockbead edge and turncatch. Access to hang the pendulum is through the removable back secured with turn catches. It has a flat iron dial, spade hands for both minute and hour, a spun bezel without a sight ring and a plastered in glass. Circa 1910.
Dimensions: Dial diameter 7⅝in., bezel diameter 8⅜in., surround diameter 10½in.
Maker: Winterhalder & Hofmeier.

A typical German going barrel movement marked on the backplate W & H Sch. Note the small movement, straight pillars, a backcock screwed on one side only and the long suspension spring with a hooked on pendulum.

Private Collection

PLATE 123

The dial marked Trade mark Dent, 4 Royal Exchange & 61, Strand, London.

A twentieth century wall clock made for Dent, of which the oak case has a carved rope design surround without any access to the movement. The cast bezel with integral sight ring is kept shut by a spring clip on the left hand side. Its small dial has seconds indications with the number 2612 and a slot within the figure twelve marked S-F for regulation. Circa 1930.

Dimensions: *Dial diameter 6in., bezel diameter 6½in., case diameter 8½in., case depth 3½in.*

The movement has straight plain pillars screwed into the backplate and a going barrel movement.

Private Collection

The small movement has a lever platform mounted on the top with a dust and protection cover over the balance and the manufacturer's trade mark of COVENTRY written within a symbol of a key and ASTRAL below with the number 8295.

Striking dial clock by Edward White.
See Plate 120 for details.

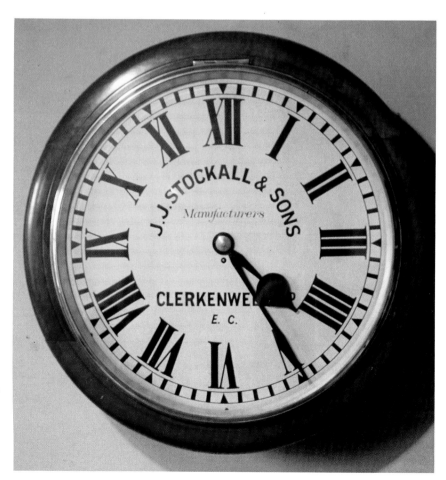

Large 24in. dial clock by J.J. Stockall &
Sons. See Plate 128 for details.

PLATE 124

A mid-twentieth century 10in. dial clock made by Smith's. The oak surround is made up from sections and screwed permanently to the back box which only has access to the pendulum through the bottom door. The spun bezel is chrome plated as is also the hand collet. Its thin aluminium dial is marked London County Council, and does not support the movement. Circa 1950.
Dimensions: *Dial diameter 10in., surround diameter 13 ¼ in.*

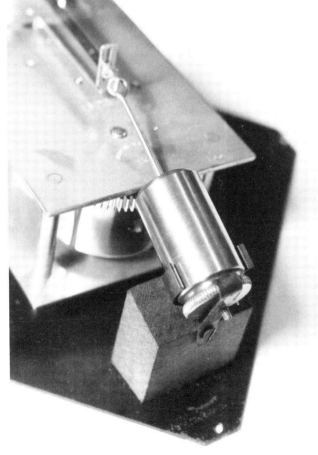

The rectangular plated movement is secured to a false plate which is screwed into the case independently of the dial, which also carries the pendulum fixing clamps. These two piece clamps hold the cylindrical bob quite securely. The bob screws completely on to the rod without a rating nut, the rod being hooked on to the long suspension spring. The backplate is stamped Smiths Empire.

Private Collection

PLATE 125

An early twentieth century slave dial clock in a drum type case. The flat iron dial, marked Gent & Co Ltd. Makers. Parsons' Patent Leicester, has aluminium hands both counterbalanced and a spun bezel with sight ring screwed permanently to the surround. There is no facility for manual time setting as this is done electrically. Circa 1910.

Dimensions: Dial diameter 11¾ in., bezel diameter 12¾ in., case diameter 15¼ in., case depth 3⅜ in.

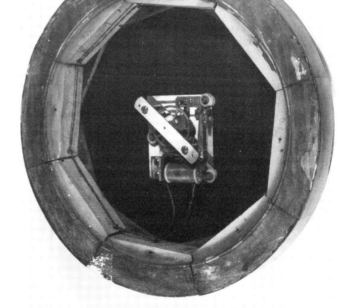

The case is made up from eight pieces of wood with the terminal blocks on top of the case. The typical slave movement is of an early design.

Private Collection

PLATE 126

A large slave dial clock made for the General Post Office. The flat iron dial is marked out with minute divisions but no minute circles, the George VI initials and crown and the letters G.P.O. The aluminium hands are both counterbalanced and the bezel is screwed permanently to the surround. One of the advantages of the appearance of these clocks is that they can be fitted close to a wall because of their small shallow movements. Circa 1950.

Dimensions: *Dial diameter 18in., surround diameter 22in., total depth 3¼in.*

Private Collection

PLATE 127

The Kings' and Queens' crests applied to the dials of clocks made for Government contract consisted of the initials and a crown above. The crowns of each reign are different and the style of lettering varies. VR, $G^V R$ and $G^{vi}R$ are normally written in fancy intertwining letters, whereas the ER for Edward and the $E^{ii}R$ for Elizabeth are normally in block capitals. Because of the brief length of the reign of Edward VII, clocks with this symbol are hard to find.

*A very large 24in. dial clock signed on the dial J.J. Stockall &
Sons, Manufacturers, Clerkenwell Rd., E.C. The mahogany
surround is made up in four sections and the heavy cast bezel with
integral sight ring and bevelled edge glass is hinged at the top. Circa
1920.*

*The heavy duty rectangular plated movement has the counterbalance
for the hour hand on the hour wheel itself and the counterbalance for
the minute hand on an arbor between the plates driven through an
extra wheel in the motionwork.*

*The trade mark of intertwined initials J.J.S. within a toothed wheel
and numbered 7296 are situated on the front plate below the winding
square.*

R.E. Rose

PLATE 129

A large good quality dial clock made for the G.P.O. Its dial has minute divisions but no minute circles and is marked in the normal place G.P.O. just below the hand centre. The convex mahogany surround is made up in sections and the cast bezel has an integral sight ring. Circa 1940.

Dimensions: *Dial diameter 18in., bezel diameter 19in., surround diameter 23½in.*

The large movement has rectangular plates measuring 7¼in. x 6in. and ⁵/₃₂in. thick and a barrel 3in. across and 1⅞in. depth. The plain pillars are secured through the backplate with large screws and brass washers. Stamped on the backplate is the number 857.

Private Collection

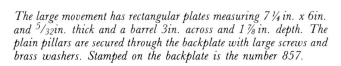

PLATE 130

One of the last fusee dial clocks to be made by Elliott's, with a flat iron dial marked G.P.O. and E^{ii}R with the crown, spade hands and no minute circles. The spun bezel has a snapped in sight ring and a mahogany surround made up in sections. The box has a solid rebated side door and a rounded bottom with access door and turncatch. Circa 1955.

Dimensions: Dial diameter 12in., bezel diameter 12⅜in., surround diameter 15in.

Maker: F.W. Elliott (see text).

The rectangular plated movement has straight pillars screwed through the backplate and is stamped Elliott London 5 EFW 55/6 25788. It is assumed that the 5 is the batch number, EFW is Elliott F.W., 55/6 is 1955/June. The ink stamp to the right of this has a crown and the letters G.P.O. AppD 2569.

Private Collection

PLATE 131

DESCRIPTION OF THE WORKS.

THE Works are situated within eight minutes walk of West Croydon station, with entrances in the Whitehorse and Union Roads. Trams from East and West Croydon and Norwood Junction stations pass the door. We are always glad to WELCOME VISITORS.

The floor area is about one acre in extent, and the following separate departments are found :—

VARIOUS DEPARTMENTS.

Iron, gunmetal, and bell metal foundries.
Heavy turret clock shop.
Small turret clock shop.
Heavy machine shop and turnery.
Smithy.
Church-bell hanging and founding.
Wheel cutting department.
Small clock making and repair shops.
Dial glazing and painting.
Pattern and clock case making.
Carpenters and packing-case shop.

From this it will be seen how many separate trades are required to produce the finished article, and by manufacturing throughout from the raw material, a close inspection and guarantee of every detail of construction can be assured.

Works entrance, Union Road, showing clock tower 100 ft. high with four 10 ft. 6 in. dials

PLANT & TOOLS. In order to meet the increasing competition by lowering the prices, and that without reducing the quality of the output, the Works have been entirely remodelled during the year 1905. The most up-to-date automatic and semi-automatic machines have been put down in order to reduce working costs. All parts are manufactured to gauge, on the interchangeable system, and assembled together for stock. By this means much greater accuracy of workmanship is ensured. Certain details in a clock, which are better finished by hand, are made by a staff of skilled workmen, some of whom have been with the firm for 40 years.

PIECEWORK. In many shops the stress of modern competition has led to the introduction of systems of pieceworking.

The management came, some years ago, to the decision that, however carefully watched, there was a danger of inferior work slipping through. All piecework has therefore been entirely abolished, the men working by the hour.

A corner of the iron foundry, showing moulds for large dials in foreground.

3

STOCK. All turret clock movements are put through in batches for stock. Deliveries can therefore be promptly made, since dials and motion work up to 10 ft. 6 in. diameter are always in stock.

MATERIALS. The materials used are of the highest quality. With our own foundries this can be absolutely guaranteed, since the raw product alone enters the Works. We would specially draw attention to the fact that no *brass* is used in the *turret clock* movements, the wheels and bushes being of a special mixture of hard *gunmetal*. This wears very much better and justifies the extra cost of material and finishing time.

TESTING. All clocks are thoroughly tested under actual working conditions for some time before being put into stock or packed for delivery ; they are guaranteed to leave the Works in perfect order.

REPAIRS. Our clock jobbing, cleaning and repair departments overhaul hundreds of small clocks yearly. Full particulars should be sent with repairs, which should be sent in *all* cases *Carriage Paid.*

GEAR CUTTING. We cut spur, bevel, and worm gears, of any shaped tooth and in any material ; accuracy of work is specially guaranteed.

Small clock testing with "seconds" regulating clock.

VISITORS TO OUR WORKS WILL BE WELCOMED !

Small turret clock testing shop, showing timepieces, striking and quarter movements under test for regulating, &c.

4

OFFICE AND LIBRARY CLOCKS.

The illustrations on opposite page show Standard Timepiece Clocks which are put through in batches. The rounds and short drops (Nos. 304, 295) are standard Government patterns. The trunk patterns (Nos. 214, 215) are railway clocks, and we have a very large variety of other clocks, photos of which will be sent on application.

They must not be compared in price with the cheap foreign made article on the market, as the movements are heavy and are fitted with bridge motion work, hard and well-polished pinions, fixed with gut or chain.

PRICES.

			£ s. d.		£ s. d.
No. 112.	12 in. diameter dial	with gut	3 0 0	with chain	3 5 0
	14 in. ,,	,,	4 0 0	,,	4 5 0
	16 in. ,,			,,	5 5 0
	18 in. ,,			,,	6 15 0
No. 115.	12 in. diameter dial			with chain	5 0 0
	14 in. ,,			,,	6 5 0
	16 in. ,,			,,	7 10 0
	18 in. ,,			,,	10 0 0
No. 140.	We have made these in two sizes only, viz.:				
	24 in. diameter dial			with chain	18 0 0
	36 in. ,,			,,	25 0 0
No. 214.	12 in. diameter dial	with gut	4 0 0	with chain	4 5 0
	14 in. ,,	,,	4 17 6	,,	5 2 6
	16 in. ,,			,,	6 7 6
	18 in. ,,			,,	8 10 0
No. 215.	Railway Platform Weight Clock, 18 in. diameter dial				14 10 0
No. 295.	12 in. diameter dial	with gut	2 15 0	with chain	3 0 0
	14 in. ,,	,,	3 5 0	,,	3 10 0
	16 in. ,,			,,	4 15 0
	18 in. ,,			,,	6 10 0
No. 304.	12 in. diameter dial	with gut	2 5 0	with chain	2 10 0
	14 in. ,,	,,	2 10 0	,,	2 15 0
	16 in. ,,			,,	3 15 0
	18 in. ,,			,,	5 10 0

In comparing these prices with those for which cheap foreign clocks can be obtained it should be borne in mind that our manufactures are not intended to compete with these in any way. We find a constant and increasing demand not only for *good* workmanship, but for the best obtainable ; the majority of our orders for clocks of this size are from H.M. Government, Post Office and War Office, the India Office, Asylums, Hospitals, Railway Companies, &c., and to none of these would we be able to supply any work or material not of the best quality possible, so rigid is the inspection enforced.

We adhere therefore to the policy of supplying the best only, and can guarantee that any clock sold singly will be identical with those supplied on the Post Office contract, &c.

Showrooms : Messrs. CALLOW, WRIGHT & HEWLETT, Ltd.,
70 Newman Street, Oxford Street, London.

28

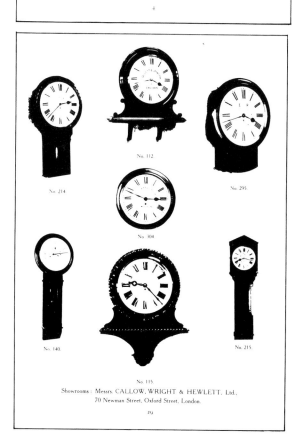

No. 214

No. 112

No. 295

No. 304

No. 140

No. 215

No. 115

Showrooms : Messrs. CALLOW, WRIGHT & HEWLETT, Ltd.,
70 Newman Street, Oxford Street, London.

29

Four pages from the 1906 catalogue of Gillett & Johnson of Croydon.

PLATE 132

JAMES JONES ELLIOTT
1886-1904

Founder of J.J. ELLIOTT & SONS
Maker of high grade Grandfather clocks
and Fuzee and chain bracket ¼ chimes

FOUR GENERATIONS | OF CLOCKMAKERS

FRANK WESTCOMBE ELLIOTT
1904-1944

Founder of F.W. ELLIOTT LTD.
Chairman and Managing Director

RONALD
JAMES
ELLIOTT 1929-1966

Director and Sales Manager

HORACE
WESTCOMBE
ELLIOTT 1919-

Chairman and Managing Director
since 1950

LEONARD FRANK ELLIOTT 1917-
Engineer in charge of clock production

RICHARD
WESTCOMBE
ELLIOTT 1966-
Electronic Engineer
and Sales Director

PETER
JAMES
ELLIOTT 1966-
Apprenticed Engineer.
Training to take charge
of clock production

of London

ANTHONY
DAVID
ELLIOTT 1954-
Apprenticed Cabinet Maker.
Director in charge of case production

217

PLATE 133

This photograph of the employees of F.W. Elliott in 1926 at Union Road shows around 100 people with a large number of women workers and youngsters sitting in the front.

PLATE 134

WHEEL AND PINION MAKING.

This photograph, also taken in 1926 at Union Road, Croydon, shows the wheel and pinion making department of F. W. Elliott.

PLATE 135

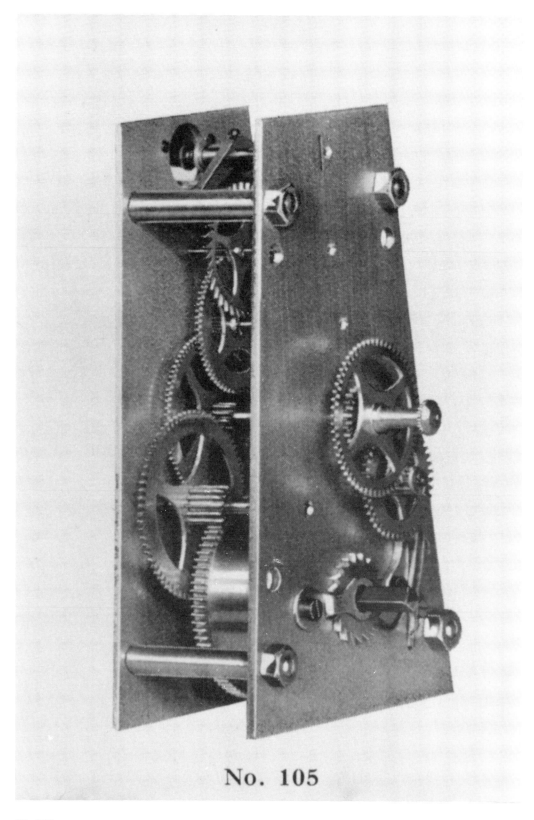

No. 105

The Elliott 14 day pendulum timepiece as used in dial clocks around the 1950s, has a going barrel movement, adjustable front pallet bush and plain pillars secured with hexagonal nuts.

PLATE 136

No. 7779 or **No. 7857**
Roundhead Office Clocks.
Oak or Mahogany cases.
8in., 10in., 12in. or 14in. round dials.

No. 7779
Spun brass bezel, box screwed to ring, doors in side and bottom.

No. 7857
Solid brass bezel, box pegged to ring at back, dovetailed joints, with rounded bottom. Doors at side and bottom.

As can be seen in the photograph from F.W. Elliott's pre-1950 catalogue the choice is oak or mahogany in four sizes with two grades of case. The cheaper case has a spun bezel, not pegged and a flat bottom, and the good quality case has a cast bezel, pegged on surround and a rounded bottom.

PLATE 137

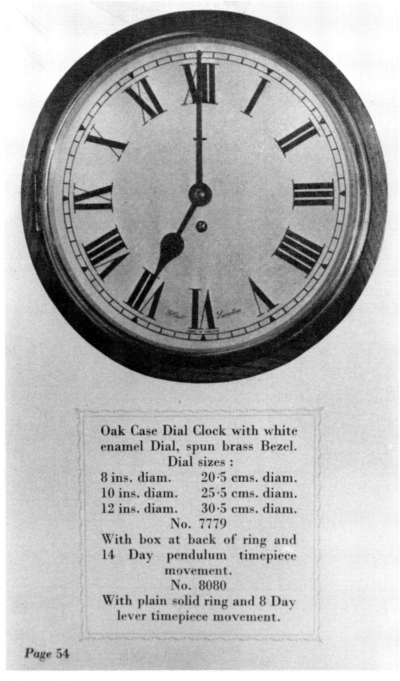

Oak Case Dial Clock with white
enamel Dial, spun brass Bezel.
Dial sizes :
8 ins. diam.   20·5 cms. diam.
10 ins. diam.   25·5 cms. diam.
12 ins. diam.   30·5 cms. diam.
No. 7779
With box at back of ring and
14 Day pendulum timepiece
movement.
No. 8080
With plain solid ring and 8 Day
lever timepiece movement.

Page 54

This photograph is taken from F.W. Elliott's 1953 catalogue, the prices for the clocks were
as follows:

			NET Trade price	25% Purchase Tax	Fixed selling price
7779 *8in.*	*Oak 14*				
10in.	*day Pendulum*		£4/12/6	£1/3/2	£8/17/6
12in.	*T/P*				
8080 *8in.*	*Oak*				
10in.	*8 day lever*		£6/5/-	£1/11/3	£12/-/-
12in.	*T/P*				

Appendix I

Reproduction of the
1797 Act of Parliament

ANNO TRICESIMO SEPTIMO

Georgii III. Regis.

* ✶✶✶

C A P. CVIII.

An Act for granting to His Majefty certain Duties on Clocks and Watches.   [19th *July* 1797.]

Moft Gracious Sovereign,

E, Your Majefty's moft dutiful and loyal Subjects the **Preamble.** Commons of *Great Britain* in Parliament affembled, towards raifing the neceffary Supplies to defray Your Majefty's Publick Expences, and making a permanent Addition to the Publick Revenue, have freely and voluntarily refolved to give and grant unto Your Majefty the Duties herein-after mentioned ; and do moft humbly befeech Your Majefty that it may be enacted ; and be it enacted by the King's moft Excellent Majefty, by and with the Advice and Confent of the Lords Spiritual and Temporal, and Commons, in this prefent Parliament affembled, and by the Authority of the fame, That, from and after the Fifth Day of **From *July* 5,** *July* One thoufand feven hundred and ninety-feven, there fhall be charg- **1797, the following annual** ed, affeffed, and paid, unto His Majefty, His Heirs and Succeffors, **Duties to be** throughout the Kingdom of *Great Britain*, the feveral Duties herein-after **paid :** mentioned ; that is to fay,

For and upon every Clock or Timekeeper, by whatever Name the fame **For every** fhall be called, which fhall be ufed for the Purpofe of a Clock, and placed **Clock, 5 s:** in or upon any Dwelling Houfe, or any Office or Building thereunto belonging, or any other Building whatever, whether private or publick, belonging to any Perfon or Perfons, or Company of Perfons, or any Body Corporate or Politick, or Collegiate, or which fhall be kept and ufed, by any Perfon or Perfons in *Great Britain*, there fhall be charged an Annual Duty of Five Shillings :

For and upon every Gold Watch, or Watch enamelled on Gold, **ForeveryGold** or Gold Timekeeper ufed for the Purpofe of a Watch, by what- **Watch, or enamelled** ever **on Gold, 10 s:**

5   19 Y 2

ever Name the fame fhall be called, which fhall be kept, and worn, or ufed, by any Perfon or Perfons in *Great Britain*, there fhall be charged an Annual Duty of Ten Shillings :

For every Silver or Metal Watch, 2s. 6d. And for and upon every Silver or Metal Watch, or Silver or Metal Timekeeper ufed for the Purpofe of a Watch, or any other Watch, or Timekeeper ufed for the like Purpofe, not before charged, of whatever Materials the fame fhall be made, and by whatever Name the fame fhall be called, which fhall be kept and worn, or ufed, by any Perfon, there fhall be charged an Annual Duty of Two Shillings and Sixpence :

The faid feveral Duties to be paid by the refpective Proprietors of fuch Clocks, Watches, and Timekeepers.

What Watches fhall be deemed Gold. II. And be it further enacted, That every Watch, of which the outer or the inner Cafe fhall be made of Gold, or fhall be enamelled on Gold, fhall be charged with the Duty hereby impofed on Gold Watches.

Duties to be under the Management of the Commiffioners of Taxes. III. And be it further enacted, That the Commiffioners authorized or appointed, or who fhall be hereafter authorized or appointed, to put in Execution the Acts relative to any of the prefent Duties placed under the Management of the Commiffioners for the Affairs of Taxes, fhall be Commiffioners for executing this prefent Act, and the Powers herein contained, with relation to the Duties hereby granted, as before mentioned, in all the Counties, Ridings, Divifions, Shires, Stewartries, Cities, Boroughs, Cinque Ports, Towns, and Places refpectively, within the Kingdom of *Great Britain* ; and that the feveral Surveyors, Infpectors, Affeffors, and Collectors, refpectively appointed or to be appointed to put in Execution the faid Acts relative to the faid prefent Duties under the Management of the faid Commiffioners for the Affairs of Taxes, or any of them, fhall be Surveyors, Infpectors, Affeffors, and Collectors, to put in Execution this prefent Act, with relation to the Duties hereby granted, as before mentioned, according to the Powers given to them refpectively by the faid Acts, or any of them, and not hereby altered, or according to the Powers given to them by this Act ; and the faid Commiffioners, and other the Perfons aforefaid, being refpectively duly qualified to act in the Execution of any of the faid Acts before mentioned, fhall and they are hereby refpectively empowered and required to do all Things neceffary for putting this Act in Execution with relation to the faid Duties hereby granted, as before mentioned, in the like and in as full and ample a Manner as they, or any of them, are or is authorized to put in Execution the faid Acts relative to the faid prefent Duties under the Management of the faid Commiffioners for the Affairs of Taxes, or any Matters or Things therein refpectively contained.

Duties to be afcertained, etc. as other Duties under their Management. IV. And be it further enacted, That the aforefaid Duties by this Act granted, fhall and may be afcertained, managed, collected, recovered, paid over, and accounted for, under fuch Penalties, Forfeitures, and Difabilities, and according to fuch Rules, Methods, Directions, and Provifions, by which the Rates and Duties now placed under the Management of the Commiffioners for the Affairs of Taxes, or any of them, are or is, or may be afcertained, managed, collected, paid, recovered, paid over, and accounted for, except as far as any of the faid Rules, Methods, Directions, and Provifions, are exprefsly varied by this

7

Act ;

Act; and all and every the Powers, Authorities, Rules, Directions Penalties, Forfeitures, Claufes, Matters, and Things, contained in any Act
or Acts relative to the faid Rates and Duties, or any of them, now in
Force, for the furcharging, mitigating, recovering, paying, and accounting for the Rates and Duties by any former Acts granted, as far as
the fame are applicable to the aforefaid Duties granted by this Act, and
not exprefsly varied, or otherwife provided for, fhall be in full Force,
and duly obferved, practifed, and put in Execution throughout the Kingdom of *Great Britain*, for furcharging, mitigating, recovering, paying,
and accounting for the aforefaid Duties granted by this Act, as fully and
effectually, to all Intents and Purpofes, as if the fame Powers, Authorities,
Rules, Directions, Penalties, Forfeitures, Claufes, Matters, and Things,
were particularly repeated and re-enacted in the Body of this Act.

V. And be it further enacted, That the faid Commiffioners hereby
appointed to put in Execution this Act fhall, in their refpective Counties, Ridings, Divifions, Shires, Stewartries, Cities, Boroughs, Cinque
Ports, Towns, and Places, for which they are or fhall be appointed
Commiffioners refpectively, meet for the Firft Time on or before the
Firft Day of *Auguft* One thoufand feven hundred and ninety-feven, or on
fuch other Day as the faid Commiffioners, or any Two or more of them,
fhall think proper to appoint, not later than the Fifteenth Day of *September* One thoufand feven hundred and ninety-feven, and proceed in
the Execution of this Act in fuch and the fame Manner as is prefcribed
by any Act or Acts with refpect to the Rates and Duties before mentioned, under the Management of the faid Commiffioners for the Affairs
of Taxes, (except where any Alteration is made by this Act); and the
faid Commiffioners fhall, at fuch their Meeting, caufe Notice to be given
to the Perfons appointed within their refpective Diftricts or Divifions to
be Affeffors or Collectors under the faid Acts before mentioned, or any
of them, that fuch Perfons are alfo appointed refpectively Affeffors or
Collectors of the Duties granted by this Act.

First Meeting of Commiffioners,

who fhall give Notice to the Affeffors of their Appointment.

VI. And be it further enacted, That the feveral Perfons appointed
Affeffors for the prefent Year fhall, within Fourteen Days after Notice of
their being appointed Affeffors of the aforefaid Duties hereby granted,
and the feveral Perfons to be hereafter appointed Affeffors fhall, within
Fourteen Days after fuch their Appointment, yearly leave Notice in
Writing at every Dwelling Houfe within their refpective Diftricts, in or
upon which any Clock, Watch, or Timekeeper aforefaid fhall be placed,
kept and worn, or ufed, or in which any Perfon liable to be affeffed to
the aforefaid Duties hereby granted fhall dwell.

Affeffors to leave Notice yearly at the Houfes of Perfons liable to the Duty.

VII. And be it further enacted, That every Notice to be left as aforefaid at any Dwelling Houfe, for the Occupier or Occupiers thereof, fhall
require fuch Occupier or Occupiers to prepare and produce, within the
Space of Fourteen Days next enfuing the Day of giving fuch Notice,
a Lift or Declaration in Writing of all the Clocks, and Timekeepers ufed
for the Purpofe of Clocks, and placed in or upon fuch Dwelling Houfe,
and belonging either to the Owner or Owners of fuch Dwelling Houfe,
or to fuch Occupier or Occupiers; and alfo of all Watches, and
Timekeepers ufed for the Purpofe of Watches, kept and worn,
or ufed, by fuch Occupier or Occupiers; and another Lift in Writing,

*Notice to re-
quire the
Houfekeepers
to prepare
Lifts and De-
clarations in
the Form con-
tained in the
annexed Sche-
dule.*

19 Z　　　　　　　　　　　　　　　　　containing

containing the Chriftian and Surnames of each and every Perfon dwelling in fuch Dwelling Houfe, whether fuch Perfons are liable to the aforefaid Duties by this Act granted or not, and whether fuch Perfon fhall be One of fuch Occupier's Family, or an Inmate or Lodger in fuch Dwelling Houfe; which Lift and Declaration fhall be made out by fuch Occupier or Occupiers in the Form in the Schedule to this Act annexed.

Houfekeepers to make out Lift and fign Declaration in 14 Days after Notice, and to require all Perfons within the Houfe to declare the Number of Clocks and Watches for which they ought to be affeffed, &c.

VIII. And be it further enacted, That every fuch Occupier for whom any fuch Notice as aforefaid fhall be left, fhall be obliged, within Fourteen Days after fuch Notice being left, to make out the Lift, and fign the Declaration before mentioned; and fhall alfo, within the like Period, caufe the Contents of the faid Notice to be read over and made known to each and every Perfon dwelling in fuch Dwelling Houfe, Office, or Building as aforefaid, liable to the aforefaid Duties; and fhall require each and every fuch Perfon to declare to every fuch Occupier the exact Number of the Clocks, Watches and Timekeepers, for which he or fhe ought to be affeffed, and to give a Defcription thereof, in fuch Manner that the Duties payable for the fame may be afcetained, or to declare that fuch Perfon has not kept and worn, or ufed, within the Time herein-after fpecified, any fuch Clock, Watch, or Timekeeper; which Declarations the faid Occupier or Occupiers fhall caufe to be entered in the Lift or Declaration to be delivered by him, her, or them, to the Affeffor or Affeffors, and fhall require each and every fuch Perfon to write or caufe to be written his or her Chriftian or Surname oppofite the Entry of his or her Clocks, Watches, or Timekeepers, or his or her Declaration as aforefaid; and every fuch Perfon, being required thereunto as aforefaid by any fuch Occupier or Occupiers, fhall be obliged to make fuch Declaration, and to atteft the fame in the Manner before directed, unlefs fuch Perfon fhall be ufually refident elfewhere, out of the Diftrict of fuch Affeffor or Affeffors where fuch Notice fhall be left, and fhall be liable to be affeffed in fuch other Place, and fhall declare the Place where he or fhe intends to be affeffed to or pay, or has been affeffed to or paid, the aforefaid Duties, which Declaration fhall be entered on the Return to be made by fuch Occupier or Occupiers, and figned as aforefaid.

Lifts for the Firft and Second Times to contain the largeft Number of Clocks and Watches liable to Duty between Aug. 1, 1797, and the Time of making them out, and afterwards during the Year ending April 5, preceding.

IX. And be it further enacted, That every fuch Lift or Declaration fhall, for the Firft and Second Times of the fame being required under this Act, contain the greateft Number of Clocks, Watches, and Timekeepers liable to the aforefaid Duties hereby granted, which have been placed in or upon his or her Dwelling Houfe, Offices, or Buildings as aforefaid, or kept and worn, or ufed, by the refpective Perfons fpecified in fuch Lift or Declaration as aforefaid, at any One Time between the Firft Day of Auguft One thoufand feven hundred and ninety-feven, and the Day of making a Return thereof refpectively, according to the Directions of this Act; and every fuch Lift or Declaration thereafter to be made fhall contain the greateft Number of fuch Clocks, Watches, and Timekeepers, fo placed as aforefaid, or kept and worn, or ufed, by fuch Perfons refpectively, during the Year ending on the Fifth Day of April preceding the Day of making fuch Return; and each Perfon mentioned in the Lift and Declaration of fuch Occupier, fhall be liable to be charged to the full Number of his or her Clocks, Watches, and Timekeepers, which fhall or ought to be inferted in fuch Lift or Declaration.

X. Pro-

X. Provided always, and be it further enacted, That it fhall and may be lawful to and for any fuch Affeffor or Affeffors, whenever he or they fhall fee Occafion, to ferve a Notice perfonally upon, or leave the fame at the Houfe where any Perfon liable to any of the aforefaid Duties hereby granted, and not being the Occupier of fuch Houfe as aforefaid, fhall refide, requiring fuch Perfon to make out, fign, and deliver a feparate Lift and Declaration of the Number of his or her Clocks, Watches, and Timekeepers in the Manner before directed; and every fuch Perfon fhall, after fuch Notice fo ferved or left, make out, fign, and deliver, a Lift and Declaration, within the Times refpectively before limited, in fuch Form and Manner as is herein directed to be done by Occupiers of Dwelling Houfes with refpect to Clocks, Watches, and Timekeepers, being their own Property refpectively, or in Default thereof a feparate Affeffment fhall be made upon fuch Perfon, in the Manner before directed with refpect to fuch Occupiers as aforefaid; and every fuch Perfon fhall be liable to be affeffed in the Diftrict in which fuch Lift and Declaration fhall be made, unlefs he or fhe fhall add to fuch Return a Declaration of the particular Parifh or Place of his or her ufual Refidence where fuch Perfon intends to pay, or has been affeffed to or paid, the aforefaid Duties.

Affeffors may ferve Notice on Perfons not being Houfeholders, requiring them to make out feparate Lifts, &c.

XI. And be it further enacted, That if any Occupier of any Dwelling Houfe at which any fuch Notice fhall be left, fhall, for the Space of Fourteen Days after fuch Notice, neglect or refufe to make out fuch Lifts or Declarations, or either of them, or fhall neglect or refufe, within the faid Period of Fourteen Days, to make known the Contents of fuch Notice to each and every Perfon dwelling in fuch Dwelling Houfe, or to require and take the Lifts or Declarations of every fuch Perfon willing to make the fame, or to infert the fame in the Declaration of fuch Occupier, in the Manner herein directed, or to deliver or caufe to be delivered fuch Lift and Declaration to fuch Affeffor or Affeffors, duly filled up and figned as aforefaid, when he or they fhall call for the fame at fuch Dwelling Houfe, at any Time after the Expiration of Fourteen Days from the faid Notice being left, and fhall not leave fuch Lift and Declaration at the Place named in the faid Notice, at the Place of Abode of One of the faid Affeffors, within Fourteen Days after fuch Affeffor or Affeffors fhall have fo called for the fame, then fuch Affeffor or Affeffors fhall, from the beft Information he or they can obtain, make an Affeffment upon fuch Occupier for or in refpect of every Clock, Watch, or Timekeeper, kept and worn, or ufed, by fuch Occupier, and upon every other Perfon dwelling in the Dwelling Houfe of fuch Occupier, for or in refpect of every Clock, Watch, or Timekeeper, kept and worn, or ufed, by fuch other Perfon; and every fuch Affeffment fo made upon the Occupier, fhall be final and conclufive upon him or her, without Liberty of Appeal therefrom, unlefs fuch Occupier fhall prove on fuch Appeal, as is herein-after mentioned, that he or fhe was not at his or her Dwelling Houfe at the Time of leaving the faid Notice, nor between that Day and the Time limited for delivering fuch Lift and Declaration to the Affeffor, or fhall alledge and prove fuch other Excufe as the Commiffioners for executing this Act fhall in their Judgement think reafonable and fufficient, and at the Time of fuch Appeal fhall produce upon Oath a true and full Lift

If Houfeholders neglect to make out Lifts, etc. the Affeffors fhall affefs them from the beft Information they can obtain, which fhall be final, unlefs certain Particulars be proved.

4

and

and Declaration, made and figned as herein required, of all Clocks, Watches, and Timekeepers, placed or being in or upon his or her Dwelling Houfe, Offices, or Buildings aforefaid, or kept and worn, or ufed, by him or her, or any Perfon or Perfons dwelling in any fuch Dwelling Houfe, Office, or Building as aforefaid, to the beft of the Knowledge or Belief of fuch Occupier; and every fuch Affeffment fo made upon any fuch other Perfon fhall be final and conclufive upon him or her, without Liberty of Appeal therefrom, unlefs fuch other Perfon fhall prove that the Contents of fuch Notice had not been made known to him or her, or that no Lift or Declaration had been required from him or her, or that fuch Lift or Declaration had been given, and neglected to be inferted in the Lift or Declaration of the Occupier, and at the Time of fuch Appeal fhall produce, on Oath, a true and full Lift and Declaration, figned by him or her, of all Clocks, Watches, and Timepieces, kept and worn, or ufed, by him or her, within the Time for which fuch Lift and Declaration are required to be given.

Affeffors, &c. if they find Omiffions in Lifts, may make Surcharges after the Rate of Double the Duties; of which they fhall receive a Moiety.

XII. And be it further enacted, That fuch Affeffors as aforefaid fhall not be bound by fuch Lifts and Declarations as fhall be delivered to them refpectively in purfuance of this Act, but that fuch Affeffors, and alfo any Surveyor or Infpector of the Duties hereby impofed, fhall be at Liberty, if he or they fhall find, on due Examination, that any Clock, Watch, or Timekeeper, liable to any of the Duties by this Act impofed, is omitted in fuch Lift or Declaration, to furcharge the fame, and make a true Affeffment upon every Perfon liable as aforefaid within their refpective Diftricts, of the real Number of fuch Clocks, Watches, and Timekeepers, liable to the faid Duties, or any of them, fubject to an Appeal, at fuch Times and in fuch Manner as is directed by the aforefaid Acts relative to the prefent Duties under the Management of the faid Commiffioners for the Affairs of Taxes, or any of them; and that in all fuch Cafes fuch Surcharge fhall be made after the Rate of Double the Duty for every Clock, Watch, or Timekeeper, fo omitted; and the Affeffor, Surveyor, or Infpector, fo making fuch Surcharge, fhall be and is hereby entitled to, and fhall have and receive, for his own Ufe, One Moiety of the Sum charged by every Surcharge which may be juftly made upon any fuch Lift and Declaration.

Firft Affeffment to be made for Three Quarters, from July 5, 1797, and afterwards for a Year.

XIII. And be it further enacted, That the Firft Affeffment under this Act, of the faid Duties hereby impofed, fhall be made for Three Quarters of a Year, from the Fifth Day of *July* One thoufand feven hundred and ninety-feven, and afterwards fhall be made for One whole Year, from the Fifth Day of *April* in every Year.

Duties to be paid Quarterly.

XIV. And be it further enacted, That the aforefaid Duties hereby granted fhall be paid Quarterly, at the Times and in the Manner following; that is to fay, on the Fifth Day of *January*, the Fifth Day of *April*, the Fifth Day of *July*, and the Tenth Day of *October*, in every Year, by equal Portions; the Firft of the faid Payments upon the faid Affeffment for Three Quarters of a Year, to be made on the Tenth Day of *October* One thoufand feven hundred and ninety-feven.

XV. And

XV. And be it further enacted, That in refpect of every Clock, or Timekeeper ufed for the Purpofe of a Clock, which fhall be erected, placed, or be in or upon any Building belonging to any Company of Perfons, Body Politick or Corporate, or Collegiate, a Notice fhall annually, as aforefaid, be left with any known Officer of fuch Company, Body Politick or Corporate, or Collegiate, who fhall certify the Contents thereof to his Superior or Superiors having the Care of fuch Clock, Timekeeper, or Building, or to whom fuch Clock, Timekeeper, or Building, fhall belong ; or if no fuch Officer fhall be known to the Affeffor or Affeffors, then fuch Notice fhall be affixed on the outer Door of fuch Building, which Notice fo delivered or affixed fhall be deemed good and fufficient Notice, and fhall be as effectual to compel the Delivery of a Lift and Declaration of the Names and Defcriptions of the Perfon or Perfons chargeable with the Duty hereby impofed on fuch Clock or Timekeeper, as if the fame had been perfonally ferved on fuch Perfon or Perfons ; and the Duty hereby impofed on fuch Clock or Timekeeper fhall be paid by the Company, Body Politick or Corporate, or Collegiate, to whom fuch Clock, Timekeeper, or Building fhall belong, and the Goods and Chattels of fuch Company, Body Politick or Corporate, or Collegiate, to whom fuch Clock or Timekeeper fhall belong, fhall be liable in Payment of the fame, in like Manner as the Goods and Chattels of any Owner of any Clock charged with the faid Duty by this Act is hereby, or by any Act or Acts herein referred to, made liable for Nonpayment of the faid Duty.

A Notice to be left with the Officer of Companies, etc. or affixed to the outer Door of the Building on which the Clock is erected, etc.

XVI. And be it further enacted, That where any Occupier of any Dwelling Houfe, or any Officer of any Company, Body Politick or Corporate, or Collegiate, or other Perfon liable under the Directions before contained to deliver fuch Lift and Declaration as aforefaid to the Affeffor or Affeffors, fhall refufe or neglect, within the Time herein-before prefcribed, to deliver or caufe to be delivered to fuch Affeffor or Affeffors, fuch Lift or Declaration fpecifying the Number of Clocks, Watches, and Timekeepers, ufed as aforefaid by fuch Occupier or Occupiers, and likewife of thofe belonging to all fuch Perfons dwelling within fuch Dwelling Houfe, Office, or Building, as fhall have refpectively made to fuch Occupier the Declaration herein-before required, or belonging to fuch Company, Body Politick or Corporate, or Collegiate ; or if any Perfon or Perfons dwelling in any Dwelling Houfe, and liable, under the Directions of this Act, to give to the Occupier thereof fuch Declaration as aforefaid, fhall neglect or refufe, on Demand, to give fuch Declaration of the Number of his or her Clocks, Watches, and Timekeepers, or to declare that he, fhe, or they has or have ufed or worn none, to fuch Occupier, and to fign his or her Name to fuch Declaration, he or fhe fo neglecting or refufing fhall, for every fuch Offence, forfeit the Sum of Ten Pounds.

Penalty of 10 l. for not delivering Lifts and Declarations, etc.

XVII. And be it further enacted, That, from and after the Tenth Day of *October* One thoufand feven hundred and ninety feven, if any Perfon fhall have, keep, and ufe, any Clock, or Timekeeper for the Purpofe of a Clock, or keep and wear, or ufe, any Watch, or Timekeeper for the Purpofe of a Watch, liable to any Duty by this Act impofed, without having declared the fame in the Manner herein directed, every fuch Perfon fhall, for every fuch Offence, forfeit and pay the Sum of Ten Pounds.

After Oct. 10, 1797, a Penalty of 10 l. for having Clocks or Watches, and not having declared the fame.

20 A　　　　　　　　　　　　　　　　　XVIII. And

The Duties on Clocks in Dwelling Houses not enjoyed by any particular Occupier to be charged upon the Landlords.

XVIII. And be it further enacted, That when any Dwelling House with the Offices and Buildings thereto belonging, shall be demised to different Occupiers in separate Apartments. the Duties by this Act granted as aforesaid, which shall become payable in respect of any Clock or Timekeeper, placed or being in or upon such Dwelling House, Office, or Building, and belonging to the Landlord or Landlords, and not exclusively in the Enjoyment of any particular Occupier, shall be charged upon the Landlord or Landlords who let or demised the same, his, her, or their Executors or Administrators, and not on the Occupier or Occupiers.

Duties on Clocks let with Dwelling Houses, &c. to be paid by the Occupiers.

XIX. Provided always, and be it further enacted, That the aforesaid Duties hereby granted, which shall be payable in respect of any Clock or Timekeeper, placed or being in or upon any Dwelling House, or any Office or Building belonging thereto, or occupied therewith, and which shall be let or demised together with such Dwelling House, Office, or Building, shall be paid by the Occupier or Occupiers thereof, his, her, or their Executors or Administrators, and not by the Landlord or Landlords, except in the Case herein-before mentioned, any Covenant, Agreement, or Contract to the contrary notwithstanding,

How Duties on Infants are to be charged.

XX. And be it further enacted, That the aforesaid Duties hereby granted, which shall become payable by any Person under the Age of Twenty-one Years, having a Parent or Guardian, or residing with any Tutor or Curator, shall be charged upon such Parent or Guardian, or such Tutor or Curator, provided the Name of such Parent, Guardian, Tutor, or Curator, shall be returned to such Assessor or Assessors of the aforesaid Duties, or in Default thereof, the said Duties shall be charged upon and paid by such Infant.

Duty not to extend to Householders exempted from the Duties on Windows and Houses, for One Clock, or One Silver or Metal Watch:

XXI. Provided always, and be it further enacted, That nothing herein contained shall be construed to charge with the Duty hereby imposed, any Person who shall inhabit any Dwelling House wholly exempt from the Payment of the Duties on Windows or Lights, by an Act of the Sixth Year of the Reign of His present Majesty, and also of the Duties on inhabited Houses, by an Act of the Nineteenth Year of the Reign of His present Majesty, in respect of One Clock, or Timekeeper to be used for the Purpose of a Clock, or having only One Clock or Timekeeper, in respect of One Silver or Metal Watch, or Silver or Metal Timekeeper used for the Purpose of a Watch; any Thing herein-before contained to the contrary notwithstanding.

Nor to Occupiers of Houses not rateable at more than Ten Windows, for Clocks not worth more than 20s.

XXII. Provided also, and be it further enacted, That nothing herein contained shall be construed to charge with the said Duty, any Person inhabiting a Dwelling House which, together with the Offices thereunto belonging, is or ought to be rated at not more than Ten Windows or Lights to the Duties on Windows or Lights, in respect of any Clock, or Timekeeper used for the Purpose of a Clock, in such Dwelling House, the Movements of which Clock or Timekeeper shall be made of Wood, or fixed upon Wood, and which Clocks are usually sold by the respective Makers thereof at a Price not exceeding the Sum of Twenty Shillings for each such Clock, or which shall not be of greater Value than

9

the

the faid Sum of Twenty Shillings; any Thing herein-before contained to the contrary notwithstanding.

XXIII. Provided also, and be it further enacted, That nothing herein contained shall be construed to extend to charge with the aforesaid Duties, any Clock or Timekeeper placed or being in or upon any Building in the Occupation of His Majesty, His Heirs or Successors, or any of the Royal Family, or of any Ambassador or Foreign Minister residing in *Great Britain*, or in or upon either House of Parliament, or any Hospital or other Building erected and maintained for charitable Purposes, nor upon any Parish Church, or any Chapel or other Place of Publick religious Worship, or any Watch or Timekeeper kept, had, used, or worn, in any House inhabited by any of the Royal Family, or by any such Ambassador or Foreign Minister.

Not to extend to the Royal Family, or Ambassadors, or to Hospital, Churches, &c.

XXIV. Provided also, and be it further enacted, That nothing herein contained shall be construed to extend to charge with the Duty hereby imposed any Servant in Husbandry dwelling with his or her Master or Mistress, in any Dwelling House exempt from the Payment of the said Duties on inhabited Houses, by the Act of the Nineteenth Year of His said Majesty's Reign, before mentioned; nor to any Non-commissioned Officer or Private in His Majesty's Army, or in the Marines or the Militia, nor to any Seaman in His Majesty's Navy, or employed in the Merchant Service.

Nor to certain Husbandmen, nor Soldiers, Marines, or Sailors;

XXV. Provided also, and be it further enacted, That nothing herein contained shall be construed to extend to charge with the Duty hereby imposed, any Maker of or Dealer in Clocks, Watches, or Timekeepers, in respect of any Clock, Watch, or Timekeeper, kept by him for Sale, or intrusted to him or his Servants or Workmen, in the Course of Trade; such Maker of, or Dealer in Clocks, Watches, or Timekeepers, being duly licensed thereunto by virtue of this Act; nor any Pawnbroker in respect of any Clock, Watch, or Timekeeper, kept for Sale or in Pledge, such Pawnbroker being duly licensed thereunto by virtue of the Laws now in Force.

Nor to the Stock of licensed Makers of, or Dealers in, Clocks and Watches, or licensed Pawnbrokers.

XXVI. And be it further enacted, That every Person using and exercising the Trade and Business of a Maker of, or Dealer in Clocks, Watches, or Timekeepers, within the City of *London*, or the City or Liberties of *Westminster*, the Weekly Bills of Mortality, the Parishes of *Saint Mary-le-Bone*, or *Saint Pancras*, in the County of *Middlesex*, or the Borough of *Southwark*, in the County of *Surrey*, and who shall take out a Licence to use and exercise the said Trade and Business of a Maker of, or Dealer in Clocks, Watches, or Timekeepers, shall yield and pay annually, to and for the Use of His Majesty, His Heirs and Successors, the Sum of Two Shillings and Sixpence; and that every Person using and exercising the said Trade and Business of a Maker of, or Dealer in Clocks, Watches, or Timekeepers, without the City of *London*, the City and Liberties of *Westminster*, the Weekly Bills of Mortality, the Parishes of *Saint Mary-le-Bone*, and *Saint Pancras*; in the County of *Middlesex*, and the Borough of *Southwark*, in the County of *Surrey*, and who shall take out a Licence to use and exercise the said Trade and Business of a Maker of, or Dealer in Clocks, Watches, or Timekeepers, shall yield and

Makers of or Dealers in Clocks and Watches, taking out a Licence, to pay annually, within certain Limits, 2s. 6d. and without, 1s.

and pay annually, to and for the Ufe of His Majefty, His Heirs and Succeffors, the Sum of One Shilling.

XXVII. And, for the better and more effectually raifing, levying, collecting, and paying the faid Duties hereby granted on Licences, be it enacted, That the fame fhall be under the Government, Care, and Management, of the Commiffioners for the Time being appointed to manage the Duties charged on ftamped Vellum, Parchment, and Paper, who, or the major Part of them, are hereby required and empowered to employ fuch Officers under them for that Purpofe, and allow fuch Salaries and incidental Charges as fhall be neceffary ; and to provide and ufe fuch Marks or Stamps, as they fhall think fit, to denote the faid Duties, and to repair, renew, and alter the fame from Time to Time as they fhall fee Occafion, and to do all other Matters and Things neceffary to be done for putting this Act in Execution with relation to the faid Duties hereby granted, in the like, and in as full and ample a Manner as they, or the major Part of them, are authorized to put in Execution any of the Laws now in being concerning ftamped Vellum, Parchment, and Paper.

XXVIII. And be it further enacted, That, from and after the paffing of this Act, any Two or more of His Majefty's Commiffioners appointed to manage the Duties charged on ftamped Vellum, Parchment, or Paper, or fome Perfon duly authorized by them, or any Three or more of them, fhall grant Licences to fuch Perfons who fhall ufe and exercife the Trade and Bufinefs of a Maker of, or Dealer in Clocks, Watches, or Timekeepers, in any City, Town, or Place within *Great Britain*, to ufe and exercife the fame within fuch City, Town, or Place, for any Space of Time as herein-after mentioned, not exceeding One Year, and every fuch Licence fhall ceafe and determine on the Fifth Day of *July*, in the Year for which the fame fhall be iffued ; and every fuch Licence taken out for the Year in which the fame fhall be iffued, fhall be in Force until and upon the Fifth Day of *July* then next following, and fhall commence from the Date thereof ; and every fuch Licence taken out for any Year fubfequent to the Year in which the fame fhall be iffued, fhall commence from the Fifth Day of *July* then next enfuing, and continue in Force until

and upon the Fifth Day of *July* in the fucceeding Year ; and that every fuch Perfon fhall take out a frefh Licence for another Year, Ten Days at leaft before the Expiration of that Year for which he fhall have been licenfed, if he fhall continue to ufe and exercife the faid Trade and Bufinefs of a Maker of, or Dealer in Clocks, Watches, or Timekeepers, and fhall in like Manner renew fuch Licence from Year to Year, paying down the refpective Sums due on fuch Licence, as long as he fhall continue to ufe and exercife the faid Trade and Bufinefs of a Maker of, or Dealer in Clocks, Watches, or Timekeepers.

XXIX. And be it further enacted, That Perfons carrying on their Trade and Bufinefs of Makers of, or Dealers in Clocks, Watches, or Timekeepers in Partnerfhip, fhall not be obliged to take out more than One Licence in any One Year for carrying on fuch Trade or Bufinefs.

XXX. And be it further enacted, That every Perfon ufing or exercifing the Trade or Bufinefs of a Maker of, or Dealer in Clocks, Watches, or Timekeepers, not having a Licence to ufe or exercife the Trade or Bufinefs

8

finefs

finefs of a Maker of, or Dealer in Clocks, Watches, or Timekeepers, who fhall, after the Firft Day of *Auguft* One thoufand feven hundred and ninety-feven, within the ·Limits herein-before defcribed, and after the Firft Day of *September* One thoufand feven hundred and ninety-feven, without the faid Limits, carry on the faid Trade and Bufinefs of a Maker of, or Dealer in Clocks, Watches, or Timekeepers, without having obtained a Licence for that Purpofe under the Directions of this Act, fhall forfeit and pay the Sum of Five Pounds.

XXXI. And be it further enacted, That One Moiety of all pecuniary Penalties and Forfeitures hereby impofed, fhall (if fued for within the Space of Three Calendar Months from the Time of any fuch Penalty or Forfeiture being incurred) be to His Majefty, His Heirs and Succeffors, and the other Moiety thereof, with full Cofts of Suit, to the Perfon or Perfons who fhall inform or fue for the fame within the Time aforefaid, and which fhall and may be fued for in His Majefty's Court of Exchequer at *Weftminfter*, for Offences committed in *England*, and in His Majefty's Court of Exchequer at *Edinburgh* for Offences committed in *Scotland*, by Action of Debt, Bill, Plaint, or Information, wherein no Effoin, Privilege, Wager of Law, or more than One Imparlance fhall be allowed.

Application of Penalties fued for in Three Months, and where they may be fued for.

XXXII. Provided always, and be it further enacted, That in Default of Profecution within the Time herein-before limited, no fuch Penalty or Forfeiture fhall be afterwards recoverable, except in the Name of His Majefty's Attorney General in *England*, or Advocate in *Scotland*, by Information in the refpective Courts aforefaid, in which Cafe, the Whole of fuch Penalty or Forfeiture fhall belong to His Majefty, His Heirs and Succeffors; and that all Penalties and Forfeitures, and Shares of Penalties and Forfeitures, incurred as aforefaid, belonging to His Majefty, His Heirs or Succeffors, fhall be paid into the Hands of the Receiver General of His Majefty's Stamp Duties for the Time being; and that in all Cafes where the Whole of fuch pecuniary Penalties or Forfeitures fhall be recovered to the Ufe of His Majefty, His Heirs or Succeffors, it fhall be lawful for the faid Commiffioners to caufe fuch Rewards as they fhall think fit, not exceeding One Moiety of fuch Penalties or Forfeitures fo recovered, after deducting all Charges and Expences incurred in re-covering the fame, to be paid thereout, or amongft any Perfon or Perfons who fhall appear to them to be entitled thereto, either as Difcoverers or Informers, in refpect of fuch Penalties or Forfeitures fo recovered; any Thing herein contained to the contrary notwithftanding.

Recovery of Penalties not fued for in Three Months.

Penalties to His Majefty to be paid to the Receiver General of Stamp Duties, out of which Informers may be rewarded.

XXXIII. Provided always, and be it further enacted, That it fhall and may be lawful to and for any Juftice of the Peace refiding near the Place where the Offence fhall be committed, to hear and determine any Offence againft this Act, which fubjects the Offender to any pecuniary Penalty, which faid Juftice of the Peace is hereby authorized and required, upon any Information exhibited or Complaint made in that Behalf, within Three Calendar Months after the Offence committed, to fummon the Party accufed, giving to each Party Three Days Notice to appear, and alfo the Witneffes on either Side, and to examine into the Matter of Fact; and upon Proof made thereof, either by voluntary Confeffion of the Party accufed, or by the Oath of One or more credible Witnefs or Wit-

Juftices may determine Offences where pecuniary Penalties are inflicted.

20 B   neffes,

neffes, or otherwife, as the Cafe may require, to give Judgement or Sentence for the Penalty or Forfeiture, as in and by this Act is directed to be divided, One Moiety thereof to the Poor of the Parifh or Place where the Offence fhall be committed, and the other Moiety thereof to the Informer or Informers, and to award and iffue out his Warrant, under his Hand and Seal, for the levying the faid Penalty fo adjudged on the Goods of the Offender, and to caufe Sale to be made thereof, in cafe they fhall not be redeemed within Six Days, rendering to the Party the Overplus (if any), and where the Goods of fuch Offender cannot be found fufficient to anfwer the Penalty, to commit fuch Offender to Prifon, there to remain for any Space of Time not exceeding Six nor lefs than Three Calendar Months, unlefs fuch pecuniary Penalty fhall be fooner paid and fatisfied ; and if any Party fhall find himfelf or themfelves aggrieved by the Judgement of any fuch Juftice, then he or they fhall and may, upon giving Security to the Amount of the Value of fuch Penalty and Forfeiture, together with fuch Cofts as fhall be awarded in cafe fuch Judgement fhall be affirmed, appeal to the Juftices of the Peace at the next General or Quarter Seffions for the County, Riding, Divifion, Shire, Stewartry, or Place, which fhall happen, after Fourteen Days next after fuch Conviction fhall have been made, and of which Appeal reafonable Notice fhall be given, who are hereby empowered to fummon and examine Witneffes upon Oath, and finally to hear and determine the fame, and in cafe Judgement fhall be affirmed, it fhall be lawful for fuch Juftices to award the Perfon or Perfons appealing to pay fuch Cofts occafioned by fuch Appeal, as to them fhall feem meet.

Application of Penalty which may be levied by Diftrefs.

Perfons aggrieved may appeal to the Quarter Seffions.

Penalty on Witneffes for not appearing or not giving Evidence.

XXXIV. And be it further enacted, That if any Perfon or Perfons fhall be fummoned as a Witnefs or Witneffes to give Evidence before fuch Juftice touching any of the Matters relative to this Act, and fhall neglect or refufe to appear at the Time and Place to be for that Purpofe appointed, without a reafonable Excufe for fuch Neglect or Refufal, to be allowed of by fuch Juftice of the Peace, or appearing fhall refufe to be examined on Oath and give Evidence before whom the Profecution fhall be depending, that then every fuch Perfon fhall forfeit for every fuch Offence the Sum of Forty Shillings, to be levied and paid in fuch Manner as is herein directed as to other Penalties.

Conviction to be made in the following Form.

XXXV. And be it further enacted, That the Juftices of the Peace before whom any Offender fhall be convicted as aforefaid, fhall caufe the faid Conviction to be made out in the Manner and Form following, or in any other Form of Words to the fame Effect, *mutatis mutandis* ; that is to fay,

' B E it remembered, That, on the   Day of
'   in the Year of our Lord   in the County of
'   A. B. of   was convicted before
' me C. D. One of His Majefty's Juftices of the Peace for
' refiding near the Place where the Offence was committed ; for that
' the faid A. B. on the   Day of   now laft
' paft, did, contrary to the Form of the Statute in that Cafe made and
' provided, [*here ftate the Offence againft the Act*] ; and I do declare and
' adjudge that the faid A. B. hath forfeited the Sum of
' of lawful Money of *Great Britain*, for the Offence aforefaid, to be dif-
                                                                    ' tributed
3

234

tributed as the Law directs. **Given** under my Hand and Seal, the Day of

Which Conviction the faid Juftice fhall caufe to be wrote fairly upon Parchment, and returned to the next General or Quarter Seffions of the Peace for the County, Riding, Divifion, Shire, Stewartry, or Place, where fuch Conviction was made, to be filed by the proper Officer there, and there to remain, and be kept among the Records of the fame County, Riding, Divifion, Shire, or Stewartry, or Place; and no fuch Conviction fhall be removed by *Certiorari* or other Procefs into any Court whatfoever

Convictions to be kept among the County Records, and not removeable into any Court.

XXXVI. And be it further enacted, That all Monies arifing by the faid feveral Duties by this Act granted (the neceffary Charges of raifing and accounting for the fame excepted), fhall from Time to Time be paid by the refpective Receivers appointed under the refpective Commiffioners of Taxes and Stamps, into the Receipt of His Majefty's Exchequer, and fhall be carried to and made Part of the Confolidated Fund.

Duties to be carried to the Confolidated Fund.

XXXVII. Provided always, and be it further enacted, That the Monies arifing or to arife of the feveral Duties before mentioned, or fo much thereof as fhall be fufficient, fhall be deemed an Addition made to the Revenue, for the Purpofe of defraying the increafed Charge occafioned by any Loan raifed or Stock created by virtue of any Act or Acts paffed in this Seffion of Parliament; and that the faid Monies fhall, during the Space of Ten Years next enfuing, be paid into the faid Receipt diftinctly and apart from all other Branches of the Publick Revenue; and that there fhall be provided and kept in the Office of the Auditor of the faid Receipt, during the faid Period of Ten Years, a Book or Books, in which all the Monies arifing from the faid feveral Duties, and paid into the faid Receipt, fhall, together with the Monies arifing from any other Rates and Duties granted or to be granted in this Seffion of Parliament, for the Purpofe of defraying fuch increafed Charge as aforefaid, be entered feparate and apart from all other Monies paid or payable to His Majefty, His Heirs or Succeffors, upon any Account whatever

Application of Duties, which for Ten Years are, with others granted for the fame Purpofe, to be kept feparate from all other Monies.

THE

THE

SCHEDULE to which this Act refers.

I *A. B.* Occupier of the Dwelling Houfe fituate at do hereby declare, That the following Lift contains the true and full Number of Clocks, and Timekeepers ufed for the Purpofe of Clocks, placed or being within or upon my faid Dwelling Houfe, or any Office or Building belonging thereto or occupied therewith; and the true and full Number and Defcription of all the Watches, and Timekeepers worn or ufed for the Purpofe of Watches, which I now keep and wear, or ufe, or have kept and worn, or ufed, fince the
videlicet,

No. of Clocks.	No. of Gold Watches.	No. of Silver or other Watches.

And I do alfo further declare, That the following Lift contains the Names of all Perfons now dwelling in my faid Dwelling Houfe, Offices, or Buildings, who ought to be affeffed to the faid Duty, to the beft of my Knowledge and Belief; and that I have caufed the Contents of the Notice left at my Dwelling Houfe to be made known to each of them; and that they have feverally made the Declaration fet oppofite their refpective Names, which Names are of their refpective Hand Writing;
videlicet,

Names.	No. of Clocks.	No. of Gold Watches.	No. of Silver or other Watches.
A. B.			
C. D.			

FINIS.

Appendix II
Wheel Trains

Common wheel trains with anchor or deadbeat escapement

Centre wheel	3rd wheel	3rd wheel pinion	Escape wheel	Escape wheel pinion	Effective length of pendulum in inches
90	78	6	27	6	4.57
78	72	6	33	6	4.78
88	80	8	40	7	5.01
88	76	6	27	6	5.03
84	80	7	36	7	5.20
84	78	7	36	7	5.47
84	78	7	35	7	5.78
84	80	7	34	7	5.83
90	84	7	30	7	5.91
84	78	7	34	7	6.13
84	72	6	27	6	6.16
84	80	7	33	7	6.19
84	78	7	33	7	6.51
88	84	7	29	7	6.62
78	72	6	28	6	6.64
84	80	8	36	7	6.79
84	76	7	33	7	6.86
84	78	7	32	7	6.92
86	74	7	28	6	7.04
88	84	7	28	7	7.10
80	76	7	34	7	7.12
92	80	7	28	7	7.16
84	68	6	26	6	7.45
78	72	6	26	6	7.70
82	78	7	31	7	7.74
80	70	6	26	6	7.75
78	70	7	36	7	7.88
72	66	6	30	6	8.08
80	78	7	31	7	8.13
88	84	7	26	7	8.24
78	72	6	25	6	8.33
78	66	6	27	6	8.50
96	76	8	33	8	8.96
84	78	7	28	7	9.04
78	72	6	24	6	9.04
82	72	7	30	7	9.70
72	66	6	27	6	9.98
86	82	8	32	8	10.20
70	60	6	30	6	10.35
84	80	8	29	7	10.47
88	84	7	23	7	10.53
88	84	8	30	8	10.56
80	72	8	38	8	10.84
84	78	7	25	7	11.34
66	60	6	30	6	11.64
77	72	7	25	6	11.64
84	80	7	24	7	11.70
84	70	7	27	7	12.08
84	78	7	24	7	12.31
72	72	7	30	7	12.58
84	80	8	30	8	12.77
80	72	8	30	7	13.31
84	78	7	23	7	13.40
84	78	8	30	8	13.44
90	84	8	26	8	13.44
84	80	8	29	8	13.67
84	72	8	28	7	13.86
78	76	7	25	7	13.86
80	80	8	30	8	14.09
78	72	8	34	8	14.24
80	78	8	30	8	14.82
80	77	8	30	8	15.20
80	72	8	24	6	15.28
78	70	7	20	6	18.75
72	72	8	30	8	21.47

Common fusee wheel counts are 84, 86, 90, 94, 96, 98, 100, 108, 110 meshing with a centre wheel pinion of 7 or 8 leaves.

Common wheel trains with verge escapements

Centre wheel	Contrate wheel	Contrate wheel pinion	Verge wheel	Verge wheel pinion	Effective length of pendulum in inches
84	76	6	27	6	5.53
84	72	6	27	6	6.15
80	70	6	29	6	6.23
84	70	6	27	6	6.51
84	72	6	25	6	7.18

Wheel count usually used for lever escapement dial clocks

Centre wheel	3rd wheel	3rd wheel pinion	Contrate wheel	Contrate wheel pinion	Escape wheel	Escape wheel pinion
64	60	8	60	8	15	7

Motion work wheel counts (dial clocks)

Hour wheel	Minute wheel	Intermediate wheel	Inter pinion	Comments
72	35	35	6	Unusual
72	36	36	6	Used in over 10 per cent of dial clocks.
72	38	38	6	Rare before 1830 but after used in 25 per cent of dials.
72	39	39	6	Unusual.
72	40	40	6	The most common throughout, used in nearly 50 per cent of dials.
72	42	42	6	Fairly common.
72	48	48	6	Very unusual.
84	40	40	7	Unusual.
84	44	44	7	Very unusual.
84	48	48	7	Very unusual.
96	48	48	8	Unusual.

Striking trains used in dial clocks

Fusee	Pin wheel	Pin wheel pinion	Gathering pallet wheel	Gathering pinion	Warning wheel	Warning pinion	Fly pinion
90	54	8	48	6	48	6	6
90	64	8	56	8	50	7	7
84	64	8	56	8	49	7	7
84	64	8	64	8	56	8	7

Tavern clock trains

Barrel	2nd wheel	2nd wheel pinion	Centre wheel	Centre pinion	3rd wheel	3rd wheel pinion	Escape wheel	Escape pinion	Effective length of pendulum in inches
80	60	16	60	12	56	8	34	7	30.47
60	64	20	64	8	60	8	30	8	39.14
144	—	—	60	7	56	8	30	7	39.14
100	64	16	60	8	56	8	30	7	39.14
80	62	20	60	8	56	8	30	7	39.14

A tavern clock striking train

Barrel	Pin wheel	Pin wheel pinion	Gathering pallet wheel	Gathering pallet pinion	Warning wheel	Warning pinion	Fly pinion
104	72	8	56	6	42	7	7

Appendix III   Thwaites Numbering 1761-1910

Up to 1842 dates of the numbering are approximate; after they are taken from actual records.

Numbers	Date	Numbers	Date	Numbers	Date
0—50	1761	4631—4820	1811	13400—13453	1863
51—100	1762	4821—5010	1812	13454—13491	1864
101—150	1763	5011—5200	1813	13492—13574	1865
151—200	1764	5201—5390	1814	13575—13697	1866
201—250	1765	5391—5580	1815	13698—13785	1867
251—300	1766	5581—5770	1816	13786—13855	1868
301—350	1767	5771—5960	1817	13856—13889	1869
351—400	1768	5961—6150	1818	13890—13942	1870
401—450	1769	6151—6340	1819	13943—13994	1871
451—500	1770	6341—6530	1820	13995—14067	1872
501—550	1771	6531—6720	1821	14068—14111	1873
551—600	1772	6721—6910	1822	14112—14157	1874
601—650	1773	6911—7100	1823	14158—14231	1875
651—700	1774	7101—7390	1824	14232—14259	1876
701—750	1775	7391—7580	1825	14260—14314	1877
751—800	1776	7581—7770	1826	14315—14382	1878
801—850	1777	7771—7960	1827	14383—14436	1879
851—900	1778	7961—8150	1828	14437—14519	1880
901—950	1779	8151—8340	1829	14520—14601	1881
951—1000	1780	8341—8530	1830	14602—14706	1882
1001—1050	1781	8531—8720	1831	14707—14840	1883
1051—1100	1782	8721—8910	1832	14841—14905	1884
1101—1150	1783	8911—9200	1833	14906—14978	1885
1151—1200	1784	9201—9390	1834	14979—15097	1886
1201—1250	1785	9391—9580	1835	15098—15210	1887
1251—1300	1786	9581—9770	1836	15211—15316	1888
1301—1350	1787	9771—9960	1837	15317—15385	1889
1351—1400	1788	9961—10150	1838	15386—15483	1890
1401—1450	1789	10151—10340	1839	15484—15539	1891
1451—1500	1790	10341—10500 1840 and	1841	15540—15601	1892
1501—1550	1791	10501—10618 1842 and	1843	15602—15700	1893
1551—1600	1792	10619—10706	1844	15701—15480	1894
1601—1650	1793	10707—10763	1845	15841—15911	1895
1651—1700	1794	10764—10830	1846	15912—16005	1896
1701—1750	1795	10831—10933	1847	16006—16143	1897
1751—1800	1796	10934—11015	1848	16144—16221	1898
1801—1850	1797	11016—11037	1849	16222—16290	1899
1851—2000	1798	11039—11119	1850	16291—16338	1900
2001—2150	1799	11120—11205	1851	16339—16398	1901
2151—2450	1800	11206—12367*	1852	16399—16423	1902
2451—2700	1801	12368—12466	1853	16424—16474	1903
2701—3000	1802	12467—12589	1854	16475—16564	1904
3001—3300	1803	12590—12712	1855	16565—16575	1905
3301—3490	1804	12713—12835	1856	16576—16592	1906
3491—3680	1805	12836—12902	1857	16593—16658	1907
3681—3870	1806	12903—12986	1858	16659—16715	1908
3871—4060	1807	12987—13099	1859	16716—16727	1909
4061—4250	1808	13100—13199	1860	16728—16734	1910
4251—4440	1809	13200—13239	1861		
4441—4630	1810	13240—13399	1862		

* Nos. 11300—12299 are missing.

Appendix IV

Thwaites Numbering of Dial Clocks 1842-1899

From the following, although incomplete tables, some idea of the percentage of dial clocks manufactured by Thwaites can be assessed. Due to the difference in terminology by the writers of the original records it has been necessary to group together the entries of Spring Dial Gray, Spring Dial, Spring Dial clock, Glassed Dial, 2nd size timepiece, 3rd size timepiece and Large Spring Dial under the general heading of Dial Clocks, even though it was very likely that some would have been used in bracket clock cases, inset dials and gallery clocks.

Dial clock numbers	Year	Double dial numbers	Dial clocks produced in year	Dial clock numbers	Year	Double dial numbers	Dial clocks produced in year
10501) 10503—10505) 10508) 10519—10520)	1842		7	10765—10767) 10769) 10775) 10777—10779) 10781—10782) 10786—10787) 10791) 10794—10795) 10800—10803) 10805—10807) 10809—10813) 10815—10819) 10820*) 10822—10830)	1846	10814	43
10527—10529) 10532—10540) 10543—10545) 10549—10550) 10553) 10555—10556) 10559—10577) 10579—10590) 10595—10596) 10600) 10610—10612) 10614)	1843	10578 10597	60				
				10831—10859) 10861—10873) 10876—10880) 10885—10889) 10892—10932)	1847		93
10621) 10628) 10630—10635) 10639) 10641—10646) 10648—10672) 10675—10676) 10678—10685) 10692) 10700) 10705—10706)	1844		54	10935—10939) 10942) 10950—10962) 10965—10968) 10970—10971) 10974—10981) 10988—10991) 10993—11015)	1848		60
10708—10711) 10723—10725) 10732—10735) 10737—10741) 10745) 10747—10748) 10750—10751) 10761)	1845	10720	23	11016) 11019—11025) 11037)	1849	11035 11038	11

* Round plates

Dial clock numbers	Year	Double dial numbers	Dial clocks produced in year
11039*)			
11040—11048)			
11049**)			
11050—11053)			
11055—11056)	1850	11057—11058	50
11059)		11060—11061	
11062—11066)		11067—11068	
11069—11077)			
11082—11088)		11090	
11091—11094)			
11154—11155)			
11159)			
11174—11177)	1851		22
11186—11191)		11193	
11194—11195)		11197	
11201—11205)			
11210—11211)		11213	
11214—11215)			
11217—11218)		11220—11223	
11224—11227)			
11229)			
11232—11233)		11235	
11236—11239)			
11242—11243)			
11247—11248)			
11259—11263)			
11267—11268)	1852	11270	117
11275—11278)		11274	
11282)			
11285—11286)			
11289—11294)			
11297—11299)			
12300—12343)			
12345—12351)			
12353—12362)			
12364—12367)			
12368—12373)			
12375—12378)			
12380—12381)		12383	
12384)			
12386—12390)			
12392—12416)	1853		76
12419—12424)			
12431—12436)			
12439—12440)			
12443—12444)			
12451—12466)			

*   Backset
** With day of month

Dial clock numbers	Year	Double dial numbers	Dial clocks produced in year
12467—12475)			
12477—12486)			
12488—12493)			
12495—12501)			
12503—12504)			
12506—12509)			
12522—12524)	1854		100
12526—12539)			
12541—12551)			
12553—12559)			
12561—12566)			
12568—12575)			
12577—12589)			
12590—12600)			
12608)			
12611—12614)			
12616—12617)			
12620—12682)	1855		93
12687)			
12699—12708)			
12712)			
12720)			
12722)		12723	
12724—12741)		12742	
12743—12753)			
12756—12761)			
12764—12770)			
12772)		12773	
12774—12778)	1856		104
12780—12783)			
12787—12791)			
12793)			
12795—12824)		12825	
12826—12827)		12828	
12829—12835)			
12841—12857)			
12861)			
12866—12872)			
12874)	1857		33
12877—12881)			
12885—12886)			
12903—12912)			
12920—12922)			
12930)			
12946)			
12949—12958)	1858		45
12965—12973)			
12975—12977)			
12979—12986)			

Dial clock numbers	Year	Double dial numbers	Dial clocks produced in year
12987—12988)			
12991—12998)			
13000)			
13002—13003)			
13011—13032)			
13034—13037)			
13039—13040)	1859		52
13045—13048)			
13050—13051)			
13059)			
13091—13092)			
13098—13099)			
13101—13104)			
13109—13113)			
13115—13120)			
13132—13140)			
13142—13145)			
13148—13161)			
13163—13165)	1860		63
13168—13169)			
13175—13176)			
13178—13186)			
13190—13192)			
13195—13196)			
13211—13212)			
13214—13215)	1861		4
13242—13244)			
13258—13259)			
13275—13279)			
13281—13282)			
13285—13286)	1862		24
13380)			
13383—13384)			
13387—13390)			
13397—13399)			
13401)			
13414)			
13416—13418)			
13426—13437)	1863		22
13439—13440)			
13442—13444)			
13455—13462)			
13464—13468)			
13471—13474)	1864		21
13480—13483)			
13497—13498)			
13502)			
13510)			
13517—13520)			
13522)			
13529—13531)	1865		34
13542—13545)			
13551—13554)			
13557—13563)		13564	
13565)			
13568—13572)			
13580—13587)			
13591)			
13593—13598)			
13601—13603)			
13605—13607)			
13610—13611)			
13614—13624)			
13628—13635)			
13638—13644)			
13646—13649)	1866		74
13652—13654)			
13666—13667)			
13669—13670)			
13672—13673)			
13676—13678)			
13682—13684)			
13686—13689)			
13694)			
13697)			
13703—13707)			
13722—13723)			
13726—13727)			
13729—13740)			
13742—13743)			
13749—13751)	1867		34
13754—13755)			
13768)			
13773)			
13781—13782)			
13784—13785)			

Dial clock numbers	Year	Double dial numbers	Dial clocks produced in year	Dial clock numbers	Year	Double dial numbers	Dial clocks produced in year
13790) 13792—13793) 13799—13801) 13806) 13813—13815) 13817—13818) 13821—13823) 13825—13826) 13835—13836) 13838—13849) 13851—13855)	1868		36	14158—14164) 14179—14181) 14183—14185) 14194) 14200) 14203—14206) 14220—14224) 14227—14231)	1875		29
13862—13865) 13869) 13873) 13878—13880) 13883—13889)	1869		16	14233) 14236—14246) 14253—14259)	1876		19
13891—13895) 13898) 13912) 13914—13916) 13918—13921) 13923—13924) 13926—13927) 13930)	1870	13896—13897	21	14264—14267) 14269) 14271—14272) 14274—14275) 14277—14278) 14281—14295) 14302) 14304—14305) 14308—14312)	1877	14296 14300	36
13955—13971) 13975—13979) 13983—13984) 13990)	1871	13950 13986	27	14316—14344) 14352—14354) 14356—14362) 14364—14370)	1878		46
14010—14011) 14015—14030) 14032—14038) 14044) 14048—14057) 14059—14064)	1872		42	14385—14406) 14408—14413) 14416—14417) 14423—14424) 14426—14430) 14432—14435)	1879	14431	42
14069) 14071) 14087—14088) 14092) 14098) 14102—14106) 14109—14111)	1873		14	14437) 14450—14465) 14467—14472) 14474—14478) 14483) 14487—14497) 14499—14509) 14511—14519)	1880		60
14113—14117) 14142—14143) 14154—14155)	1874	14130	10	14520—14527) 14529) 14533—14534) 14538) 14541) 14543) 14545—14549) 14552—14579) 14584—14599)	1881		63

Dial clock numbers	Year	Double dial numbers	Dial clocks produced in year
14602—14605)			
14608)			
14611)			
14616—14631)			
14633)			
14637)			
14639—14642)			
14644—14654)			
14658—14660)	1882		72
14664—14666)			
14668—14674)			
14678)			
14680)			
14687—14700)			
14702)			
14704—14706)			
14707—14725)			
14732—14757)	1883	14773	97
14771)			
14776—14825)			
14841)			
14844—14847)			
14849—14852)			
14855—14857)			
14870)	1884		36
14872—14874)			
14877—14889)			
14894—14899)			
14904)			
14907—14909)			
14911—14926)			
14928—14929)			
14931—14933)			
14936—14950)			
14961)	1885		51
14964—14969)			
14972—14973)			
14975—14976)			
14978)			
14981—14987)			
14990)			
14993—14996)			
15001)			
15003—15016)	1886		103
15018—15051)			
15055—15057)			
15059—15095)		15096	
15097)			
15110)			
15114—15115)			
15117—15120)		15129—15131	
15132—15144)		15145	
15146—15155)			
15159)	1887	15160	81
15161—15175)		15176	
15177—15182)			
15184—15189)			
15194—15209)		15210	
15211—15243)			
15248—15249)			
15256—15263)			
15266)	1888		50
15308—15309)			
15312—15315)			
15318—15330)			
15334—15344)			
15346—15351)			
15354—15359)		15360	
15361—15362)	1889		53
15366—15369)			
15371—15372)			
15377—15384)			
15386)			
15388)		15389	
15392—15396)			
15398—15404)			
15406—15418)	1890		80
15423—15428)			
15430—15436)			
15438—15476)			
15484—15487)		15488	
15493—15498)		15491	
15500—15502)			
15504—15506)			
15509—15511)	1891	15512	38
15513—15515)			
15518—15521)			
15527—15535)			
15548)			
15550)			
15552—15554)			
15556—15565)			
15567—15569)	1892		31
15572—15575)			
15577—15579)			
15596—15601)			

Dial clock numbers	Year	Double dial numbers	Dial clocks produced in year
15602—15608)			
15610—15614)		15615	
15618—15637)			
15643—15645)			
15647—15648)			
15650—15658)	1893		65
15669—15671)			
15678)			
15682—15689)			
15691—15696)			
15702—15711)			
15718—15720)		15721	
15722—15736)			
15743—15754)			
15756—15767)			
15769—15787)	1894	15789	113
15790—15791)			
15798—15800)			
15802—15821)			
15823—15826)			
15829—15839)			
15841—15843)			
15845—15857)		15858	
15859—15868)	1895		68
15871—15911)			
15912—15976)			
15981—15983)			
15989)	1896		81
15992—16000)			
16003—16005)			

Dial clock numbers	Year	Double dial numbers	Dial clocks produced in year
16007—16015)			
16019—16024)			
16028)			
16031—16041)			
16050—16051)		16053	
16060—16062)			
16069—16072)			
16079)	1897		69
16088—16099)			
16106)			
16108—16118)			
16126—16127)		16128	
16133—16134)			
16137—16138)			
16144—16146)		16147	
16148—16150)			
16152)			
16154—16159)			
16163—16169)		16170	
16171—16175)			
16177—16187)	1898		67
16189—16191)		16192	
16193—16196)			
16199—16204)			
16206—16214)			
16216—16220)			
16223—16225)			
16227—16231)			
16233—16242)			
16245—16246)			
16248—16254)	1899		43
16256—16261)			
16263—16265)			
16272—16274)			
16287—16290)			Total 2978

Appendix V

Makers worked for by Thwaites

The numbers given represent the total number of jobs known to have been done for each maker

ALLAM & CLEMENTS	7	DUTTON & SONS	1
ANDREWS, Nathaniel James	1	DUTTON, ? Matthew	4
ARNOLD, John	1	DWERRIHOUSE & CARTER	3
BAIRD, John	3	DWERRIHOUSE, John	33
BAIRD, W. & J.	6	EARNSHAW, Thomas	8
BAKER, Edward	1	EDWARDS, George	1
BANKS, Robert	8	ELLICOTT & CO.	38
BARRAUD, John	26	ELLICOTT, John & Son	183
BARRAUD, Paul	74	EMANUEL, Joel	2
BAYLEY, Barnard	6	EVANS, James	6
BECK, Christopher	1	EVIL, William	3
BELDON	9	FIDGETT, William	1
BERTHOUD, ? Pierre Louis	1	FIELD, Thomas	41
BIDEN	2	FISHER & SONS	27
BIRD, Edward	2	FLADGATE, John	6
BONNINGTON & THORP	73	FORSTER, Joseph	3
BORRELL, Henry	1	FOWLDES, Andrew	39
BOWEN, Thomas	1	FRANKCOM, Charles	1
BRAY, Thomas	2	FRENCH, Edward	4
BREARLEY, ? James	2	GANTHONY, Richard	2
BRINKMAN, George	44	GOODFELLOW, William	2
BROWN, John	1	GOUT, Ralph	14
BROWN, Thomas	51	GRAHAM, James	2
BUCKLAND, Thomas	1	GRANT, John	31
BUNYON, Robert	4	GREAVES, William	1
CADE & ROBINSON	1	GUNTER, Richard	28
CARPENTER, William	50	HALEY & MILNER	76
CATHERWOOD, Joseph	66	HALEY, Charles	22
CHASSEREAU, Edward	10	HARE, Alexander	1
CHAUBAUD, F. & A.	13	HARPER, Thomas	1
CLARKE & SON	11	HARRISON, Thomas	10
CLEGHORN, Samuel	10	HAWKINS, Thomas	2
COLLETT, John	4	HAYLOR, ? Charles	1
COWARD & CO.	4	HAYNES, William	3
CRIBB, William	1	HEDGE & SON	12
CUMMING, Alexander	15	HEDGE, Nathaniel	9
DAVENPORT, James	4	HIGGINSON, John	1
DENNETT, Richard	2	HIPKINS	28
DESBOIS, Phillipe	3	HOUGHTON, James	4
DODD & LESLIE	1	HOWARD, ? John Jarvis	1
DODD, Joseph	3	HOWE, James	10
DORRELL, William	5	HYNAM, Robert	81
DRURY, James	3	IMLAH, Peter	2
		JACKSON, Edward	9

JACOBS, Judah	8	RIGBY, Joshua	2
JAMISON, George	58	ROBINS, John	3
JARDIN, John	1	ROBINSON, Owen	1
JEFFERIES, Isaac	3	ROCHAT, Jean Marc David	1
JONES, William	3	ROGERS, Isaac	4
JOYCE, S. & C.	23	ROOKE, John	1
JULLION, Francis	4	ROSKELL, Robert	19
KEATES, William	1	RUSSELL, Charles	1
KEELEY, Thomas	1	RUSSELL, John	1
KING, James Frederick	4	RUTH, Carl	1
LAMBERT, John (1)	1	SADLER, Stephen	6
LAMBERT, John (2)	5	SALMON, Edward	1
LANCASTER, Francis	1	SANDERSON, Henry	8
LE COQ & HAYES	24	SCOTT & IDLE	2
LE COQ & SON	127	SCOTT, James Amos	5
LEROUX, John	8	SELBY, Peter	2
LESLIE & PRICE	3	SHEAF, Thomas	6
LINDLEY, ? James	5	SHIRLEY	36
LOCK & SON	2	SHUTTLEWORTH, Francis	7
MAKEPIECE, Robert	2	SIMPSON, Archibald	8
MANGIN, Thomas	69	SIMS, Henry	2
MASON, John	1	SKINNER, John	12
MERRILL, Charles	6	SPENCER & PERKINS	106
METCALF, George Marmaduke	39	SPENCER, William	3
MILES, Thomas	26	STARLING, Charles	1
MITCHELL & RUSSELL	2	STEPHENSON, George	3
MITCHELL, William	1	STIRLING, John	6
MOORE, William	3	STONE, George	3
MORISET & LUKINS	9	TATE, Ruth	1
NEALE, John	1	THOROGOOD, Richard	11
NEWTON, John	3	THWAITES, Joseph	7
NICHOLLS, John	10	TOMLIN, Edward	69
NICOLL & SON	2	TOULMIN, Samuel	4
OAKLEY, William	4	TRAVERS, William	2
ORE, Thomas	1	TREGENT, James	16
PEACHEY, ? John	1	TUTET, Edward	21
PERIGAL & DUTTERRAU	21	TWYCROSS & SON	3
PERIGAL & SON	9	TWYFORD, Robert	6
PERIGAL, Francis	69	UNDERWOOD, Robert	1
PRATT & SON	1	UPJOHN, Peter	4
PRENTISS & SON	12	VALE, HOWLET, CAR & ROTHERHAM	1
PRENTISS, Daniel	13	VALENTINE, John	2
PRICE, William	1	VULLIAMY, Benjamin & Justin	3
PRIOR, Edward	101	WALL & SON	1
PRIOR, George	42	WALL, John	1
PYBUS, William	8	WEBB, Edward	3
RADFORD, James	1	WEEKS	2
RAE, Charles	4	WICKES, John	3
RECORDON & DUPONT	1	WIGHTWICK & MOSS	76
RECORDON, Louis	2	WILD, James	2
RIACH, Hugh	1	WISWALL & CO	2
RICE, Thomas	1	WOODWARD, Joseph	6
RICHARDS, Thomas	1	YONGE, George	27

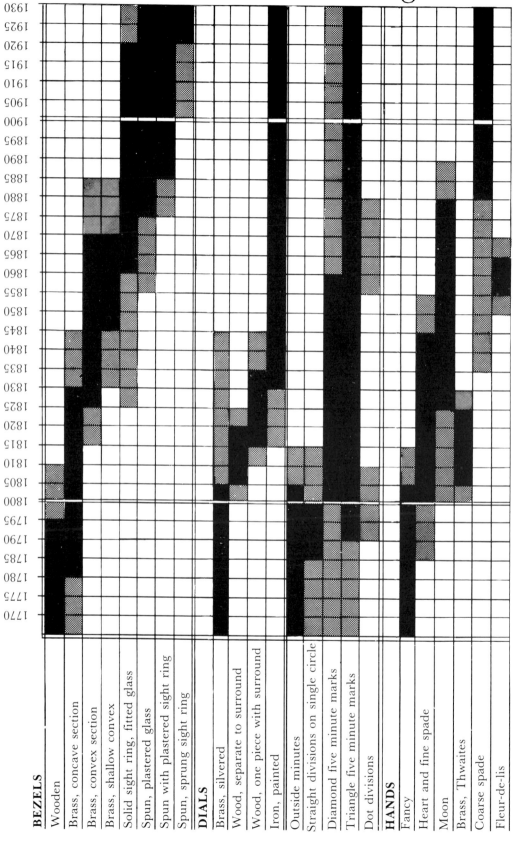

CASES
- Salt box
- Rounded bottom
- Drum and octagonal
- Chisel foot drop
- Curved foot drop
- Rounded bottom drop

SURROUNDS
- Concave section
- Convex section

PLATES
- Tapered
- Round or round topped
- Rectangular
- Straight chamfered shoulders
- Convex shoulders
- Concave shoulders
- Shaped shoulders

ESCAPEMENTS
- Verge
- Anchor
- Dead beat

Years (column axis): 1770, 1775, 1780, 1785, 1790, 1795, 1800, 1805, 1810, 1815, 1820, 1825, 1830, 1835, 1840, 1845, 1850, 1855, 1860, 1865, 1870, 1875, 1880, 1885, 1890, 1895, 1900, 1905, 1910, 1915, 1920, 1925, 1930

■ Main period of manufacture

▨ Build up and tailing off period of manufacture

Index

255

CARTER,
Cornhill,

LONDON.